Politics in
WEST GERMANY

A COUNTRY STUDY

Politics in
WEST GERMANY
Second Edition
A Revision of *Politics in Germany*

Lewis J. Edinger
Columbia University

Boston   Toronto
LITTLE, BROWN AND COMPANY

To

MONICA   **SUSAN**
Class of 1974   *Class of 1976*

Preface

This book is not an up-dated version of my *Politics in Germany* under a different title. That text was written in the 1960s, and a revision incorporating some cosmetic alterations might have been the easiest and quickest way to meet demands for a new edition. However, I felt compelled to do more than that and ended up writing an entirely new study. An introduction to contemporary West German politics for American undergraduates today appeared to require changes in organization and content.

First, I sought to write a text for students who share neither the memories nor, so it would seem, many of the views of their predecessors. Second, political developments in the German Federal Republic seemed to call for perspectives and interpretations rather different from those applied to earlier periods. Finally, my learning experiences since writing the previous study indicated the need for an approach that would place West German politics and policies more distinctly in a comparative framework for the analysis of advanced industrial societies.

I have found writing this short introductory text in some ways a more difficult, but also a more challenging undertaking than composing a lengthy scholarly monograph for specialists. One can all too easily forget that young people who were not yet born at the time of the Berlin Blockade and were at most infants during the Cuban Missile Crisis, do not share the personal recollections of older readers. They could not be assumed to be familiar with my subject and the theories and methods involved in its treatment. Furthermore, I realized that American students were likely to approach politics in another advanced industrial society from viewpoints shaped by recent and contemporary political developments in the United States.

At the same time I have been keenly conscious of the expertise of my professional colleagues standing ready to roast me over the fires of their critical disdain for errors of omission and commission. As I sought to simplify complex matters, I realized only too well that my generalizations slighted details that others might feel should have been included, that current affairs might be interpreted from a different theoretical stance, and that new information and future developments might not support my analysis.

I have attempted to resolve the attendant dilemmas by choosing a middle road, sacrificing on the one hand some of the educative advantages of simplification and on the other some of the illuminating advantages of specificity in matters of detail. Thus, I have endeavored to be as factually accurate as the available evidence would permit while keeping description and analysis from becoming mired in details.

The direction and extent of political change in the Federal Republic also indicated the need for new perspectives. When I wrote *Politics in Germany,* prevailing attitudes appeared too ambivalent, the state and its regime too new, to permit more than very cautious estimates of trends. By now, more firmly established political patterns seem to provide a stronger basis for explanations and projections.

In *Politics in Germany* I noted that many — perhaps I should have said most — contemporary observers analyzed developments in the Federal Republic largely in terms of earlier German political experiences. Particularly insofar as such historical perspectives were informed by the Nazi era, they appeared to me to risk slighting or distorting indications of significant differences in ongoing developments. In the light of subsequent events I have come to feel even more strongly that "the lessons of history" may not only guide, but misguide our analysis of present patterns and future trends. Looking backward, as Lot's wife discovered, can lead to very solid, but also rather inflexible perspectives.

It seems to me the time has come to reexamine the relevance of the past for an understanding of politics in the Federal Republic and to ask ourselves to what extent reference to increasingly remote historical events disorients our efforts to comprehend present developments. After all, the dissolution of the *Reich* and the emergence of its two successor states lie more than thirty years back. And much that has happened since then suggests that the distance of time has been magnified by discontinuities in the concerns and quality of West German political life. The long process of adjustment to a modern industrial society has evidently ended, as a distinguished British historian has noted, and the attendant problems that troubled German politics over the last century have spent their force.[1]

If this is so, a different benchmark is indicated for studying the current scene. In order to compare the political system of the Federal Republic with others in the contemporary world, it would appear to be more instructive to look to emerging patterns rather than to German developmental crises of the past. From this perspective, the structures and processes of political management in this particular advanced industrial society assume greater importance in my analysis than the fact that in former times Germans demonstrated little capacity for democratic government.

My description and analysis of contemporary West German politics thus center on public policy processes in a complex modern society. Readers of *Politics in Germany* will find that this focus has led me to sound a somewhat different methodological tune than in that study. I have placed greater emphasis on organizational structures directly related to governmental activities and less on indirectly related cultural patterns. I particularly shy from the notion that we can attribute distinctive features of collective political behavior in the Federal Republic to the typical traits of a peculiarly German "national

[1] George Barraclough, "A New View of German History," *N.Y. Review of Books*, November 16, 1972, p. 29.

character." To me this concept appears to hinder rather than help comparison with politics in other countries and to provide at most a catch-all category for otherwise inexplicable cultural differences.[2]

I have omitted extensive footnote references from this text because much of the pertinent literature is in German and most readers are unlikely to be familiar with that language. Further, many of my published and unpublished sources are not likely to be easily available to undergraduates. More accessible items are included in the Suggestions for Further Reading at the end of the book.

Directly or indirectly I am deeply indebted to the work of far too many persons to be named here. I feel however obligated to single out a few individuals and organizations to whom I owe a very special debt of gratitude. Kendall A. Baker, Gerard Braunthal, Paul J. Cassidy, Mark Kesselman, Gerhard Loewenberg, Paul Luebke, and Stanley Rothman offered critical comments and constructive suggestions that helped me enormously. I learned a great deal about the less visible aspects of West German politics in recent years from my conversations with Kurt Biedenkopf, Karl Dietrich Bracher, Peter Corterier, Klaus von Dohnanyi, Alfred Grosser, Reimut Jochimsen, Leisler Kiep, Peter von Oertzen, Hermann Schmitt-Vockenhausen, and Manfred Schüler. Elisabeth Noelle-Neumann and Rudolf Wildenmann generously supplied unpublished opinion poll data, and Donald Kommers allowed me to read the draft manuscript of his study on the West German

---

[2] The "national character" approach, derived from studies of small, tightly-knit, and encapsulated communities, seems to me to have limited value for understanding and comparing political relationships in large, pluralistic, and complex industrial societies. My own work, and that of others, has made me increasingly suspicious of both intuitive "insights" and more "scientific" efforts to capture the essence of such relationships in this manner. They tend, all too often, to posit a modal type of behavior, based either implicitly or explicitly on rather questionable assumptions and measures of centrality, and then to slight or consider aberrant significant deviations from the observed mean. In a society with extensive cross-cutting cleavages, as well as shifting and overlapping political alignments, one encounters multiple role and reference group identifications that cannot be captured in this fashion. We have little evidence that "nationality" discriminates over time between the political behavior of large populations under different jurisdictions more than "transnational" variables, such as age, education, and expendable income.

Constitutional Court. Arie Bucheister, Linda Garcia, Phillip Godwin, Laura Reanda, Robert Sorensen, and Howard Stoffer deserve much thanks for assisting in the composition of this book; and Kathryn Daniel and Janet Beatty of Little, Brown and Company for seeing it through to publication. Inter Nationes and the Foreign Office of Bonn, and the Consulate General and Information Service of the Federal Republic in New York, jointly and separately, provided personal contacts and source materials that would otherwise not have been available to me. Finally, I want to express my appreciation for financial support from the John Simon Guggenheim Foundation and from the Ford Foundation through a grant to the Institute on West Europe of Columbia University.

L.J.E.

Contents

Figures and Tables

Politics in
WEST
GERMANY

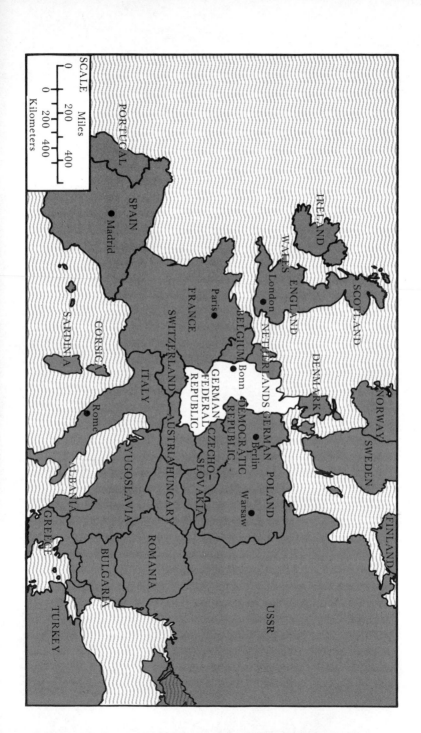

CHAPTER I

Introduction

PERSPECTIVES

Suppose for a moment that you are forced to bail out of a crippled aircraft and try to find out where you are after you hit the ground. What language do the people speak? You hear "Ja" and "Nein" and conclude that German is the native tongue. However, what country is this? It could be Austria or Switzerland, but you decide that most likely you are in Germany. You are only half right, an official-looking person tells you: "the German nation" is divided into two states; and this is the German Federal Republic, not the German Democratic Republic.

You should let your loved ones know you are alive and well. A short message on a picture postcard will do. "This is Frankfurt," you might write, "and I feel quite at home here." Big modern buildings line the noisy city streets, the highways are crowded with cars and trucks, and the countryside is dotted with factory chimneys belching forth acrid fumes. Familiar tunes drift from bars and record shops, department store windows are filled with modern appliances and mannequins in familiar clothing, and neon signs lighting up the nighttime sky advertise familiar consumer products.

However, you might also find yourself in a more unfamiliar setting. "This is Rottenburg," you tell your family, "a very quaint old town." The houses are medieval, the streets narrow

1

and crooked, and there are churches all over the place. Things here seem to be rather different than at home.

Both descriptions would give a very superficial picture of life in the Federal Republic, based on limited observations. Should you remain a while and look closer and further, you would quickly discover that although some things are much the same as in the United States, others are only something like it or quite different. In social and economic activities as well as in political affairs you will find both similarities and differences.

This, then, is a book about politics in a state that is not a nation-state, about West German politics but not politics in Germany, and about politics in some respects similar to those in other countries and in other respects dissimilar. It will not tell you everything there is to know about anything that might be called political in the Federal Republic. Its purpose is rather to identify general features that will help you to understand political processes there and allow you to make informed comparisons. What sort of comparisons? That depends on what you are looking for, what you see, and what you make of it. Proceeding from a conception of what seems important, you may observe and describe and, perhaps, analyze similarities and differences in the manifestation of particular phenomena in various political systems.

Governmental stability, for example, has seemed to many scholars a significant measure of the extent and intensity of partisan conflict in political systems. They have noted that the Federal Republic has been fairly stable, and have contrasted this stability with past political turmoil in Germany, or with contemporary instability in other parts of the world. Both are descriptive comparisons.

Analytical comparisons take us a step further in search of explanations for the observed variance. Why has the Federal Republic had only five chiefs of government in almost three decades, whereas other governments in Germany and elsewhere have followed each other in rapid succession? Here some scholars have attributed such differences primarily to specific constitutional arrangements, others to existing circumstances, and still others to leadership factors. The lack of governmental stability in previous periods and in other countries is said to be due to the absence of one or another of these determinants.

How one approaches politics in the Federal Republic thus depends on one's point of view and consequent comparative points of reference. What therefore seems particularly important to some observers is for others quite unimportant. One scholar may not consider economic or sociocultural phenomena that another scholar feels are crucial. An "insider" involved in German politics may see matters quite differently than an outsider. The way indisputable facts are selected for emphasis and interpretation may vary with different theoretical perspectives, political value preferences, or both.

Take, for instance, differences in the treatment of past events. Some observers hold that these events have little bearing on contemporary politics and that it is quite enough to know about more immediate developments to understand what is going on. Others maintain that German politics in our own day can be comprehended only in terms of a causal chain of changing or unchanging configurations that go back as much as a century or more. Communist writers in the German Democratic Republic, for example, embrace historical determinism. They conclude that whereas in their Germany the oppressed working people have after a long struggle assumed control of their own destiny, the traditional ruling class continues to dominate in the "capitalist" Federal Republic. Quite to the contrary, assert historians there. From their view of German history, the politics of the "liberal" Federal Republic reflect the realization of previously frustrated demands for liberty and social justice. "Over there," on the other hand, the autocratic patterns of the past are seen as preserved in a new form.

Both the writers and the readers of books such as this one need therefore to be aware of the variety of comparative perspectives and personal values that are brought to the study of its subject. Do we see political conflict as a pathological or healthy characteristic of a political system? Do we consider a democratic regime better than an autocratic one, and, if so, what standards are we using to make the distinction and how do we apply those criteria to evaluating political conditions in the Federal Republic? Do we assume that the political life of a people is rooted in distinctive cultural traits? Or do we think that their politics are more or less typical of those found in other advanced industrial societies with representative forms of government?

If you keep questions such as these constantly in mind, they will help you discern the perspectives of the author and assess your own reaction to what is presented and how. For in learning about the points of view of others and about politics in another country, one may arrive at a clearer awareness of one's own political outlook and come to see politics in one's own country somewhat differently than before.

POLITICS AND PUBLIC POLICY

To put it briefly, our subject is politics with a German accent. In the broadest sense of the term, politics deal with matters of public concern, and political issues focus on what these matters are, what should be done about them, and who should do it. A somewhat narrower and specific definition will, however, be more useful for our purposes. Politics, in this sense, revolve around governmental activities that affect relations between and within independent states. Within such states, they center on the choice and execution of public policies that may, to a greater or lesser extent, involve the entire population and, perhaps, its descendants.

But though there are politics everywhere, they are obviously not everywhere the same. They vary in time and place with differences in the organization of political life and the environment for public policies. They vary, too, due to differences in the outlook, relationships, and style of behavior of the involved actors. And they vary with public policy issues that may lead to or result from governmental actions in different contexts and settings.

To begin with, then, the Federal Republic is defined by the boundaries and qualities of an independent West German state. That is, it is a formal organization of people living in a particular territory who are bound together by exclusive and inclusive rules of public law and government. Ultimate responsibility for the formulation and enforcement of those rules is vested in public officials, such as government leaders and civil servants, whose formal authority extends throughout, but not beyond the confines of the sovereign state.

In this state, as in others, the scope and natures of public authority are formally defined by the rules of the regime, its form of government. Basic constitutional norms and derivative principles of public law set standards for the proper relationship between governors and governed and delineate the realm of public policy. In the Federal Republic these norms and principles call for popular participation and control through elections and representative bodies as well as for compliance with the decisions of officials charged with the formulation and execution of public policies. They also provide for the distribution of public authority among various branches and levels of government and between elected and appointed officials of the state. These formal arrangements will be described in the next chapter.

Public policies are the products and sources of political developments within and beyond the boundaries of independent states. They vary however not only with differences in the nature of the political systems, but with differences in the economic, social, and cultural setting. Trade relations as well as diplomatic relations with other states may give rise to political issues and demands for government action, and foreign and domestic affairs may be influenced by what the government does or fails to do. We shall consider the external and domestic socioeconomic environment for public policy in the Federal Republic in Chapter III. In some respects, as we will see, this setting closely resembles that in other advanced industrial societies, and resulting political issues are therefore only variations on common themes. At the same time, particular circumstances have led to politically relevant attitude and behavioral patterns that distinguish politics in West Germany from those in otherwise kindred societies.

Beginning with Chapter IV we will focus on explicitly political processes that shape and are shaped by public policies in the Federal Republic. In Chapter IV we shall first examine the current relevance of German experiences with earlier political systems and then consider how contemporary West Germans relate to the present regime. In Chapter V we will look at learning processes that shape ongoing political attitudes and behavior patterns and then analyze the prevailing structure of political participation and influence. Chapter VI deals with partisan organizations that serve primarily to recruit political leaders and to mobilize support for or opposition to their policies. In Chapter VII we will examine the nature of pressure group politics and the particularly important role of a few key interest associations.

In the last three chapters we will bring all of these elements together to study the interaction between politics and public policies in the Federal Republic. In Chapter VIII the emphasis will be on policymaking, whereas in Chapter IX it will be primarily on the consequences of policy decisions. We will conclude our analysis of West German politics in Chapter X with a brief review and a look at future problems and prospects.

CHAPTER II

Organization of the State

THROUGHOUT THIS BOOK we will be concerned with the interaction between state and society and between the constitutional regime and the political system in the Federal Republic. A state, like other organizations, encompasses more or less enduring membership positions which are occupied by different individuals over the course of time. And in every sovereign state there are formal regime rules defining the nature and relationship of such positions, the qualifications needed to occupy them, and the "lawful" conduct of citizens, public officials, and aliens. These rules vary with the organizational structure of different states and with the dynamics of their political processes.

Formal arrangements are often observed more in theory than in practice, and constitutional and other legally mandated procedures may be honored more in the breach than in the observance because political actors do not respect them. However, in the contemporary political life of the Federal Republic, attitudes and behavior are widely patterned by the formal framework for selecting and processing public policies. It is therefore particularly appropriate that we begin by seeing how the present state and regime came to be constituted and how they are structured.

THE BASIC LAW

The Federal Republic and its constituent "Basic Law" of 1949 are the products of the defeat of a united Germany in

World War II and the inability of the conquerors to agree on the form of its political reconstruction. Although the leaders of the four powers that in 1945 assumed control over its territory in separate American, British, French, and Russian zones of military occupation pledged themselves initially to collaborate in establishing a democratic regime for all of Germany, their ideas of what this meant and how it might be attained proved irreconcilable. Within two years the American and British zones were merged into an embryonic West German state which, with the addition of the French zone, became in 1949 the German Federal Republic. The Soviet Union responded by sponsoring the establishment of the German Democratic Republic as a second successor state to the former German *Reich*. The old capital city of Berlin, in the middle of that state, continued to be nominally under the control of all four powers. However, one section became in fact the capital of the Democratic Republic while the rest was associated with but not formally incorporated into the Federal Republic. West Berlin remains to this day under joint American, British, and French jurisdiction and protection and is therefore outside the sovereignty of the Federal Republic. Former German territories east of the Democratic Republic became part of Poland and the Soviet Union (see Figure II.1).

The Basic Law of 1949, according to its preamble, was supposed to provide a temporary organization for a temporary state, pending the reunification of Germany and the ultimate incorporation of the entire country in a European union. It was drafted by the representatives of the three occupation powers — the United States, Britain, and France — and those of West German leaders acceptable to them in the name of the entire "German people," including "those Germans to whom participation was denied" because they lived in the area controlled by the Soviet Union. According to Article 146, it was to "cease to be in force on the day on which a constitution adopted by a free decision of the German people comes into force."

The declared object of the framers of the Basic Law of 1949 was thus "to give a new order to political life for a transitional period," as the preamble puts it. The lengthy docu-

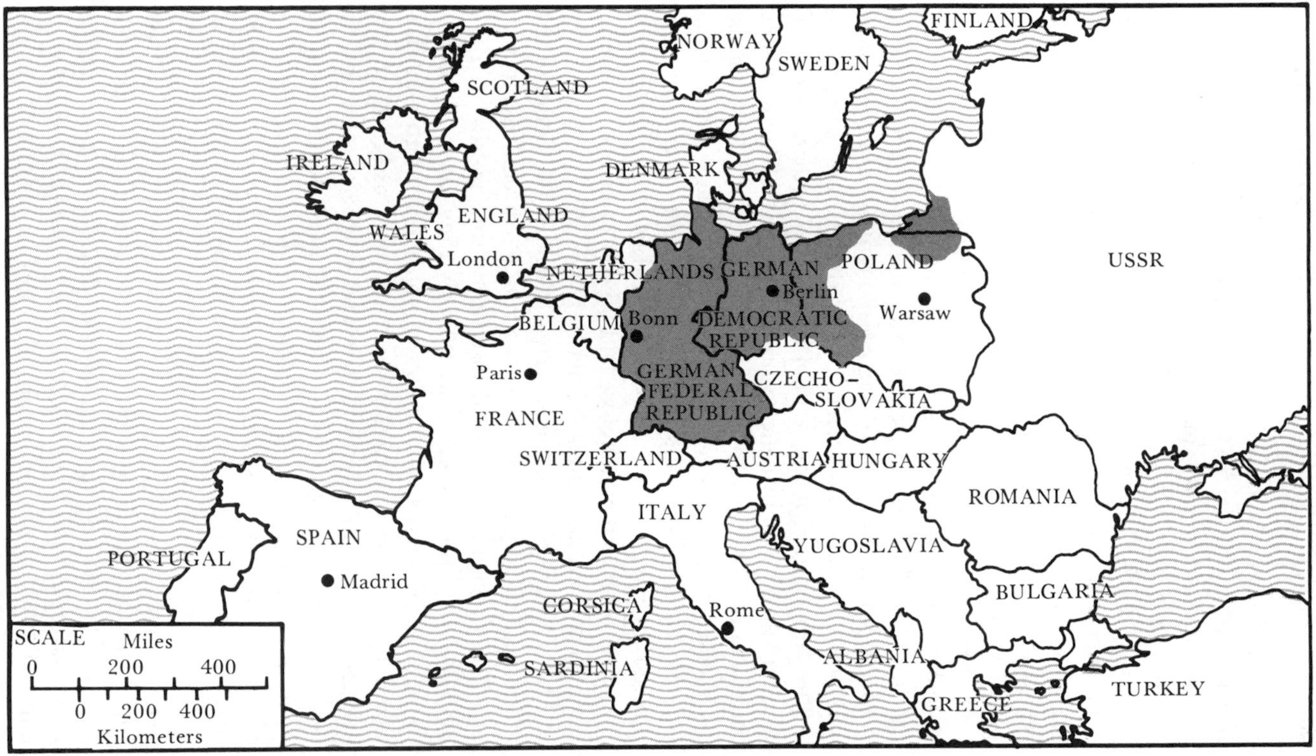

Figure II.1. *1937 German Frontiers*

ment they drew up was not an expression of prevailing political norms in Western Germany but a compromise between
the various views of the members of the constituent assembly
and of the American, British, and French military governors
and their advisers. Based on constitutional theories derived
from German and non-German political philosophies and
experiences, it was never put to a direct popular test in a
referendum and remained to be "bought" by the affected
population.

By specifying in considerable detail how the new political
system was to work in a "democratic and social federal state,"
the founding fathers sought to structure future relationships
between political actors, among component parts of the state,
and between state and society. Their design was intended to
ensure long-range political stability and to provide ironclad
legal safeguards against the recurrence of developments which
they believed had led to the failure of previous German ex-
periments with democracy. To guide Germans along what
was expected to be a difficult road of transition from an authoritarian past to a firmly established democratic order in a
pluralist society, they therefore laid down rather precise norms
of political conduct under the new regime.

The roles assigned to the governed reflected the belief of the
authors of the Basic Law that too much "direct" democracy
was likely to lead to political instability and, possibly, to the
destruction of their design. Accordingly they carefully sought
to regulate popular participation in politics through organizational arrangements that for the most part assigned to the
average citizen only intermittent and indirect roles in the
policymaking processes of a "representative" democracy. Implied in the governmental structures that were established was
the expectation that strong governmental leadership would
need to ensure the smooth operation of the new system and to
create political orientations that would give the regime legitimacy among the mass of the population. An educative
function was thus linked to a stabilizing function of the constitution by the assumption that the efficient operation of the
organization of the state would in time induce its citizens to
embrace the role assignments and norms set forth in the

Basic Law, and thus institutionalize the new political order.

The roles assigned to the governors were designed to provide for a democratic state ruled by law and under law by responsible public officials (a *Rechtstaat*). Toward this end, the framers of the Basic Law first anchored a bill of fundamental human and civil rights and provisions for representative government in constitutional doctrine. Second, to prevent the concentration of governmental powers, they provided for the dispersion of public authority through a complex system of checks and balances among various organs of government. Here their design called for the fusion of a federal with a parliamentary form of government and a balance between executive, legislative, and judicial powers at various levels of government.

Under the constitutional principles of 1949 governors as well as governed were obliged not only to respect but, if need be, to defend the established regime. The rules of responsible citizenship imposed on the governed the obligation to obey the legitimate decisions of public officials and actively to oppose illegitimate acts of governmental authority. In turn, principles of responsible government imposed on the agents of the state an obligation to observe and uphold the formal rules for their selection, their conduct, and the scope of their authority. And although the Basic Law subordinated individual and group interests to the "public interest," the state and its officials were to serve rather than dominate the people. Majority rule was to prevail, but it was not to give representative governments a mandate to ignore the constitutional rights of minorities in the name of the popular will or "interests of state."

Amendments to the Basic Law require a two-thirds majority in each of the two houses of the federal parliament. The constitution has been altered more often in twenty-five years than the American in two hundred. Especially over the last decade, sections have been deleted, changed, and added, and in 1970, a constitutional commission was established to consider further alterations. However, political leaders have on the whole avoided tampering with the constitutional essence of the regime. The original provisions remain essentially the formal foundations of the political system of the Federal Republic, and both past and contemplated alterations have generally been directed to adapting the Basic Law to changing conditions and policies without affecting its fundamental principles.[1]

SOURCES AND SCOPE OF PUBLIC AUTHORITY

"All state authority emanates from the people," according to Article 20 of the Basic Law. "It shall be exercised by the people by means of elections and voting and by specific legislative, executive, and judicial organs." This key provision introduces four basic distinctions in the constitutional order of the Federal Republic. One is between citizens and noncitizens, the second between citizens who are entitled to vote and those who are not, a third between the enfranchised population and public officials who exercise state authority in the name of "the people," and a fourth among different governmental agents of that authority.

Every "domestic juristic person" is considered subject to the authority of the state under the Basic Law. That term applies not only to individuals, but to organizations such as political parties, interest associations, religious associations, and business enterprises. All of these "persons" are expected to pay taxes levied on them by public authorities, to respect the laws of the Federal Republic, and to follow the instructions of duly authorized public officials.

Anyone living within the Federal Republic and any organization subject to its jurisdiction is thus supposed to obey its laws or suffer the penalties set for the infraction of those laws. But not everyone who has these legal obligations is entitled to claim all the basic rights set forth in the constitution. Some rights are for "everyone," but others apply only to the "Germans." Everyone is for instance declared to be entitled to the human rights of liberty, legal equality and redress, and free-

---

1 Updated texts of the Basic Law are regularly published in English by the Press and Information Office of the Government of the Federal Republic. For a good analysis of the constitutional changes to 1970, see Ulrich Scheuner, "Das Grundgesetz in der Entwicklung zweier Jahrzehnte," *Archiv des oeffentlichen Rechts,* 1970, pp. 353–408.

dom of religion and expression. But only Germans are granted the civic rights of assembly, association, and travel within the territory of the Federal Republic.

Who then is a citizen? The most obvious answer, anyone born or naturalized in the Federal Republic, would at present exclude the majority of the people, for most of them were born before the establishment of the state. Article 116 of the Basic Law therefore bestows automatic citizenship on all who were citizens of Germany before its division, or who were admitted to its 1937 territory as refugees of "German stock," or who are the wives or descendants of such persons. Strictly interpreted, this article might mean that citizenship extends not only to anyone in the German Federal Republic who meets these criteria, but to all those who are thus defined as Germans but live in former German territories now parts of Poland and the Soviet Union.

Here the language of the Basic Law reflects the unwillingness of its authors to recognize the legality of a second successor state to the old German Reich and the legality of annexation by conquest. However, as with other articles, this one applies only "unless otherwise provided by law." In the course of regularizing "intra-German" relations with the East German Democratic Republic and "foreign" relations with Poland and the Soviet Union, ordinary legislation and treaty arrangements have actually limited the claim to citizenship in the Federal Republic to Germans on its territory.

Any citizen, male or female, who is eighteen years or older may not only vote but run for public office. However, the basic law provides that a candidate must possess the necessary "aptitude, qualifications, and professional achievements" which, in effect as we shall see, restrict entry into elective positions.

No constitution, however detailed its provisions, can specify exactly how it is to be applied in every instance. The Basic Law of the Federal Republic allows key public officials considerable flexibility in the choice and implementation of public policies by qualifying constitutional principles or leaving their interpretation in the hands of the legislative, executive, and judicial organs of the state. Accordingly, parliamentary acts, governmental regulations, and court decisions have over the years defined and redefined the scope of public authority more explicitly.

Article 6 of the Basic Law, for example, provides that "marriage and the family shall enjoy the special protection of the state." It calls the upbringing of children "a natural right . . . and duty" of parents, but it also stipulates that "the national community shall watch over their endeavors." This provision has been interpreted by public authorities as giving them the license to set and enforce standards for the "proper" care and treatment of children at home, as well as the responsibility for seeing to their education in schools under the supervision of the state. Article 2 provides that the inviolability of personal freedoms may be curbed by law in the public interest, and here the provisions of the Criminal Code have been used to impose authoritative restraints on the exercise of such freedoms. Article 18 bars the "misuse" of the freedom of expression. This provision has permitted governmental agencies to confiscate "seditious" literature and to censor publications on the grounds that they corrupted "public morals" or threatened the sanctity of marriage and the family. Under articles 9 and 21, public authorities have the power to curb freedom of association and ban organizations found to be directed against the constitutional order. Accordingly, groups and individuals accused of supporting "subversive" causes have been prosecuted in the courts, and barred from public service employment and in the 1950s both the Communist and a radical right-wing party were outlawed.

AGENTS OF PUBLIC AUTHORITY

Public officeholders are defined by the positions that constitutional and derivative public law assigns to them among the organizational components of the machinery of the state. When a person is elected or appointed to a public office, he is invested with some elements of the authority which by the Basic Law is delegated by the people to legislative, executive, and judicial instruments of public policy. Correspondingly, when a parliamentary deputy, policeman, or judge is not acting in his proper official capacity, or ceases to exercise his public function, he is divested of that authority and the legal responsibilities and privileges that go with his position.

In terms of the formal organization of the state, what matters here is thus the office and its relationships to other positions, such as those of citizen, voter, and resident alien. It is the office that distinguishes the officeholder from other members of the organization and involves him more directly in the making or implementation of public policies. And it is the office that identifies the extent of his legal authority over others and of others over him.

In the Federal Republic one individual may hold several offices in various areas and at different levels of authority. For example, a person can at the same time be an elected federal legislator, an appointed federal minister, and a member of the nonfederal civil service as a university professor. Each position carries a title, and rights and duties, which under law go with being a member of the legislature, the cabinet, or the public administration. These rights and duties do not overlap, but they may be accumulative. Thus, parliamentary immunity does not permit the professor to libel his professional colleagues and students in the academic community; however, a minister may accumulate pension rights above and beyond those due to him as a member of parliament and the civil service.

DIVISION AND FUSION OF PUBLIC AUTHORITY

Federalism and the Federal Council. Among the major states of Europe, the Federal Republic is the only one with a federal rather than a centralized organization of government. As in the United States, legislative, executive, and judicial authority is dispersed among various geographic units. The essential jurisdictional division is between the organs of the Federation (the *Bund*), the national parliament, government, and judiciary, and those of its ten constituent states (the *Länder*). (See Figure II.2.)

As in every other federation, the component regions are subject to national regulations. The Basic Law thus gives the central government the responsibility to enforce its provisions in the constituent states of the Federal Republic. Federal law

Figure II.2. *Organization of the Federal Republic*

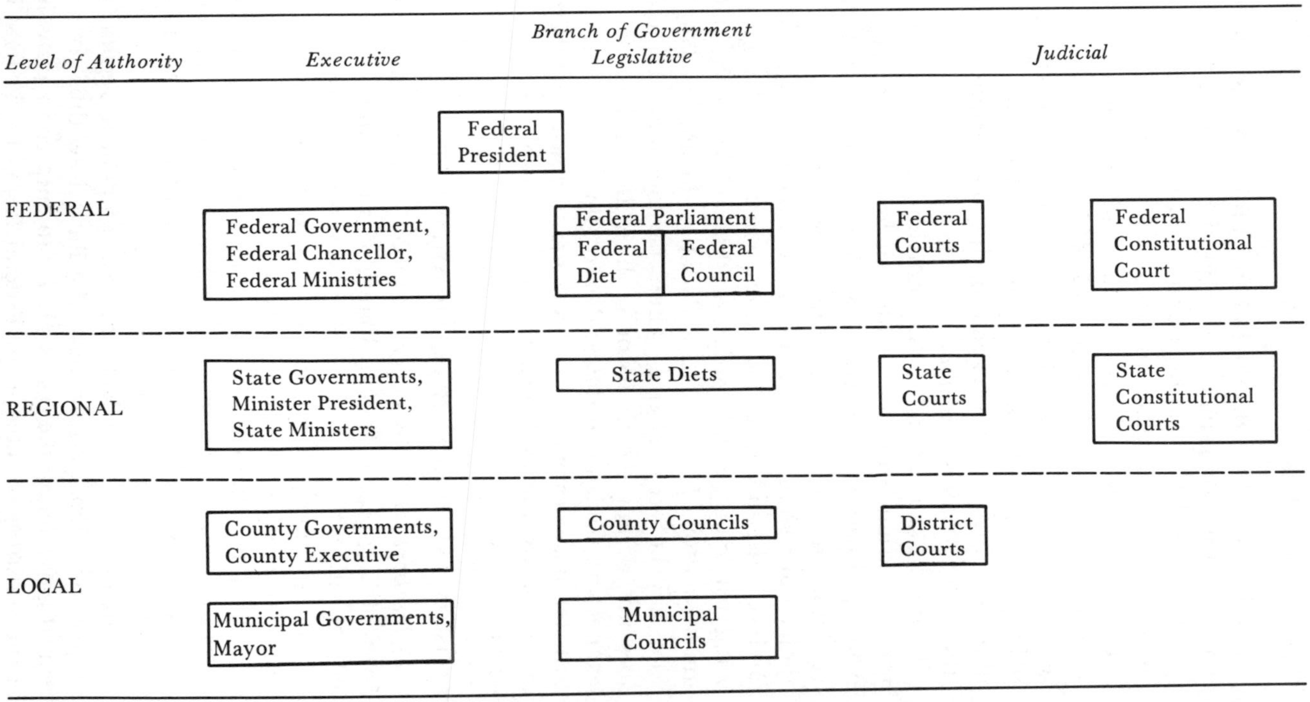

Level of Authority	Branch of Government		
	Executive	*Legislative*	*Judicial*
FEDERAL	Federal Government, Federal Chancellor, Federal Ministries	Federal Parliament — Federal Diet | Federal Council	Federal Courts — Federal Constitutional Court
	Federal President		
REGIONAL	State Governments, Minister President, State Ministers	State Diets	State Courts — State Constitutional Courts
LOCAL	County Governments, County Executive	County Councils	District Courts
	Municipal Governments, Mayor	Municipal Councils	

has preeminence over state law, the human and civil rights set forth in the Basic Law must be respected by authorities in the states, and the constitutional order of the states must conform to the principles of "republican, democratic, and social government based on the rule of law" laid down in the federal constitution. For example, since the death penalty is outlawed by the Basic Law it may not be imposed in any of the states and their local governments must include legislative bodies "chosen in general, direct, free, equal, and secret elections" by the enfranchised population.

Legislatures, governments, and courts in the constituent states are constitutionally responsible for the uniform application of federal laws and regulations. Powers that are not specifically assigned to the states under the Basic Law — for the most part affecting educational and cultural matters — are either the exclusive preserve of the Federation, like defense and foreign policy, or shared in the form of concurrent legislative authority. Subject to these provisions, public officials of the states control most of the public administration, the police, radio and television stations, and the disbursement and use of public funds by county and municipal authorities.

To balance the obligations of the states and the limitations on their autonomy, the Basic Law assigns to their elected representatives key positions in federal politics. They participate in selecting the federal president and the justices of the principal federal courts and, more importantly, they have a very significant voice in the making and implementation of federal policies through the Federal Council (*Bundesrat*).

The Federal Council — which is actually a council of the constituent, nonsovereign states — is the upper house of the Federal Parliament and formally one of the strongest second chambers in the world. Unlike the lower house, it cannot be dissolved; and its constitutional powers are far greater than, for instance, those of the French Senate and the British House of Lords, and, in some respects at least, equal to those of the American Senate. However, in contrast to that body, membership in the Federal Council is not by direct election and the constituent states are not equally represented. The forty-one seats are allocated to the various states roughly on the basis of their population, and vary from five for the most populous of the ten states to three for the smallest. The corresponding votes are cast in a unit on the instructions of state governments chosen by and responsible to popularly elected state Diets.

The Federal Council is a vital link in the constitutional relationship between national and regional authorities, between the federal executive and the lower house of the Federal Parliament, and between the central government and local governments. For example, federal officials may not bypass or overrule state authorities without the express approval of a majority vote in the Federal Council. The Federal Government must submit all of its legislative drafts to the upper house before they go to the lower, and most bills passed by the latter need the consent of the former.[2] All federal executive ordinances must be approved by a majority in the Federal Council, and emergency executive government without the participation of the lower house must have the support of the upper chamber.

The Federal Presidency. Whereas under American principles of division of powers national executive authority rests in a single office, the Basic Law provides for a dual executive. Like the American president, the president of the Federal Republic (*Bundespräsident*) is not a member of the legislature, but unlike him he is not the head of the Federal Government as well as of the state. As in all countries with a parliamentary form of government, the chief of state has no significant policymaking responsibilities — at least under normal conditions — and in no respect does the federal president have the more far-reaching constitutional authority of the French president. He is enjoined from engaging in "partisan" activities, bound to accept the decisions of the Federal Government, Federal Parliament, and courts, and largely restricted to the exercise of ceremonial functions.

In contrast to the hereditary chiefs of state in parliamentary

---

[2] Either by a simple plurality or, in the case of constitutional amendments and certain key legislation, by a two-thirds majority.

monarchies, the federal president holds an elective office for a fixed period; but unlike the French president he is not directly chosen by the people. Instead he is selected for a five-year term by the Federal Convention (*Bundesversammlung*) — an electoral college composed of the deputies of the lower house of the Federal Parliament and an equal number of delegates elected by the state Diets on the basis of proportional representation. Actually, the choice lies in the hands of the leaders of the political parties who control the Federal Convention. An incumbent may be reelected for a second, but not a third term.

All of the president's "public acts" — including his official letters, speeches, and publications — formally require the approval of the politically responsible executive, the federal chancellor (*Bundeskanzler*). He cannot veto actions of the Federal Government or Federal Parliament and must sign all legislation, decrees, and letters of appointment and dismissal submitted to him by the chancellor or ministers. At the same time he does not enjoy the political immunity of the British monarch; impeachment proceedings before the Federal Constitutional Court may be initiated by a two-thirds majority in either house of the Federal Parliament against a president believed to have violated his constitutional responsibilities.

The occupant of the office must therefore be extremely circumspect in observing the formal limits of his authority. He may try to warn and admonish policymakers in statements designed to express or mobilize public opinion and he may attempt to exploit his constitutional right to be informed and consulted by the chancellor to influence governmental policy. Experience has shown, however, that governmental leaders supported by solid parliamentary majorities will not and need not accept presidential interference and advice.

In the opinion of some German constitutional lawyers the president may possess some reserve powers to block or, at least, delay policy decisions and exercise greater influence under exceptional circumstances. As yet untested provisions of the Basic Law might allow a president so inclined to play a more independent and decisive role in a conflict between government and legislature by using his rather limited power to dissolve the lower house or support a minority government.

The Federal Government. Constitutional provisions for a system of checks and balances between the Federal Government *(Bundesregierung)* and Federal Parliament call for the fusion as well as separation of executive and legislative authority. Here the framers of the Basic Law sought to legitimate as well as restrict majority rule in a representative democracy by formal arrangements regulating the interplay between government and opposition parties and elected and appointed public officials. The politically responsible governing leaders were made less dependent on the constant support of a legislative majority than in a pure parliamentary system but more so than in an American-type presidential system. In this way indirect popular control of the executive branch through the legislative representatives of the electorate was to be ensured and arbitrary government to be avoided. At the same time, these arrangements were to provide for strong and stable governmental leadership under emergency conditions and in situations when irreconcilable conflicts among the popularly elected representatives produced a deadlock in the legislature.

Government actions and statements are usually announced in the name of the Federal Government as a whole, but constitutional responsibility rests with its chief. The Basic Law provides neither for executive leadership by a committee chosen by the legislature, as in Switzerland, nor for a collegial cabinet government whose members are collectively responsible to parliament, as in England. Executive authority and majoritarian government are primarily linked through the position of federal chancellor. He alone is chosen by the popularly elected Federal Diet *(Bundestag)*, and he alone is accountable to it for the conduct of all members of the Federal Government.

Unless a chancellor resigns or dies in office, a candidate for the position is normally nominated by the federal president immediately after the election of a new Diet. The nominee, who need not be a member of either house of the Federal Parliament, must obtain more than half of the votes in the lower house to obtain the office. If its deputies reject him they can, by a similar absolute majority, nominate their own candidate, and then the president must appoint him. Should no one manage to gain such support, a simple plurality will suffice to elect a candidate of the Federal Diet, but in this case the president need not appoint him and can, if he wishes, dissolve the chamber on his own authority.

Once in office, a chancellor cannot be impeached, nor can he be forced to resign unless an absolute majority of the Federal Diet elects a successor under a unique constitutional provision requiring a "positive vote of no confidence." Should a majority refuse to give him a vote of confidence, but at the same time be unable to agree on a replacement, he may either ask the federal president to order new Diet elections, or continue to govern up to six months if he has the support of the Federal Council and president.[3] However, these rights lapse as soon as the lower chamber elects a new chancellor.

The exclusive constitutional responsibility of the chief of the Federal Government is formally matched by exclusive powers that give him primary authority over the formulation of governmental policies and over the activities of his associates in the Federal Government. Neither the president nor parliament can legally compel the chancellor to include anyone in his cabinet or to dismiss any of his ministers or advisers; the decision is officially his own. He may appoint them or remove them as he sees fit. The chancellor also controls the federal bureaucracy subject to civil service regulations, and he exercises considerable discretion in the distribution of public funds and the implementation of legislation. And although the chancellor ordinarily needs the approval of one or both houses of the Federal Parliament for his policy proposals and budgetary requests, he may legally withhold information requested by the legislature, ignore its wishes and expression of disapproval, and veto budgetary appropriations that exceed his requests.

Like the American president and other chief executives,

---

[3] In the states, which have no dual executives and only unicameral legislatures, the failure of a positive vote of no confidence in the chief of government in some instances permits him to order new elections and in others requires the state Diet to dissolve itself.

the chancellor is aided in the conduct of his office by a staff of trusted advisers. Most are public officials attached to the Federal Chancellery (*Bundeskanzleramt*), headed at various times either by a federal minister or senior civil servant. Its members assist the chancellor in planning and coordinating government policies and supervising the activities of the entire Federal Government. They may also serve as emissaries to other agencies of government and foreign leaders, and to non-governmental associations and political parties.

The federal ministers are formally not the chancellor's peers but his subordinates, and are responsible to him rather than to the Federal Parliament. They are appointed and dismissed by the president on the chancellor's recommendation; their terms of office end automatically with the death, resignation, or replacement of the chancellor, and they can neither be censured nor singled out for special vote of confidence by the legislature. The number of ministers and their specific field of responsibility is left to the chancellor's discretion by the Basic Law. There have been as many as twenty and as few as twelve; there have been ministers with and without specific portfolios. One of them is usually appointed deputy chancellor; other key posts correspond to the major constitutional responsibilities of the Federal Government for foreign, defense, and economic policies.

Under the constitution and the standing rules of the Federal Government, its ministers have four primary policymaking responsibilities. First, as members of the cabinet, they may participate in formulating decisions which the chancellor has the formal right to accept or reject. Second, they may individually advise the chancellor on policy matters, but he is entitled to ignore or overrule their recommendations. Third, they are charged with supervising and planning policy within their departments if they are not ministers without specific portfolios. Such responsibilities may include not only preparing bills for consideration by the cabinet and parliament but, more directly, formulating administrative and legal ordinances (*Rechtsverordnungen*) that spell out in detail the application of federal laws. Fourth, ministers have the formal authority to supervise the implementation of federal policies by subordinate officials, including state officials responsible for administering federal laws and derivative ministerial regulations.

Serving under the chancellor and the members of his cabinet are parliamentary secretaries, who are members of the Federal Diet, and state secretaries who are senior career officials of the Federal Civil Service. These officials may represent their chiefs in Federal Parliament and its committees and serve as their delegates in various other capacities. All of them are formally political appointees — like most deputy and assistant secretaries in the United States government — and may be removed from their positions at the discretion of their superiors. The parliamentary secretaries are in effect junior members of the Federal Government without cabinet rank, and their term of service ends with that of the chancellor. The state secretaries, on the other hand, remain members of the public administration beyond the tenure of any particular government. However, they may be moved to another position or temporarily pensioned if a federal chancellor or cabinet member wants someone else to advise and assist him.

The Federal Diet. The parliamentary elements in the constitutional order make the Federal Diet (*Bundestag*) formally the more important of the two chambers in the national legislature. According to the design of the Basic Law, it is to be the primary lawmaking organ for the entire country and the principal representative body for popular control over the Federal Government. The deputies of the Diet are elected directly by enfranchised West German voters, normally every four years, whereas the federal president, chancellor, and the members of the Federal Council representing the state governments are elected indirectly.

Under the West German system of checks and balances the official authority of the Diet is greater than that of the French National Assembly, but in some ways not as great as that of the British House of Commons or the United States House of Representatives. Unlike the legislative powers of the House of Commons, those of the West German Diet are curbed by the federalist features of the Basic Law, by judicial review, and by the right of the executive branch to exercise a veto when the Diet goes beyond its budgetary proposals. And in contrast to the House of Representatives, the chamber may be dissolved by the president when it is deadlocked with the executive branch and unable to elect a new chief of government.

Collectively the deputies of the countrywide electorate have an equal voice with the representatives of the states in the selection of the federal president and chief justices of the federal judiciary, but have sole control over the selection of the federal chancellor. Constitutional amendments and bills that fall under the joint legislative authority of the Federation and its member states require the consent of the Federal Council, but legislation on policy matters within the exclusive jurisdiction of federal organs does not. International treaties, for instance, must only be ratified in the Diet. Under the Basic Law a conference committee of the two chambers is to resolve differences over legislation requiring the approval of both of them. All told, the approval of a majority of the Diet is needed to give constitutional legitimacy to federal policy under all but exceptional emergency conditions.

The Basic Law charges the federal deputies with supervising the federal executive on behalf of the people through debates, questions, and investigations as well as by binding legislation. They have the right to summon members of the Federal Government to appear before the Diet and its committees, but cannot compel them to disclose information, reply to questions, or debate an issue. On the other hand, the chancellor, ministers, or their representatives may attend plenary and committee sessions — even if they are not deputies — and present their views any time they wish. The same applies to members of the Federal Council.

Like the Federal Council and Federal Government, the Federal Diet operates under formal rules of organizational procedure which have changed little over the years. By these rules the business of the lower house is conducted under the direction of a Council of Elders. It includes the Diet's president, its vice-presidents, and about fifteen other deputies and sets the agenda for the chamber and supervises its proceedings.

Most of the legislative work of the deputies is conducted in committee sessions. Except for the Committee on Defense, none of the nineteen or so regular or standing committees has the formal investigatory powers of congressional committees in the United States. Under Article 44 of the Basic Law special committees of inquiry, empowered to conduct open or secret hearings, must be established on the motion of one-fourth of the deputies. This provision allows a minority of the deputies to initiate an investigation into the conduct of the executive, but committees of inquiry have no subpoena powers and their ability to extract information from the Federal Government depends on its cooperation.

Public Policy Administration. Formal responsibility for the application of governmental policies is shared by central, regional, and local authorities. Federal ministries exercise direct constitutional control primarily over policy implementation in foreign relations and defense and over interregional services, such as the countrywide public transportation and communications networks. Federal monetary policies are administered by the central Federal Bank and social service policies by independent federal administrative agencies similar to the Social Security and Veterans Administration in the United States. Most other administrative tasks are assigned to state and local authorities. (See Figure II.3.)

In the implementation of most routine domestic policies that directly affect the average citizens of the Federal Republic, the state governments exercise primary administrative authority. In addition to seeing to the enforcement of laws and regulations within their exclusive jurisdiction, the state ministries and their respective bureaucratic infrastructures occupy strategic intervening positions between central and local authorities in the application of federal legislation and ministerial ordinances.

Whereas the countrywide system of public administration for the Federation is thus for the most part regionally dis-

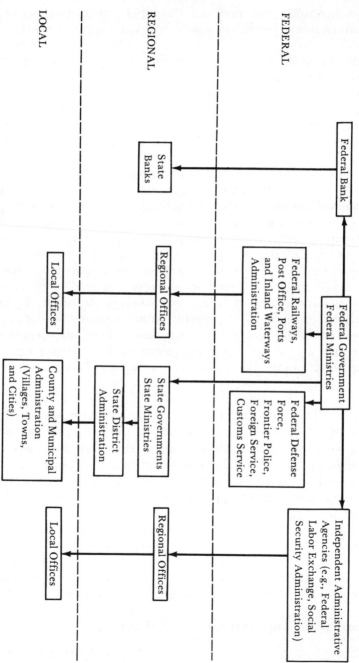

Figure II.3. *Organization for Policy Implementation*

FEDERAL

REGIONAL

LOCAL

Federal Bank

State Banks

Federal Government
Federal Ministries

Federal Railways,
Post Office, Ports
and Inland Waterways
Administration

Regional Offices

Local Offices

Federal Defense
Force,
Frontier Police,
Foreign Service,
Customs Service

State Governments
State Ministries

State District
Administration

County and Municipal
Administration
(Villages, Towns,
and Cities)

Independent Administrative
Agencies (e.g., Federal
Labor Exchange, Social
Security Administration)

Regional Offices

Local Offices

persed among the ten constituent states, the administrative organization within the states is highly centralized. Here the lines of authority run from the state governments, especially their ministries for interior and educational affairs, through state district administrations to county and local government agencies. In the last analysis, most laws and administrative regulations are executed by local officials directly or indirectly accountable to appropriate state authorities and not by the comparatively few local agents of the Federal Government. The collection of all income taxes, for example, rests with the state governments who strictly supervise the policy implementing functions of local authorities.

The Basic Law grants self-governing communities far less autonomy than enjoyed by their counterparts in the United States. Although it allows them to regulate their own affairs "within the limits set by law," this provision gives local governments little policymaking authority. Under the federal and state constitutions, schools, police departments, social services, in fact almost all but local public transportation and utility services, are controlled by state authorities.

Corresponding to this distribution of administrative responsibilities, the public administration is composed of several distinct but interlocking structures and interdependent but not overlapping bureaucratic hierarchies. In 1974, these took in close to one out of ten employed West Germans. Most public employees are, however, not government officials, whereas the civil servants (*Beamten*) represent governmental authority by virtue of their executive position.

Most civil servants, including university professors, are career officials employed by the state governments and, directly or indirectly, subject to their control. As teachers, policemen, tax collectors, and the like, they provide the general population with most of its immediate contacts with public authorities. The small federal ministerial bureaucracy is on the whole not involved in such relationships. Apart from exercising those domestic tasks falling under their immediate jurisdiction, its members primarily plan and supervise the uniform implementation of federal policies throughout the country (see Table II.1).

Table II.1.   *Public Administration Personnel in the German Federal Republic in 1974 (in rounded percentages)*

	Civil servants & judges	Salaried employees	Wage earners	Total
Federal[a]	3.4	3.9	4.4	11.7
State[b]	32.2	17.5	6.2	55.9
Local	5.3	16.9	10.2	32.4
Total (N = 2,551,925)	40.9	38.3	20.8	100.0

[a]Not including about 1 million employed by public enterprises, such as the federal railways and the federal postal, telegraph and telephone service, and members of the armed forces.

[b]Including teachers and university professors who constituted 43.1 percent of state personnel and 24.1 percent of all public administration personnel in West Germany.

Source: *Statistisches Jahrbuch für die Bundesrepublik Deutschland*, 1975, pp. 412-13.

The Judiciary. Under the constitutional system of checks and balances judicial authority is vested in an independent judiciary. Ordinary courts are divided horizontally into a number of functional hierarchies, each of which is closely integrated vertically through a network of local, regional, and supreme federal courts (see Figure II.4). The constitutional courts in the Federation and states are coequal with the executive and legislative branches of government and have the authority to overrule them and other courts within their jurisdiction.

German jurisprudence distinguishes among universal, general, and absolute principles of justice (*Recht*) and relativist, particular, and finite principles of law (*Gesetz*). By the prevailing rules of a democratic Rechtstaat the courts are supposed to combine both sets of principles and render equal justice under law. Constitutional provisions stipulate that judges shall base their verdicts on what the law provides as well as on their interpretation of desirable or established social values. Trial by jury is rare. Most courts are collegial bodies, and the verdict of a majority of their members is handed down in the name of the entire bench. Individual

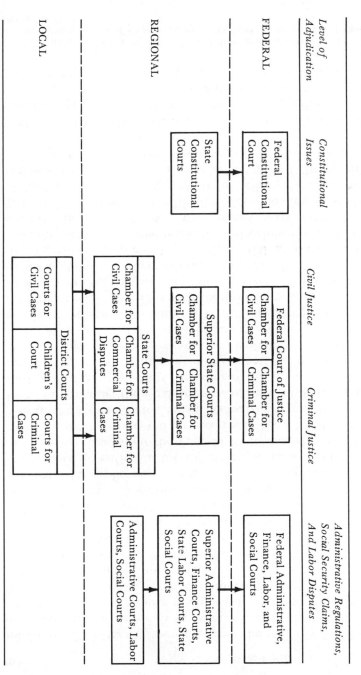

Figure II.4: *Organization of the Courts*

Level of Adjudication	Constitutional Issues	Civil Justice	Criminal Justice	Administrative Regulations, Social Security Claims, And Labor Disputes

FEDERAL

State Constitutional Courts → Federal Constitutional Court

Federal Court of Justice — Chamber for Civil Cases | Chamber for Criminal Cases

Federal Administrative, Finance, Labor, and Social Courts

REGIONAL

Superior State Courts — Chamber for Civil Cases | Chamber for Criminal Cases

State Courts — Chamber for Civil Cases | Chamber for Commercial Disputes | Chamber for Criminal Cases

Superior Administrative Courts, Finance Courts, State Labor Courts, State Social Courts

LOCAL

District Courts — Courts for Civil Cases | Children's Court | Courts for Criminal Cases

Administrative Courts, Labor Courts, Social Courts

opinions supporting or dissenting from the majority decision are usually not made public or recorded, as in the American judicial system.[4] Anonymity is supposed to protect the courts against outside interference and reinforce the prestige of the judicial organ of public authority.

The judicial pyramid of the regular court system is topped by the Federal Court of Justice (*Bundesgerichtshof*), an appellate court. As in other continental European countries, civil and criminal procedures and penalties are governed by codes of law, and review proceedings before higher courts concern only the application of uniform rules to specific cases. For instance, penalties for the infraction of traffic regulations are the same throughout the Federal Republic, whereas they vary from state to state and city to city in the United States.

As in the United States, an individual or organization indicted for violating the legal order is assumed to be innocent until proven guilty in court. In other respects, however, legal procedures are rather different and do not rest on common law traditions. A person arrested for violating the criminal code and bound over for trial by an examining magistrate may be incarcerated for months if the official believes that the accused might interfere with the pretrial investigation by the state's prosecuting attorney. Both judges and prosecutors are legally bound by their offices to ascertain the facts in the case objectively in pretrial as well as trial proceedings. In court they jointly examine witnesses and exhibits to ascertain whether the criminal code has indeed been violated as charged. The counsel for the defense is not, however, a public official but a private attorney. It is his task to show that the evidence does not warrant a conviction, or that the specific section of the criminal code under which the accused is tried does not apply in this case.

The pyramid of the administrative court system consists of chambers staffed jointly by professional and lay judges and is capped by the Federal Administrative Court (*Bundesverwaltungsgericht*). As elsewhere in Europe, these courts allow an

---

[4] The single exception is the Federal Constitutional Court whose individual concurring and dissenting opinions have been published since December 1970.

individual to seek redress from the state for alleged injuries caused by the administrative actions of its official representatives. Their justices are supposed to decide whether a government agency or one of its officials conformed with proper administrative procedures in the performance of their legal responsibilities in such cases. The issue to be adjudicated may be whether a policeman had the formal right to make an arrest, or whether a teacher followed correct procedures in meting out punishment to an unruly pupil. A businessman may claim that he suffered damages through the error of a postal clerk and a worker that an injury sustained on his job was caused by the inadequate enforcement of governmental safety regulations.

The administrative court system also allows government agencies and officials to appeal the decisions of superior authorities on the grounds that these violated administrative regulations. And in cases that do not involve constitutional issues, the Federal Administrative Court may rule on disputes between state governments, between federal and state executive organs, and among various administrative agencies.

Other segments of the judiciary deal with specialized issues of public and private law. Industrial disputes, for instance, are dealt with by federal labor courts, usually composed of an equal number of employer and employee representatives plus a professional specialist. Or, to take another example, disputes over unemployment benefits, social security payments, and workmen's compensation claims fall under the jurisdiction of the system of federal social courts.

The Federal Constitutional Court (*Bundesverfassungsgericht*) is modelled after the American Supreme Court but deals exclusively with constitutional issues. The sixteen judges of its two chambers are bound only by the Basic Law and may, on appeal, set aside the verdict of any other court — including the constitutional courts of the states — if they find it to conflict with the spirit or the letter of the Basic Law. The court has original jurisdiction in the constitutional disputes between the Federal Government and state governments, between the federal executive and parliament, between different states, and between other courts. It may also consider — and reject —

complaints by individuals and organizations who claim that their constitutional rights have been violated by public authorities and that they have no other recourse for redress. And, it may outlaw organizations and practices deemed to be inconsistent with the constitutional order and the duties of responsible citizenship.

ORGANIZATIONAL FORMS AND POLITICAL DYNAMICS

The formal patterns of positions and relationships we have surveyed provide the general organizational setting for public policy processes in the Federal Republic. Particular actors, issues, and events provide the more dynamic ingredients of political life. As we noted at the beginning of this chapter, and as we shall observe more closely in later chapters, contemporary political attitudes and actions need to be seen in terms of the profound influence of the formal arrangements and rules of the regime. For the participating actors, constitutional principles structure as well as legitimate the interplay between shifting electoral, interest group, and leadership alignments. Above all, party government, the outstanding feature of present-day politics in the Federal Republic, is both sanctioned and restricted by the principles of the Basic Law.

CHAPTER III

The Policy Environment

THE CONSTITUTIONAL PRINCIPLES of the Basic Law differentiate between state and society, public and private matters, and domestic and foreign affairs. Such formal distinctions are of basic importance for the legal regulation of West German politics, but they also tend to obscure the dynamic interaction between policy processes and policy context. Some observers consider them merely traditional vestiges of earlier versions of the Rechtstaat that have little or no real significance today. According to a prominent West German political scientist, everything now touches on or is touched by government and practically all aspects of life but the weather are therefore politically relevant.[1] If we tried to carry analysis too far, it would be easy to obliterate any meaningful distinction between the organization and operation of the political system and its policy environment. Therefore, to obtain a clear understanding of contextual conditions and relationships a more differentiated approach is advisable.

A POLYCENTRIC URBAN SETTING

The Federal Republic is one of the most densely settled and urban among the larger world powers.[2] In area it is only the

[1] Christian Graf von Krakow, "Mehr Demokratie — weniger Freiheit?" *Die Zeit,* March 2, 1973. If everybody talks about the weather but nobody does anything about it, as Mark Twain observed, it is because the weather is as yet uncontrollable. Should it become controllable, as it may in the not too distant future, weather regulations will no doubt become another issue in domestic and international politics.

[2] The data in this chapter are derived and calculated from too many sources to be cited in extensive footnotes. Principal sources include the

Table III.1.   *Major Countries: Area and Population*

Country	Area (in 1,000 sq. km.)	1973 Population (in millions)	Population density (per sq. km.)	Projected population 1980 (in millions)
G.F.R.[a]	248	62.0	249	63.0
France	547	52.2	95	55.3
U.K.	244	55.9	229	59.5
Italy	301	54.9	182	57.9
Japan	370	108.4	293	116.3
U.S.	9,363	210.4	22	235.2
U.S.S.R.	22,402	248.0[b]	11[b]	270.6
China	9,561	798.9	84	911.3
India	3,045	563.5[b]	172[b]	717.4

[a] Incl. West Berlin.

[b] 1972 data.

Source: *Statistisches Jahrbuch für die Bundesrepublik Deutschland*, 1974, pp. 24*-26*, p. 31*.

size of Oregon — about the same as Britain but smaller than France — but the country ranks tenth in the world and first in Europe in population (see Table III.1).

Unlike Britain, France, and Japan, the Federal Republic has no single center for its political, socioeconomic, and cultural affairs. These activities are dispersed among the major metropolitan clusters. About twenty-four clusters extend from the Hamburg area on the North Sea to the Munich area near the foothills of the Alps (see Figure III.1). Bonn, the federal capital, is the seat of the central government and parliament and focus of foreign relations. However, other key federal agencies — such as the central bank and the top federal courts — are located in other cities. Most of the public administra-

---

following: *Statistisches Jahrbuch für die Bundersrepublik Deutschland 1975, Bulletin der Bundesregierung* (1960–76), *Bericht der Bundesregierung und Materialen zur Lage der Nation, 1971, Basic Statistics of the European Community 1972,* and various opinion polls and statistical data reported by *Inter Nationes, Die Zeit, The German Tribune, Der Spiegel,* and various other newspapers, periodicals, and books in German. For further references see Contemporary Society, Economy, and Culture in the Suggestions for Further Reading at the end of this book.

Figure III.1. *States and Major Urban Centers*

tion and, to a considerable extent, domestic policymaking are regionally dispersed among the capital cities of the ten states of the Federal Republic. Nongovernmental activities are also directed from centers scattered throughout the country. For instance, the headquarters for the great industrial and commercial empires, and for the principal media of mass communication, are not in Bonn but in Frankfurt, Hamburg, Munich, Cologne, and other cities.

These polycentric and regional patterns support the geographic division of formal governmental authority, particularly in domestic politics. At the same time, however, the relative smallness of the Federal Republic and the excellence of its communications facilitate the operation of countrywide networks of formal and informal relationships, especially among leaders in various sectors of public life.

The geographic distribution and mobility of the population accentuates the political significance of interregional and rural-urban distinctions in the Federal Republic. In 1972, two-thirds of the people lived in just three of its component states and in communities with more than 5000 inhabitants (Table III.2). Over the preceding decade the population of the southern regions had increased disproportionately, that of medium size cities and towns by as much as 40 percent, whereas rural areas registered a continuing population loss. Demographic projections indicate more of the same in years to come. By current estimates, three-fourths of the population will be urbanized in 1985, and a much larger proportion than now will reside in the southern parts of the Federal Republic. If so, geographic political alignments identified with policy concerns of urban and suburban areas and with regional interests in the southern states may very well assume increasing importance.

By and large, geographic mobility has not so much been interregional as intraregional. People who move tend to remain in the general area.[3] Although about 30 million persons

[3] For some interesting comparative survey data on this matter see the report of a study sponsored by the Commission of the European Community on *L'Opinion des Europeens sur les Aspects Regionaux et Agricoles du Marché Commun* (Brussels, December 1971).

Table III.2.   *The States of the Federal Republic:*
                Area and Population in 1974[a]

	Percentage of total area	Population density (per sq. km.)	Percentage of total population	Percentage of change in population size 1961–74
Federal Republic	100[b]	260	100[c]	+10.0
Northern States				
Schleswig-Holstein	6.3	159	4.3	+11.5
Hamburg	0.2	2,571	2.9	– 4.9
Bremen	0.1	1,750	1.2	+ 3.0
Lower Saxony	17.2	149	12.1	+ 9.4
Central States				
No. Rhine-Westphalia	13.6	496	28.7	+ 8.4
Hesse	8.5	255	9.3	+16.0
Saar	1.0	423	1.8	+ 3.3
Rhineland-Palatinate	7.9	184	6.1	+ 8.2
Southern States				
Baden-Württemberg	14.4	248	15.4	+19.1
Bavaria	28.4	148	18.1	+14.0

[a]Not including West Berlin.
[b]248,000 km^2.
[c]60.0 million.
Source: *Statistisches Jahrbuch für die Bundesrepublik Deutschland*, 1975, pp. 49–50.

— one for every two inhabitants of the Federal Republic — changed their places of residence between 1961 and 1972, most of these evidently did not go very far. Any regional political orientations and attachments were most likely not affected by these moves.

Generational differences in geographic mobility are of some importance in contemporary German politics. The older and generally more conservative generations are likely to stay put, whereas the younger generations tend to be on the move. According to a 1972 survey, young adults without children have been going to the big cities to further their educational or occupational objectives, or to join a spouse. Young families with children, on the other hand, are leaving inner-city apartments for larger suburban homes. Older people are more firmly rooted and prefer to remain in small towns and rural villages.

Geographic mobility has thus widened the gap not only between the sizes of urban and rural population, but has caused a greater imbalance in their age structure. In the villages and provincial towns of the more sparsely settled and economically stagnant areas — such as the northeast corner of Bavaria — one sees comparatively few young persons and a disproportionate number close to, or past the age of retirement. The style of life there is on the whole more tranquil and unchanging than in the urban clusters, social relationships are more intimate, and traditional cultural and political values are more deeply entrenched. Foreign tourists may be enchanted by the gabled houses and crooked streets of the "old" Germany, and pensioners find such communities restful havens from the hectic pace of city life; but the younger generations consider them rather dull. They prefer to live in a less parochial urban environment.

In the urban centers one may pass from one municipality to another, even across state boundaries, without ever leaving built-up areas. Here pastoral scenes exist only in pictures on museum walls. And here, too, one encounters the conditions that have pushed urban problems to the forefront in domestic politics.

These problems are to a considerable extent the fruits of a vast, but poorly coordinated reconstruction process after World War II. Practically every city and factory town had suffered immense damage, and a severe housing shortage was further aggravated by an influx of some 12 million refugees from Eastern Germany and Eastern Europe. Industrial and home construction could not wait for the development of comprehensive urban and regional planning programs; buildings were erected in a hurry wherever there was space. Zoning laws were either weak or nonexistent and generous governmental tax incentives and subsidies encouraged speculators to take advantage of the availability of cheap real estate. Thousands of profitable new office and factory buildings went up in and around the cities and some 12 million new homes were built under public and private auspices within 25 years — one for every five inhabitants of the Federal Republic.

The result has been a radical transformation of the urban landscape over a fairly brief period. In the inner cities luxury apartments, parking garages, and department stores now occupy the sites of former parks and residential buildings. Further out, huge industrial and housing developments have replaced peripheral greenbelts and farm lands, and once remote towns and villages have become sprawling suburban bedroom communities. Streets and highways are choked with the cars of commuting office and factory workers and trucks thundering through by day and night. Industrial waste pollutes the air and waters, and noisy factories add to the roar of the cities.

Urban migration and expansion have proven to be a mixed blessing. On the one hand, persons who did not even have homes after World War II or lived in dank city tenements and antiquated farmhouses are now a lot more comfortable. By and large, urban homes are neat and modern and equipped with all sorts of conveniences; the sordid city slums one still finds in many other industrial societies do not exist in the Federal Republic. On the other hand, urban renewal has evidently aggravated rather than alleviated some of the familiar problems of cities and suburbs in technologically advanced societies. To judge by the evidence of opinion polls, the public concern with such problems is on the increase. As long as urban noise, congestion, pollution, and the like seemed to be unavoidable by-products of a *quantitative* increase in homes, jobs, and private cars for them, people apparently felt they had to be tolerated. Lately, however, proposals for governmental measures that will improve the *quality* of urban life have gained wide support — in part, no doubt, just because reconstruction was so successful.

These patterns of polycentrism and geographic mobility have had a marked effect on political orientations in the Federal Republic. But most of the geographic influence on political processes is affected by occupational distinctions. Self-employed farmers, artisans, and shopkeepers generally live in rural areas; industrial and service workers in urban ones. Except in small towns and villages and a few of the states, notably Bavaria, traditional local and regional loyalties appear to have greatly weakened. In the urban clusters policy-relevant relationships revolve largely around work groups and small family units, rather than around any particular geographic component of society. Apart from matters directly relating to their place of work and their families (transport and educational facilities, for example) urban residents take little interest in civic affairs at the grassroots level. Most of them do not feel particularly attached either to the community where they live or work, or to their often temporary neighbors. Well-established neighborhood action groups do not thrive in the socioeconomically amorphous urban residential areas and suburban housing developments.

POLITICAL ECONOMY

The Federal Republic is today one of the world's leading economic powers. It ranks fourth among the top industrial states and second only to the United States in per capita income and volume of foreign trade. A strong demand for its industrial exports and extensive foreign investments have given the country a key position in international economic relations, and the Deutsche Mark has been a favorite currency in international financial transactions. These circumstances have, particularly in recent years, conditioned foreign policy in the Federal Republic as well as the policies of other states toward that country.

Technological developments and changes in the patterns of production and consumption are producing shifts in the economy that are increasingly significant in politics. Industrial production is still the most important economic sector, especially the manufacture of steel and steel products, chemical goods, and electrotechnical products (see Table III.3). The share of the private and public service sector has, however, been rapidly growing and that of the agricultural sector declining. Although agricultural production tripled in volume between 1950 and 1971, its contribution to total economic output dropped at the same time from 10 to 3 percent. As with the related patterns of urbanization, these trends are having

Table III.3. *Economic Profile of Major Non-Communist Industrial Countries*

	G.F.R.	U.K.	France	Japan	U.S.
Gross domestic product, 1973 (in billions of dollars)	$ 276.1	$ 137.9	$ 199.8	$ 331.7	$1,038.0
Per capita income, 1973 (in market prices)	$5,040	$2,503[a]	$3,403[a]	$3,292	$5,554
Output by economic sector, 1972[b]					
Agriculture[c]	3.1	2.2	6.3	5.4	3.0
Industry[d]	52.5	41.6	47.1	40.6	33.0
Services[e]	45.6	56.2	50.3	51.8	63.6

[a]1972 data.
[b]Data in rounded off percentages.
[c]Includes forestry, hunting, and fishing.
[d]Includes mining, manufacturing, and construction.
[e]Includes trade, finance, transport, and utilities.
Source: *Basic Statistics of the European Community*, 1973-74, pp. 22, 25. *United Nations Statistical Yearbook*, 1974, pp. 644-49.

a decided effect on sociocultural factors that enter into politics, and on the scope and nature of governmental policies in the Federal Republic.

As in other non-Communist industrial countries, the economy is a mixed one dominated by big private and public enterprises. The private sector takes in a larger proportion of key economic enterprises than in Britain, France, and Italy, but a smaller one than in the United States and Japan. Most farms, banks, industrial firms, and commercial concerns are owned by private individuals and corporations. Some of the largest industrial establishments in the Federal Republic are however state controlled. More importantly, practically all public utilities, employment agencies, and other key economic services are government operated.

This combination is in line with patterns going back a century or more that were formally reaffirmed by the Basic Law. The present mix is, however, not immutable under the constitution. The right to private wealth and its uses for personal gain in a competitive market economy are safeguarded only as they do not conflict with the general welfare. In fact, the constitution provides for the expropriation of private property in the public interest.[4] In the last analysis overall coordinative and regulatory control of the economy is the constitutional responsibility of the agencies of the West German state and its officials.

How the balance between private enterprise and public control has been struck, and to what effect, has been due to economic as much as political factors. On the whole the trend has been toward extending governmental control and tightening the interdependent relationship between the private and public sectors. These developments have posed new issues about the role of big business on the one hand and big government on the other in the formulation and implementation of domestic and foreign economic policies.

German big business has adapted to and survived several drastic changes in the political order — including the rise and fall of the Nazi regime — and it played a major role in the economic reconstruction after World War II. Rapid recovery was the order of the day and was associated by dominant policymakers with free enterprise capitalism rather than with state ownership of the means of production and government planning. Under the leadership of Chancellor Konrad Adenauer (1949–63), and with the active support of various American governments, political means were employed for economic ends in the belief that the new state and regime had to rest on solid material foundations. Large concerns were not expropriated, as in the German Democratic Republic, nor were key economic enterprises transferred to public ownership, as in Britain, France, and Italy. They were, on the contrary, encouraged to expand by governmental policies that promised large profits to venturesome businessmen and committed the resources of the state to the support of private trade and industry. Mass unemployment, swollen by the influx of millions of refugees, provided an abundant supply of cheap labor, and

---

[4] Article 14 guarantees the right to private property, but Article 15 permits land, natural resources, and the means of production to be transferred to public ownership.

vast American financial assistance provided investment capital. What had been an impoverished, war-devastated country staged a very rapid recovery in what came to be known as the spectacular "German Economic Miracle" of the 1950s.[5] Most significantly, much of the credit for the feat was given both at home and abroad to the drive and initiative of West German private enterprise.

The fact that the present regime got its start during an explosion of collective and individual prosperity in this manner had a lasting effect on policy-relevant attitudes and relationships. For most West Germans, the new political order became identified with a thriving capitalist economy that might be tempered, but not too much tampered-with, by governmental policymakers. Higher incomes, full employment, and abundant surplus resources for the mass consumption of goods and services were linked to the expansion of domestic production and foreign trade. And here close cooperation among governmental agencies, big business, and trade unions was thought to be of critical importance. The structural switches had been thrown and policy choices locked into courses of action that promised to keep the capitalist economic train on track at maximum safe speed.

On the whole, the people of the Federal Republic have come to enjoy one of the highest standards of living in the world. They may eat more starches than Americans, but they are for that not less well fed; overnourishment has in fact become a major health problem. In 1973, 67 percent of all families owned a car, 61 percent a washing machine, 77 percent a TV, 91 percent a refrigerator, and 89 percent a vacuum cleaner. There are no beggars in the streets; the unemployed and those unable to earn a living for reasons of health or age have received compensation incomes and services that have kept West Germans well above the official poverty level in most other countries.

West Germans expect their political leaders to sustain their

---

[5] Between 1950 and 1961, the gross national product of goods and services expanded by 123 percent, industrial production by 162 percent, and per capita income by 152 percent. The number of employed persons increased by a third between 1950 and 1963, and wages and salaries 115 percent between 1949 and 1964.

country's prosperity through appropriate domestic and foreign policies. Few question the desirability of further economic growth; for most it is the basis of greater personal affluence and collective economic power. Political leaders, for their part, are attuned to the intimate relationship between changes in economic conditions and changes in the political order and are correspondingly sensitive to developments at home and abroad that might threaten the material foundations of the prevailing regime.

Economic growth, stability, and security are thus generally considered necessary, though not altogether sufficient conditions for the smooth operation of the present political system. In foreign affairs such perspectives have pushed policy issues involving international trade and finance to the forefront. In domestic affairs the question has been how to sustain the momentum of economic expansion without overheating the engine, and how to balance investments in future growth with the satisfaction of pressing consumer demands for goods and services.

It is in this context that other political issues involving economic relations have developed, for instance, over ways to reconcile greater economic democracy with free enterprise capitalism, the gains of technological advancements with their ecological and human costs, and military security considerations with the expansion of foreign trade. And it is in this context, too, that political differences over proper distribution and redistribution of the fruits of economic growth have arisen among voters, parties, interest groups, and governmental policymakers. How should available resources be allocated among different geographic regions and socioeconomic sectors? And should they be primarily devoted to improving present conditions, through larger public welfare services for example? Or should more emphasis be placed on long-range projects, such as educational reforms and scientific research? And last, but not least, to what extent should economic policy be directed toward social ends, such as a more equitable distribution of goods and services and changes in general lifestyles? It is in matters of this sort that economic and sociocultural conditions merge in the policy setting for politics in the Federal Republic, as they do in the United States.

POLITICAL SOCIOLOGY

Interrelated and frequently overlapping social distinctions are of major importance in the political life of the Federal Republic. Continuity and change in the relative significance of different aspects of social relations are reflected in voting patterns, in the activities of parties and interest groups, in the kinds of policies that are demanded and supported, and in the policies that prevail at the governmental level.

Some of these distinctions are based on birth: sex, age, family background, nativity, and religion. Others are based on acquired characteristics: residence, occupation, income, and education. Some of them have come to carry less weight in politics, others have remained significant or become more important. Religious distinctions in particular, matter far less today than ten or twenty years ago.

Nominally the West German population is almost equally divided between Protestants and Roman Catholics. Under the prevailing laws most people are born into one or the other faith; it is marked on their birth certificates and, unless they legally opt out, they will pay a tax to their church for the rest of their lives. But except among a diminishing minority of devout citizens — predominantly elderly Roman Catholic women in rural areas — religious identification is no longer a major source of political cleavage. Organized religion continues to exercise considerable influence as a pressure group in some policy areas, especially on matters relating to public morals and the constitutional obligation of the state to safeguard the sanctity of marriage and the family. However, when it comes to partisan alignments and the selection of policymakers, religious distinctions are today clearly subordinate to secular differences such as occupation, income, or age.

Occupational Patterns. In the early years of the Federal Republic it seemed for a time that profound changes in the political order were accompanied by equally basic changes in the social order. Widespread poverty and general social dislocation in the wake of World War II suggested that far more social and political equality would now prevail. Former members of the upper strata were reduced in social status and former members of the lower strata elevated. An American sociologist found social mobility to be very high in the mid-1950s and a German colleague saw "a relative[ly] equal and uniform social class" emerging from a "far advanced breakdown of social distinctions." [6] In the view of 72 percent of the respondents in a 1958 opinion poll, a capable child of poor parents no longer faced serious obstacles to social advancement. A poll of young West German adults taken fifteen years later presented a very different picture: 72 percent of the respondents now thought that an individual's future station in life was virtually determined by his parents' occupation and his family background.

The leveling of social differences turned out to be not nearly as far-reaching as it had seemed in the early years. Economic recovery reestablished a distinct social hierarchy; what had been taken to be an almost revolutionary transformation of West German society proved to be a continuation of long-range evolutionary changes extending over different regimes. Technological developments have produced a high rate of both upward and downward occupational mobility for individuals over the last fifty years — about as much as in the United States — but for working people as a whole the chances for social advancement have not changed appreciably.[7]

Less than half of the people of the Federal Republic work for their living and most of the rest depend on those who do. As indicated in Table III.4, the general characteristics of the working population are much like those in other countries with a similar political and economic order. Two interconnected trends that have accompanied the evolution of the prevailing regime are of particular political significance — a

[6] See Morris Janowitz, "Social Stratification and Mobility in West Germany, "*American Journal of Sociology,* 64 (July 1958): 6–24 and Helmut Schelsky, "Elements of Social Stability" in *German Social Science Digest* (Hamburg: Claasens Verlag, 1955), p. 115.
[7] See G. Kleining, "Struktur-und Prestigemobilitaet in der BRD," *Koelner Zeitschrift fuer Soziologie und Sozialpsychologie* 23, no. 1 (March 1971).

Table III.4. *Profile of Working Population in*
Major Non-Communist Industrial Countries

	G.F.R.	U.K.	France	Japan	U.S.
Working population, 1971					
Percentage of total population	44	46	42	52	42
Percentage of male population	54	60	55	63	54
Percentage of female population	30	32	29	39	30
Distribution by economic sectors, 1972[a]					
Agricultural[b]	8	3	13	15	4
Industrial[c]	49	43	39	36	31
Service[d]	43	54	48	49	65
Unemployed	1	3	2	1	6

[a]Data in rounded off percentages.
[b]Includes forestry, hunting, and fishing.
[c]Includes mining, manufacturing, and construction.
[d]Includes trade, finance, transport, and utilities.
Source: *Statistisches Jahrbuch für die Bundesrepublik Deutschland*, 1974, passim. *Basic Statistics of the European Community*, 1973-74, passim.

decline in family- and self-employment and a growth of employment in white-collar service occupations.

Between 1950 and 1971, the proportion of the working population engaged in agricultural production and related activities dropped from 22 to 8 percent, and employment in the service sector increased from 33 to 44 percent. Not only has the percentage of persons who derive their principal income from the operation of small farms been declining, but so has the proportion of self-employed businessmen and small family enterprises (see Table III.5). Moreover, the urban

Table III.5. *Shifts in Form of Employment in the Federal Republic*
(as percentage of total employed)

	1950	1974
Self-employed and assisting family workers	31.4	15.7
Wage earners	48.6	44.8
Salaried employees	15.8	31.4
Civil servants	4.2	8.1
Total	100.0	100.0

Source: *Die Zeit* (January 9, 1976), citing data from Federal Statistical Office.

migration of young people who prefer to work in blue-collar or, as numerous studies have shown, better yet, white-collar service jobs, indicates that many self-employed or family workers are older people whose children are unlikely to follow in their footsteps. And it is precisely these aging "petty bourgeois" who have traditionally constituted the mass of the politically most conservative groups in Germany. The growth of employment in private and public service occupations, especially in clerical and administrative jobs, has had a countervailing political effect. For it is particularly from younger people in these occupations that the proponents of government-directed change in West German society have received disproportionate support in recent years.

Forecasts indicate that manual employment in both agricultural and industrial production will further decline, but that employment will continue to grow in nonmanual service occupations. These trends are typical for a technologically advanced society and are largely attributable to increasing automation and the economic advantages of large-scale operations in a mass-consumption economy.

Income Patterns. As in the United States, personal incomes in the Federal Republic are derived primarily from employment, pensions, and profits. Most persons rely either directly or indirectly on wages and salaries to meet their living expenses; about 15 percent depend on pension payments; and only a small minority receives most of its income from investments in property and business ventures.

On the average, as we have seen, the people of the Federal Republic are today more prosperous than those in most other countries, and all income groups are appreciably better off than in the early years of the present regime. Income from employment increased by 147 percent between 1960 and 1970, and income from profits by 83 percent. In the past few years the average income of West Germans has grown more slowly, but it has more than kept up with rising prices.

Average income figures do not, however, tell the whole story; they tend to obscure the persistent *relative* deprivation of different income groups. Although everybody's income has gone up over the years, everybody has not benefited equally

Table III.6. *Distribution of After-Tax Income in*
Major Non-Communist Countries (in percentages)

	G.F.R. 1973	U.S. 1972	Japan 1969	U.K. 1973	France 1970
Share of richest 10 percent of households	30.3	26.6	27.2	23.5	30.4
Share of poorest 10 percent of households	2.8 ·	1.5	3.0	2.5	1.4
Share of middle income households	66.9	71.9	69.3	74.0	68.2
Total	100.0	100.0	100.0	100.0	100.0

Source: Malcolm Sawyer, "Income Distribution in OECD Countries" *OECD Occasional Studies*, July 1976, p. 14, Table 4.

from an expanding per capita income in the Federal Republic. In fact, inequalities in the distribution of personal wealth are about the same today as they were forty or more years ago, with a few having the most. In 1969–70 less than two percent of all households owned 31 percent of all the private wealth and 3 percent of all taxpayers 42 percent of all the taxable wealth.[8] And though the distribution of personal incomes after taxes has become somewhat more evenhanded, it favors the rich more than in other major non-Communist countries (see Table III.6).

In the view of radical critics of the present socioeconomic and political order these disparities testify to the social in-

[8] See Karl W. Deutsch, "The German Federal Republic," in Roy C. Macridis and Robert E. Ward (eds.), *Modern Political Systems: Europe,* 3d ed. (Englewood Cliffs, N.J.: Prentice-Hall, 1972), p. 372; and Kurt Sontheimer, *The Government and Politics of West Germany* (New York: Praeger, 1972), pp. 45–46. Although precise comparative data are not available, the figures we have indicate a similar constant distribution in the United States, but a decided shift in Britain. The richest 5 percent of Americans received 18 percent of all income in 1947 and 16 percent in 1972; the richest 20 percent received 43 percent in 1947 and 41 percent in 1972. In Britain, on the other hand, redistributive governmental policies reduced the share of the richest 1 percent from 12 percent of all income in 1939 to 4 percent in 1972, and the wealth of the richest 10 percent from 88 percent to 51 percent.

justices inherent in a capitalist economy. In the opinion of its more conservative supporters they merely reflect variations in monetary rewards for different levels of achievement in an open, competitive society.

In some respects, certainly, present conditions seem to offer considerable opportunities for getting ahead to those who will seize them. Traditional barriers to socioeconomic advancement are fewer and far less rigid than they once were in Germany and still are in many other countries. Religious discrimination in employment has pretty well disappeared and a title of nobility is no longer an "open sesame" to high positions. Still, significant inequalities remain in the structure of opportunities. Ambition alone is not enough to move a person from a lower to a higher level of income and social status; one also needs the necessary resources — skill, wealth, or better yet, both — and these are unequally distributed.

From the top to the bottom of the contemporary social pyramid we find a recurring theme: highly valued occupational skills will bring monetary and status rewards, and wealth will beget more wealth. Or, to put it another way, those who have more of what it takes get more of what is wanted. Persons who have large funds to invest in profitable real estate and business ventures earn more than individuals who depend primarily on wages, salaries, or pension payments. They are economically more secure in a time of rising prices and better able to see their children through a long period of educational training for the best jobs. And in a technologically advanced economy, persons who have much needed skills are paid more than those who do not, and individuals with investments in growth enterprises receive more than those who work in declining sectors of the economy. Industrial workers have fared better than small marginal farmers; skilled workers better than unskilled ones. Many wage earners in the Federal Republic today can afford a higher standard of living than general office workers or minor civil servants, and such highly trained professionals as doctors and airline pilots earn many times over the income of hospital workers and flight attendants.

Such disparities in the size, sources, and benefits of personal incomes are at the bottom of most current domestic political issues. According to its Basic Law, the Federal Republic is "a democratic and social" state. But just how this declaration should be interpreted and implemented, to what extent and in what manner public policy should assure everybody of a "fair share" of the monetary and nonmonetary fruits of national prosperity, divides political factions. Reduced to its essentials, the problem is to strike the right balance between political and economic democracy, and between technological progress and social justice.

The people who have profited the most from the present social order are quite naturally content to leave well enough alone. Conservative business leaders and their political allies point with pride to the Federal Republic's overall material accomplishments — particularly in drawing unfavorable comparisons with living conditions in the Communist German Democratic Republic. Their message to those further down in the socioeconomic hierarchy is that all of us Germans here are a lot better off than those over there.

At the opposite extreme are the proponents of radical change, especially younger social scientists who never knew the poverty of the postwar era. In their view, to compare conditions in the Federal Republic with those in earlier times and other countries is either irrelevant or pernicious. To them this begs a pressing policy question: How can we achieve substantially greater social equality here and now? The answer, they claim, is a drastic redistribution of economic power and benefits.

Most of the dominant political leaders now take a far more moderate, centrist position. They grant that more could be done to lessen socioeconomic inequities and they do not share the conservative view that the present form of West German capitalism is the best there is and can be. But they are not prepared to carry reforms to the point of changing basic societal and economic structures that would drastically alter the prevailing political order.

Educational Patterns. In the Federal Republic, as in the United States, political interest, social status, and earning power are closely related to schooling. A good education is virtually essential for the more prestigious and better-paying jobs. And the better educated a person, the more likely he or she is to feel capable of influencing the course of public policy, and to take part in politics.

The West German school system is generally less egalitarian than the American and also contains a much stronger built-in bias against late bloomers and culturally deprived children from lower social classes. From primary school to university, a process of competition and selection ostensibly based on objective criteria places even the brightest students from lower social strata at a distinct disadvantage. The parents of such students may work long hours and have neither the time nor the resources to help their children. Students from financially and educationally better endowed homes will probably get more encouragement at home; either parents or tutors are likely to help them with the demanding homework and prepare them for the stiff school examinations.

A child's future occupational career is ordinarily settled quite early under a rather unique "two-track" system. After four years of common primary schooling students are sorted out for one or another type of secondary education on the basis of past performance and apparent promise. Those judged capable enter a university-preparatory course at the gymnasium, the most prestigious and generously financed of the secondary schools. Less capable students are dispatched to prevocational secondary schools. Rigid barriers between the two secondary systems make it exceedingly difficult for a child to change from the vocational track to the academic, once he has been placed (see Figure III.2).

Secondary schooling is specifically designed to prepare students for sharply stratified socioeconomic positions in adult life. About three out of four secondary students end up on the vocational track and most of them attend the upper elementary school. This school is generally viewed as the place where the least educable can complete their formal education without too much effort. Most of these are likely to proceed through a poorly-paid apprenticeship and a once-a-week occupational school to become skilled manual workers, sales-

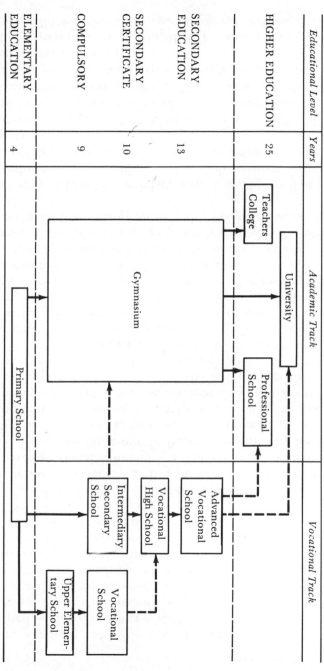

Figure III.2. *Organization of the Education System*

people, secretaries, and the like; the rest can expect to be employed as skilled or semi-skilled labor.

The remaining students on the vocational track are in the more prestigious intermediary secondary school leading to a secondary school certificate — not quite the equivalent of an American high school diploma. With this certificate, they may enter advanced vocational schools to become middle-range white-collar employees, such as social workers, nurses, and laboratory technicians.

One-fourth or so of the secondary students are on an academic track in a gymnasium. But not all will make it past the final *Arbitur* examination into a university or professional school. Many will flunk out or drop out voluntarily for lack of interest or money. Even those who are certified by the Arbitur can not count on automatic admission to an institution of higher learning because overcrowding in many of the popular fields has led to more restrictive admission policies.

Who, then, makes it to the top of the ladder — the institutions of higher learning? A relatively small, predominantly male minority that is willing and able to get the education needed for all the best white-collar jobs in the Federal Republic. Consider that in the 1970s, six out of ten university and professional school students were the children of white-collar employees — about half of them children of civil servants. On the other hand, only about one out of eight was the child of an industrial worker — compared with one of two in the United States. Only about a third of the students were women.

The wide availability of scholarship aid suggests that previous educational opportunity, rather than financial resources, is the major reason for the underrepresentation of the lower social strata.

Pressures for rapid and extensive changes in the educational system have made its reform one of the hottest policy issues in recent West German politics. The central questions are to what extent, for what purposes, and in what manner the system should be changed.

The conservatives maintain that no major changes are warranted because the structure and content of West German education uphold cherished cultural and social values. The proponents of change run a wide gamut but fall essentially into two groups. One advocates a more or less radical leveling of educational structures toward a more "humane," egalitarian, and democratic political system. The other is more concerned with raising the *quality* of West German education and advocates the introduction of curriculum reforms that will provide more scientific and technical expertise to deal with pressing problems in a period of dynamic technological change.

The most conspicuous changes in the educational system have thus far taken place at the elite level of higher education — resulting in more universities, more money, more students, and more "participatory democracy." In recent years, however, pressure has also mounted for changes in the vocational schools and apprenticeship programs. Students are no longer content to follow a preordained track into low-status occupations; they want a better education that will allow them to move upward into more socially esteemed jobs. In addition, the governmental policymakers are confronted by the challenge of more far-reaching equality that exists in the educational system of the Communist German Democratic Republic. Such pressures have led to more coordinated educational planning and control by the states and the Federal Government.[9]

The Status of Women. Equal rights for men and women is a cardinal principle of the constitutional order of the Federal Republic; according to the Basic Law "no one is to be prejudiced or favored because of his sex." Public policy has been directed toward the complete emancipation of women from their traditionally inferior position in German society. If men, nonetheless, seem to have more rights than women it is "not so much due to legal discrimination against women as to social prejudices," in the words of a 1972 report of the Federal Government.

[9] These factors were underscored in a 1971 report by an international committee of examiners to the Education Committee of the Organization for Economic Cooperation and Development, and by the 1970 Educational Report of the German Federal Government.

A vast number of laws have been passed to eradicate all sex discrimination in fact as well as form. Husbands no longer have the legal right to govern the family and control its property: wives no longer need their husbands' permission to take a job. Divorce settlements no longer favor the male, and sex discrimination in education and employment have been outlawed. Women are entitled to six weeks of paid vacation before and after childbirth and to more equitable opportunities for on-the-job training for the better jobs.

Social change has, however, lagged behind public policy and traditional patterns of sex discrimination are only slowly yielding to governmental pressures for change. West German men still embrace the time-honored notion that women belong in the home as mothers and housewives and do not need schooling for life-long occupational careers. To the great distress of West German feminists, women tend to accept these role assignments with varying degrees of enthusiasm or resignation. Important women's organizations — as in the United States — are virtually nonexistent, and women liberationists are looked on as oddities even by members of their own sex.

The lag between formal rules and actual practice is particularly notable in the status of employed women. Most of these come from and marry into lower social strata, are poorly educated, and hold jobs because they need the money. Women from more affluent homes are usually better educated and tend either not to take jobs at all or to quit them when they marry. Consequently, most women who work start as and remain unskilled and semi-skilled workers at the bottom of the occupational ladder — usually in blue-collar or clerical occupations requiring little or no vocational training. They usually have neither the incentive nor the training to compete on an equal basis with men.

In the 1970s, only one West German woman in ten had sufficient training to qualify for a better job, still fewer worked in middle-range supervisory and administrative positions, and only a very small minority were able to pursue a professional career in the upper level of the occupational hierarchy. Practically every top position in private and public employment remained, as in the past, a male preserve. Not many women held positions as judges or university professors, few were in the civil service, and women were not prominent in the upper echelons of West German corporations or in trade union leadership. Compared to the United States, West Germany had far fewer female lawyers and teachers; compared to Russia, far fewer women physicians and scientists.

Sex discrimination is less pronounced when it comes to equal pay for equal work — due in no small part to changes in public policy. In 1972, 48 percent of women doing the same work as men also received the same pay, whereas in Italy it was only 6 percent, 13 percent in Belgium, and 23 percent in the Netherlands. The fact that women's earnings have on the average not kept pace with overall increases in wages and salaries (see Table III.7) is thus largely due to the pronounced underrepresentation of women in higher-paying jobs.

Table III.7. *Shifts in Distribution of Income from Employment by Sex (in Deutsche Marks)*

			Net monthly income in DM				
	Under 800		*800–1199*		*1200–1800*		*Over 1800*	
	Men	*Women*	*Men*	*Women*	*Men*	*Women*	*Men*	*Women*
1964	62%	90%	31%	9%	5%	1%	2%	—
1972	19%	70%	46%	22%	24%	6%	11%	2%

Source: *Statistisches Jahrbuch für die Bundesrepublik Deutschland,* 1974, p. 143.

What is of more immediate political significance is that sex distinctions have gradually become less important in electoral behavior. Thus, the vote of women has not reflected greater pressures for equality. Still, it may in time lend more support to feminist demands if present socioeconomic disparities persist. West German politicians are certainly sensitive to this possibility, but are evidently not particularly troubled by it. However, many, if not most, politicians consider all sex discrimination morally indefensible and socially untenable in a truly democratic society.

The Alien Underclass. Some 2 million foreign workers —
along with their dependents — have stirred a good deal of
public controversy in the Federal Republic. The economies of
a number of other advanced industrial countries in Western
Europe — notably France, Belgium, and Switzerland — also
have come to depend on foreign labor from less developed
Mediterranean countries. Social rifts between natives and
aliens, however, are particularly pronounced in West Germany. Too many migrants have come from too many countries
in too short a time to a state that has yet to develop a distinct
national identity. Unprecedented unemployment in the mid-
1970s accentuated this issue.

Expansionist economic policies led to a shortage of native
workers in the 1960s — particularly in labor-extensive enterprises where labor-saving technological changes were not
feasible. For every person seeking a job, there were on the
average four or five vacancies, most of them in menial occupations shunned by West Germans. The policy response
to this problem was the importation of "guest workers" — an
official euphemism designed to avoid unpleasant associations
with the slave laborers brought in by the Nazis from captive
countries. By 1972, foreign workers comprised 11 percent of
the labor force — a tenfold increase in a decade. Key export
industries, such as automobile production, came to depend on
them for unskilled and semi-skilled labor. In many cities
foreigners provided most menial services, such as collecting
garbage and burying the dead.

Economically, this arrangement proved for some years to
be mutually beneficial. Foreign workers could earn much
higher wages in West Germany than in their native countries.
In addition, they were eligible to receive unemployment compensation and other welfare benefits. At the same time they
contributed to the economic well-being of the West Germans.
Their tax payments and those of employers drawing profits
from their labor provided money for public expenditure.
Their contributions to the social security system subsidized
West German pension and welfare benefits.

What was an economically beneficial arrangement produced, however, less desirable social consequences. Foreign

workers and their families — for the most part Turks, Yugo-slavs, Greeks, Spaniards, and Italians — have become social out-casts at the bottom of the West German status hierarchy. Most of them speak little or no German, live in crowded "guest workers' ghettos," pay exorbitant rents for dilapidated hous-ing, and are limited to social contacts with their own kind. Moreover, since they do not enjoy the same political rights as West Germans, they have little or no say about policies affect-ing their future.

Particularly in cities with large concentrations of "guest workers" (as many as one out of five employees in highly in-dustrialized areas), their local hosts tend to view them as extra burdens on already overtaxed public services. Many West Germans also dislike their alien ways and believe that they are more prone to steal and murder than West Germans.

As social relations between natives and aliens have gone from bad to worse, West German policymakers have felt in-creasing pressure to resolve the problem. The situation was further aggravated by an economic downturn in the mid-1970s. As the rate of unemployment among West Germans increased, foreign workers were considered competition for fewer jobs. Consequently, pressure on government leaders to halt or even reverse the inflow of foreign workers became even more pronounced. But how could this be achieved?

Every proposal to deal with the matter has encountered telling counterarguments. For instance, the suggestion that only foreign workers without dependents be admitted, as in Switzerland, has encountered the argument that this would only make their social integration more difficult. A proposal for a wider dispersion of the alien population in order to re-duce social tension has been resisted by employers of foreign workers who would have to relocate their operations.

Initial attempts to limit the number of aliens entering the country failed to stem the tide. During the recession of the mid-1970s, the Federal Government banned the further re-cruitment of foreign workers. But many unemployed aliens remained. The question was still whether they should and could be encouraged to go home. Many evidently felt at home in West Germany and would like to remain there indefinitely.

Residence visas for foreign workers are usually granted for only one year. But they are often extended. If aliens stay for five years they can apply for permanent visas; if they stay for ten, they may petition for naturalization. Public authorities have not encouraged foreign workers to overstay their welcome, but have avoided forced expulsion and offer no financial enticements to hasten their departure.

What can and might be done is not, moreover, simply a domestic issue; foreign workers involve foreign relations. For example, the Federal Republic can not legally block the entry of workers from members of the European Community, now notably Italy, and, prospectively, Spain and Greece. An agreement with Turkey actually promotes the inflow of workers from that country. External factors limit policy choices on this as on many other issues in West German politics.

THE EXTERNAL SETTING

Foreign relations intrude on domestic politics in every country in this age of electronic warfare, interlocking national economies, and global mass communications. But in few, if any, major industrial states are internal and external affairs as closely enmeshed as in the Federal Republic. Here governmental and nongovernmental relations with other states, with supranational organizations, and with multinational corporations cast a tightly woven net over policy processes. Its strands extend down to local politics and far beyond the borders of the Federal Republic to remote areas of the world that trade with West Germany.

British and Japanese politics reflect centuries of insular isolation, whereas West German politics show an intensive involvement in the wars, commerce, and cultural exchanges of continental Europe over the last 2000 years. In France a traditional sense of national exclusiveness still colors domestic and foreign policy processes, but policy in the Federal Republic is much more a product of changing international conditions. And although the size and resources of the United States have provided Americans with a sense of military security and economic independence, West Germans closely identify their welfare with external circumstances largely beyond the control of their own policymakers.

The Maintenance of Peace. Peace in Central Europe has been a primary and undisputed principle of West German policy that transcends constitutional and treaty limitations on the use of force by the Federal Republic. Memories of past wars and destruction and fears of future cataclysms have deprived West Germans of any taste for military ventures and for leaders who might involve them in such. They neither possess nor seek nuclear arms to deter or repel an attack, knowing that a few such weapons could wipe out their population. Yet they are also keenly aware that here their leaders have had to adapt to international developments.

The two Germanies have been focal points in the shifting patterns of East-West and, above all, Soviet-American relations. Nowhere else have the two superpowers confronted each other as immediately and continuously over the last three decades, and nowhere else has there been as massive a concentration of awesome military power at the command of foreign governments. The Federal Republic has come to be the keystone of the American-dominated NATO alliance and the German Democratic Republic that of the Soviet-controlled Warsaw Pact. The leaders of both superpowers have considered their countries' defense and political interests bound up with the military security of their respective German allies.

Most West Germans want the protection afforded by the Western military alliance, but they do not want to risk involvement in war. Time and again an anxious public has dreaded that a clash between the superpowers in this or some other part of the world might suddenly unleash the forces of its destruction. The question of what might be done to reduce the risk has provoked a good deal of controversy. Some groups favor an international arms control agreement that would lead to the gradual withdrawal of all foreign forces and weapons from Central Europe. Others maintain that American forces in the Federal Republic provide an essential guarantee against Soviet aggression or nuclear blackmail. A small neutralist minority — particularly on the extreme left of the political spectrum — asserts that the notion of a Soviet threat is a myth designed to uphold the power of American and West German ruling groups in the Federal Republic.

Over the years, varying perceptions of West German security needs have conditioned the course and tenor of these domestic controversies and the reactions of the mass public. The greater the fear of a Soviet attack, the greater too have been the feelings of military weakness and dependency on American protection. Conversely, the greater the sense of security from war and aggression, the greater has been the ready willingness to support disarmament proposals. But, in the last analysis, peace and security for the Federal Republic are generally believed to rest first on the maintenance of a worldwide balance of terror between the superpowers, and second on a Soviet-American understanding to preserve stability in Central Europe.

In this context, West German policymakers have had few options and little maneuverability. Their opportunities for pursuing an independent course of action have been particularly restricted in periods of high tension in East-West relations and greater in times of lowered tension.

A climate of high tension prevailed during the early years of the Federal Republic in the era of the Cold War. The failure of the United States and the Soviet Union to find a mutually acceptable solution to the "German Problem" and increasing friction between them in other parts of the world led to the rearmament of their two hostile German client states. American demands for a German military contribution to the "defense of the West" overrode the objections of a substantial minority in West Germany; the Federal Republic was locked into the NATO alliance; and German reunification became, in effect, a dead issue. West German troops joined those of their new allies in guarding the eastern frontier against the troops of the Soviet Union and its German cohorts. West German governments embraced the prevailing American hard line against concessions to the Soviet Union and so did most West German voters. As it happened, every federal election from 1949 until 1965 was preceded by a Cold War crisis and a majority of the electorate responded by supporting the ticket they believed to be most acceptable to the United States.

The easing of East-West tensions from the mid-1960s onward allowed a new set of West German policymakers to seek an accommodation with the Communist states of Eastern

Europe. As a first step they met Soviet demands for the Federal Republic's adherence to the nuclear test ban and nuclear nonproliferation treaties, which reaffirmed West Germany's status as a minor military power. This step opened the way for a series of treaties in the early 1970s that "normalized" relations with Russia and its allies. With these agreements, the West German leaders formally accepted the political order and territorial arrangements that had emerged in Central Europe in the wake of World War II, above all the division of Germany and the incorporation of its former territories into Poland. Public opinion turned with the tide. Opponents of the new "Eastern Policy" were overwhelmed in the federal election of 1972 and its proponents given a strong endorsement.

Whether these developments reflected only a temporary easing of East-West tension or initiated more enduring patterns in the external environment for West German politics only time will tell. Present indications are that the late 1960s mark a watershed between two eras and that for the foreseeable future policy issues will focus more on international economic relations and less on defense problems. If so, the economic strength of the Federal Republic may very well become more important than its military weakness and its diplomatic activities and trade ties more than its alliance ties.

The Need for Trade. The Federal Republic's leading position in world trade is a measure of its economic strength as well as its economic vulnerability. West Germany plays a key role in international commerce and finance, but it is also highly susceptible to external political and economic developments that might undercut its vital trade ties.

The Federal Republic ranks second only to the United States in exports and imports (see Table III.8). Exports represent only a small share of the American gross national product, but they constitute about a fifth of West Germany's. Moreover, for West Germany — as for Japan and the United Kingdom — the need and competition for the sale of industrial goods in foreign markets is far more important than for the United States. Whereas a large part of American exports is

Table III.8.   *Comparison of Major Trading Countries*

	U.S.	*G.F.R.*	*Japan*	*France*	*U.K.*	*Total*
Exports as percentage of GNP (1971)	4	19	11	13	16	—
Percentage of world exports (1973)	13	12	7	7	6	45
Percentage of world imports (1973)	12	10	7	6	7	42

Source: *Basic Statistics of the European Community*, 1972, p. 77. *Statistisches Jahrbuch für die Bundesrepublik Deutschland*, 1974, p. 72*.

made up of agricultural products, those of the Federal Republic consist almost entirely of industrial and capital exports. In 1972, for example, 42 percent of West German automobiles, 32 percent of chemical products, and 28 percent of steel products went abroad.

Imports are also far more crucial in the West German than in the American economy. Key industries in general and export industries in particular require basic foreign raw materials, such as copper and iron. In contrast to France, the Federal Republic has become increasingly dependent on agricultural imports; in contrast to Britain, it has no natural gas and oil resources that might diminish its reliance on foreign energy supplies; and in contrast to Japan, it has imported a substantial amount of foreign labor as we noted. For other industrialized countries and less developed nations West Germany has become a leading customer for semi-finished products and many consumer goods, such as cars, home appliances, and clothing. Foreign investments have continued to pour into the West German economy, mostly from other European countries and the United States, but also of late from oil-rich states. Iran is now a major stockholder in the Krupp industrial empire and Kuwait in the Mercedes Benz corporation.

Foreign trade is both an objective and an instrument of West German public policies. In international relations it concerns not merely questions posed by economic cooperation and competition with other states but diplomatic and military problems. In domestic politics, both specific interest group demands and more general ideological and socioeconomic cleavages are involved.

It is a generally accepted policy principle that West German economic strength, growth, and prosperity rest largely on favorable competitive conditions in world markets. The need for policies that will provide ready access to foreign customers and suppliers has been beyond dispute. All West German governments, whatever their partisan complexion, have sought to remove impediments to trade expansion. But what particular policies should be pursued to promote favorable trade conditions and obtain the best deal — and with whom and for whom — has occasionally engendered a good deal of political controversy. For example, some groups have favored international agreements that would bring in more and cheaper imports, whereas others have opposed them for fear that they would injure domestic producers. Political disputes have arisen over foreign policy priorities, especially when economic, military, and ideological objectives conflict. For example, should the need for intimate military ties with the United States override economic differences with that country? Should the Federal Republic make economic concessions to the Communist countries for the sake of improved diplomatic relations? And should West Germany put closer relations with the countries of Western Europe ahead of closer ties with the East German Democratic Republic?

The Federal Republic's most extensive and intensive trade ties are with its partners in the European Community (EC). The proportion of West German trade with the other five founding members of the Common Market increased vastly between 1962 and 1972, because of the abolition of internal custom barriers and the introduction of a common tariff on goods from outside countries, and because West Germans were cut off by the Cold War from former markets and suppliers in East Germany and Eastern Europe (see Table III.9). The result has been a high degree of economic integration. Common Market countries are today the most important customers and suppliers of the Federal Republic, but sales to and purchases from West Germany also have great economic significance for those countries (see Table III.10).

Table III.9.   *Direction of West German Trade (1960–73)*

Countries	Percentage of exports		Percentage of imports	
	1960	*1973*	*1960*	*1973*
EC countries[a]	29	46	29	51
United States	8	8	14	8
Other non-communist industrial	36	26	27	18
European communist[b]	4	6	4	4
G.D.R. (East Germany)	2	2	2	2
Other countries	21	12	24	17
Total	100	100	100	100

[a]European Community: in 1960, France, Italy, Belgium, Netherlands, Luxembourg; in 1973, also Great Britain, Ireland, and Denmark.

[b]U.S.S.R., Poland, Czechoslovakia, Romania, Hungary, Bulgaria.

Source: *Statistisches Jahrbuch für die Bundesrepublik Deutschland*, 1974, pp. 306–10.

Table III.10.   *The Federal Republic as a Seller and Buyer (1972)*

	Percentage of imports from G.F.R.	Percentage of exports to G.F.R.
World trade	11	9
European trade	14	12
EC trade	19	20
Netherlands	27	34
Belgium-Luxembourg	24	25
France	22	21
Italy	20	23
Other major trading partners		
Austria	42	22
Switzerland	30	15
Greece	21	22
Denmark	19	12
Norway	14	13

Source: *Statistisches Jahrbuch für die Bundesrepublik Deutschland*, 1974, p. 73*.

These interdependent ties have reinforced the effect of joint European Community policies on West German economic and political relations at home. For example, EC agricultural policies have catalyzed the decline in the number and political influence of West German farmers. West German policymakers, in turn, have sought wider and deeper EC ties. The government of the Federal Republic promoted and welcomed the inclusion of Britain, Denmark, and Ireland on the grounds that this would strengthen the viability and political potential of the Common Market. And it has pushed for closer collaboration among the member states in finding solutions to mutual economic problems, such as their relations with less developed countries and their differences with the United States and Japan on trade and monetary issues.

The changes in the external military and political environment that led in the early 1970s to improved diplomatic relations between West Germany and the Communist states of Eastern Europe also added a potentially significant economic element to that environment. In previous years the patterns of trade had conformed closely to prevailing East-West cleavages. Compared to the Federal Republic's extensive commercial relations with the United States and other Western industrial countries, trade with the Soviet Union and its East European allies was not very important (see Table III.9). More recently, however, West German policymakers have sought political as well as economic benefits for their country through more extensive and intensive trade relations with the Communist countries.

For their part, the Communist governments have been most ready to cooperate. West German industrial products and technical assistance are very much sought after in the Soviet Union and the rest of Eastern Europe. The Federal Republic has furnished the largest share of Western imports flowing into COMECON — the East European counterpart of the Common Market — including about a third of Soviet imports from non-Communist countries. Ideological differences have not stood in the way of such collaborative ventures with capitalist West German business firms as the construction of a pipeline that delivers natural gas from Russian oil fields to

the Federal Republic. Within five years after the signing of
the West German-Soviet agreement on August 12, 1970, bi-
lateral trade increased threefold.

Whether the liberalization of these trade relations and the
advance of substantial purchase credits to the East European
countries will pay off over the long run is a question that
divides West German leaders. Some predict substantial economic benefits in the form of profitable new export markets and sources of raw materials, whereas others question the
willingness and ability of the Communist countries to meet
West German trade needs. Some expect that more trade will
further improve political relations; others fear that it will
make the Federal Republic more vulnerable to Soviet pressure and undermine its bonds with Western countries. Depending on their outlook, political and opinion leaders are
therefore committed or opposed to more eastern trade,
whether as an objective or as an instrument of West German
foreign policy. What complicates the issue all the more is that
it is inseparable from the course of so-called intra-German relations (relations with the East German Democratic Republic).

The Problem of the Other Germany. The notion that someday, somehow, the former Reich might be reunified has been a
constant theme with many variations in West German politics.
The Basic Law calls on "the entire German people . . . to
achieve in free self-determination the unity and freedom of
Germany" and these words have been sung to different tunes
by different singers — sometimes loudly and sometimes softly.
By all present indications, reunification is, however, not even
a remote possibility.

It has been more than thirty years since the old Germany
was divided and almost as long since the creation of its two
successor states. Former political ties between East and West
Germany have been severed and each has developed new and
intimate bonds with other states. The Federal Republic has
become an integral part of the Western NATO alliance and
of the West European Community; the German Democratic
Republic has been tightly integrated into the East European
Communist bloc. The Democratic Republic is today a key

component of the Warsaw Pact military alliance as its forward bastion in Central Europe. It is, moreover, the second largest industrial power after the Soviet Union in the East European economic community and the leading source of industrial products for the other member states. The Soviet Union is East Germany's principal customer, and East German policies are shaped by Soviet policies.

In short, the German Democratic Republic is a cornerstone of the East European Communist system, and Soviet leaders have continually emphasized the necessity of a loyal East Germany for the cohesiveness of that system. The Western associates of the Federal Republic consider West Germany no less important to their side and have shown no enthusiasm for the re-creation of a state in Central Europe that would vastly exceed — in size, population, and economic strength — all but the two superpowers. Constitutional principles notwithstanding, West German policies toward East Germany are therefore restricted.

The Federal Republic's Basic Treaty of 1972 with the Democratic Republic was an important milestone in the relationship between the two Germanies. Over vehement protests from the opposition, the government of Chancellor Willy Brandt abandoned the claim of its predecessors that the Federal Republic was the only legitimate German state and formally recognized a regime that earlier West German governments had repudiated as an illegal instrument of Soviet control over East Germany. According to the Brandt government the agreement was a necessary step in its efforts to "normalize" relations with the East European Communist states and provided the basis for closer collaboration between the two Germanies after two decades of belligerent confrontation.

For the rulers of East Germany, the treaty brought the international acceptance they had long sought. Both Germanies were admitted as equals to the United Nations and the Democratic Republic was recognized as a sovereign state by countries that had previously refused to establish diplomatic relations with it in deference to West German wishes. Whether the treaty also provided a breakthrough from mutual hostility to peaceful coexistence between the two German states should become more apparent in the coming decades. In addition to the problems mentioned earlier, prevailing differences between East and West German policymakers pose major obstacles to closer collaboration.

To begin with, West and East German policymakers proceed from very different positions. When the two Germanies joined the United Nations in 1973, Chancellor Brandt emphasized the goal of reunification when he declared "My people live in two states but continue to think of themselves as one nation." But the East German spokesman asserted on the same occasion that "reunification between the German Democratic Republic and the Federal Republic will never be possible." The official West German position is that the Democratic Republic is not a foreign country with a German-speaking population, like Austria, but a part of one — though for the moment politically divided — country. Common historical experiences and cultural characteristics are asserted to be stronger than political rifts between the two regimes, and economic affinity greater than ideological differences. Accordingly, West German policy has emphasized closer cultural and trade associations in what are officially designated "intra-German" rather that international relations with the Democratic Republic.

East German leaders, to the contrary, maintain that theirs is a separate country whose people are first and foremost citizens of a "socialist" state rather than brethren under the political skin of the Germans in the Federal Republic. Accordingly, they consider the political and ideological differences preeminent and emphasize East Germany's ties to other European Communist states — above all the Soviet Union. From this point of view, cultural bonds between the two Germanies are overridden by acute and persistent differences.

The present East German leadership thus shares the view of those West Germans who believe that irreconcilable differences in their regimes will at best permit the two Germanies to live together but not to grow together. Hard-line Communists in the Democratic Republic, like militant anti-Communists in the Federal Republic, consider the very existence of the other political system a threat to their own and believe that German reunification will be possible only if one or the other is overthrown. Vigilance against such an event is the watchword on both sides of the border. Although the East German leadership has given overt and covert financial support to groups in the Federal Republic that want to introduce some if not all the elements of East German socialism, it has taken stringent measures against West German subversion of its own regime. In the face of West German efforts to increase private travel between the two states, the East German government has, for example, maintained severe restrictions on interpersonal contacts, in part to limit defections from the Democratic Republic and in part to keep West German agents out of the Democratic Republic. The border between the two states is heavily guarded on the East German side to prevent unauthorized crossings, and the importation and possession of illegal West German literature draws heavy penalties.

The most prominent symbol of the East German exclusion policy is the Berlin Wall, which divides the former capital of united Germany and cuts off East Berlin, the capital of the Democratic Republic, from West Berlin. The latter is closely linked to the Federal Republic by political and economic ties, but separated from it by 110 miles of East German territory. Its status as a nonsovereign entity under control and protection of the United States, Britain, and France was reaffirmed by a 1971 agreement between these powers and the Soviet Union, but its associations with the Federal Republic remain a point of friction between the two Germanies and their respective allies.[10] West German leaders are determined to preserve these bonds and will, for that reason, do their utmost to maintain the Western guarantees and troops that protect the city against East German efforts to change its status — a factor that plays a major role in the Federal Republic's relations with its allies. The East German leaders, on the other hand,

[10] Under the terms of the agreements, West Berliners are represented by officials of the Federal Republic in their relations with foreign countries but by their local government in their relations with the two German states.

consider West Berlin a source of covert West German threats to their security and therefore seek to loosen, if not sever, its ties to the Federal Republic.

None of these factors is necessarily insurmountable. In time, East German leaders may become more relaxed about relations with West Germany and the status of West Berlin, particularly if the Federal Republic's relations with the Soviet Union and other East European countries continue to improve. Toward this end West German policymakers have held out the lure of trade and financial benefits to the East Germans and their Communist allies.

Here they proceed on the assumption that West German trade with and through the Democratic Republic is so important to the Communist bloc that political differences will give way to economic needs. West German industrial imports have played no small part in East German economic growth and have consistently exceeded the Democratic Republic's exports to the Federal Republic, its second largest trading partner. West German governments have encouraged this commerce with subsidies and credit arrangements and have insisted that intra-German trade be exempted from the customs barriers imposed by the Common Market. As a result, East European Communist countries have been able to avoid Common Market tariffs by funneling their trade through East Germany.

A new economic agreement in the wake of the Basic Treaty calls for a significant expansion of intra-German trade, which had already increased tenfold between 1963 and 1972 and doubled between 1967 and 1972. And though for the Federal Republic this amounted to less than 2 percent of its total trade, and therefore had little economic importance, it represented 10 percent for the Democratic Republic and most of its trade outside the Communist bloc.

Whether and how the two Germanies will develop a more harmonious relationship has far-reaching implications for West German as well as international politics. Can the two rival regimes overcome their differences or are these differences too deep and the elements for conflict too numerous? Will West Germans continue to see East German Communism as a threat to their own political order and, if so, what kind of policies will be advocated and selected to meet such a challenge? And if it should prove possible to forge closer bonds to the Democratic Republic, how will they be reconciled with the Federal Republic's membership in the Western alliance system and the European Community? If a choice must be made, which ties will appear to be the more important to the West Germans and their leaders?

CHAPTER IV

Political Orientations: The Collective Past and the Present Regime

THE FORMAL ORGANIZATION of the state and the nature of the policy environment affect political relationships and behavior according to how they are perceived and evaluated by the involved actors. That is, "objective" circumstances are "subjectively" interpreted in line with personal beliefs, values, and sentiments. A social scientist may divide the West German population into classes on the basis of official figures on income or occupational differences. But it takes a sense of class consciousness on the part of that population to translate such statistical distinctions into policy-relevant attitudes and interest alignments.

A West German's view of governmental and nongovernmental components of the political system is correspondingly shaped by his orientations toward the state and its regime. In aggregate, such individual orientations form the underlying psychological "climate of opinion" for West German politics, and over time they reflect continuities and changes in common attitudes. Thus, when we speak of "typical" patterns of collective political beliefs, values, and sentiments in the Federal Republic we refer to generalized habits of thought and long-range attitudinal dispositions.

Differences in the policy processes of countries with similar socioeconomic and political structures are often attributed to cultural differences. Decision making under the Japanese parliamentary system, for instance, is said to be particularly slow and cumbersome because cultural norms call for extensive consultation, and ultimate agreement, between opposing factions. And though Americans and Englishmen share to a large extent a common legal tradition, their methods of law enforcement are said to differ because Americans are more likely to resort to violence than Englishmen.

Such cultural differences are in turn frequently associated with distinct historical memories transmitted across generations. American politics are said to reflect to this day the divisive legacy of a civil war that occurred more than a hundred years ago; English politics, centuries of constitutional continuity and domestic peace; and French politics, cleavages dating back to the revolution of 1789. The question before us, then, is to what extent and in what manner "unique" historical experiences have a bearing on contemporary West German politics.

HISTORICAL OBJECT LESSONS

West Germans, like other people, perceive and react to contemporary events in terms of past experiences and transmitted history. For example, we noted that memories of past wars and their destructiveness have led to strong pacifist sentiments in the Federal Republic. Such "lessons of history" as West Germans derive from what they *believe* to have happened in earlier times — what they personally remember and what they have been taught — provide guidelines for their political thoughts and actions. To some degree at least their expectations and their views about present developments represent negative or positive reactions to a shared historical legacy. For some the collective past is rather blurred and forms only vague pictures in their minds. For others it provides sharply engraved images that serve as reference points for their political attitudes and behavior.

For most West Germans, firsthand political experiences do not extend back much further than the lifetime of the Federal

Table IV.1. *Age Distribution of the West German Population*
(1975-80)

	Age				
Year	Under 15	15-21	22-40	41-60	Over 60
1975	24.1[a]	8.9	28.9	22.0	16.1
1980	22.2	10.2	27.1	26.3	14.3

[a]In percentages.
Source: Population projections based on 1970 census, reported in *Statistisches Jahrbuch*, 1972.

Republic. About two-thirds of West Germans living in the mid-1970s were born after 1934 (Table IV.1), which means that they were at most children when the state was established. They must depend on the testimony of others for information about what happened previously. Some of this testimony might come from those who are old enough to remember what they saw and were taught in earlier times. But for the most part, and to an increasing extent, West Germans must rely on written history, especially for information on their collective past before the beginning of the present century.

What sort of clues can West Germans derive from their transmitted past for what they should do and expect in contemporary politics? Perhaps the most basic lesson conveyed by most of their history books is that political controversies can lead to pathological conflicts but that autocracy is no cure. They can learn that the "German people" were divided for centuries by profound cultural differences and fratricidal conflicts and were only briefly united in a single state. The Protestant Reformation of the sixteenth century provoked long and bitter religious wars, and political controversies that extended into the twentieth century; the particularism of innumerable princely states — and the policies of more united countries, such as France and England — prevented the unification of "the Germanies" until it was achieved through war in the late nineteenth century. Then, the industrialization of united Germany led to two military catastrophes and intense political conflicts between rural and urban interests, employers and employees, and ideological factions committed to sharply divergent, exclusive dogmas.

Their history books also tell West Germans that the management of domestic and foreign conflicts became identified with a powerful state, strong executive leadership, weak legislatures, and minimal popular participation in policymaking. Except in some of the German cities, autocracy was the rule and majoritarian government the exception. The principles of government usually exalted the need for political order and stability in the state and assigned the formulation and enforcement of rigid legal norms to paternalistic public authorities. Harmonious relationships among individuals and groups were to be ensured more through suppression than through the free expression of differences, and more through popular compliance with formal rules handed down to them than through a popular consensus based on political bargaining among the people and their elected representatives.

Imperial Germany. A popularly chosen assembly of liberal democratic intellectuals failed to establish a united Germany governed by elected leaders in the mid-nineteenth century. The effort was ridiculed by conservative monarchists and frustrated by their superior military power. When unification finally came in 1871 it was imposed through a policy of "blood and iron" (war and force) identified with Otto von Bismarck, the founding father of Imperial Germany.

Formally a federation and a parliamentary monarchy, the German Empire (1871–1918) was in fact a thinly disguised autocracy controlled by the rulers of Prussia, its most powerful member state. Under the constitutional order devised by Otto von Bismarck, Prussia's prime minister, and Imperial Germany's "Iron Chancellor," the authoritarian Prussian regime was superimposed on the new political system. The Hohenzollern king of Prussia was also the emperor of Germany, the Prussian military establishment controlled the German armed forces, and the "nonpartisan" Prussian bureaucracy became the classic model for the German civil service. The popularly elected Imperial Diet was for the most part little more than a democratic fig leaf that barely concealed the naked exercise of political power by Prussia's landed aristocrats and big businessmen.

The elitist rule of this civil-military oligarchy was supported by rigid social stratification patterns anchored in law, and legitimated by prevailing political orientations. For nearly half a century Germans were imbued with the notion that only a powerful imperial state could safeguard the unity and survival of their national community and protect it against internal and external enemies. German political and legal philosophy glorified a personified state. Liberty was associated with the freedom of the state from restraints on its organic growth, and not with the freedom of the individual Germans to pursue their private interests. The principal duty of all members of the state was said to be service to the German nation. Political parties intervening between the patriarchal German family and the sovereign state were declared to be unimportant, if not disruptive elements in public affairs. From this point of view public authority was exercised by the executive and administrative officials *(Obrigkeit)* who served the interests of the state rather than the people. The role assigned to the ordinary citizen was that of the state's law-abiding subject *(Untertan)*.

Over the objections of a small minority of nonconformist liberal democrats and the leaders of the emerging socialist labor movement, every German was taught these principles in the schools of Imperial Germany. Every conscript in its mass armies was indoctrinated with them, clergymen preached them in the churches, and the nationalist conservative press fed them to its readers. The cultural product was a deeply ingrained political orientation that gave support to the Imperial regime. Most Germans either could not or would not see its structural weaknesses and accepted it more or less enthusiastically. The world prestige, military might, and industrial growth and economic prosperity of Imperial Germany were taken as proof that its autocratic structures worked as well, if not better than, Western parliamentary systems.

Contemporary West Germans have been taught that the Imperial regime failed to facilitate the smooth integration of preindustrial habits of thought and action with those produced by the industrialization of Germany. At home, cleavages among a plurality of interest groups were obscured rather than alleviated; in foreign affairs rational calculations yielded to nationalist emotions. Bismarck's design for internal and international conflict management — tailored to fit the man rather than his formal position — worked reasonably well for the twenty years he was in charge of its execution. But thereafter the attempt to fuse traditional conservatism with integral nationalism under the auspices of an autocratic state proved increasingly unequal to internal and external pressures. The policymaking stratum effectively resisted domestic demands for democratic reforms and committed the country to a foreign policy that exceeded its capabilities. The constitutional order underwent no substantial adaptive changes until 3 million German lives had been lost in World War I and defeat was imminent. By then political disintegration had proceeded too far to reform the system, and the Imperial regime collapsed in 1918.

Republican Germany. The second attempt to establish a democratic regime in a united Germany was initiated in 1919 by a popularly elected constitutional assembly meeting in the little town of Weimar. The framers of the new political order were for the most part democratic socialists and liberals who believed that government should rest on the consent of the governed and compromise between political factions. The experiment did not work, and the fourteen years of the Weimar Republic are presented to contemporary West Germans as an object lesson in the failure of democracy in Germany. The Weimar regime got off to a bad start. By some accounts it was a stillbirth. According to others the regime died in infancy because it lacked the strength to surmount conditions unfavorable to its institutionalization.

With the collapse of the Imperial regime, responsibility for making peace and establishing a new political order was suddenly thrust on its former critics, who had no governmental experience. Confronted by chaotic conditions at home and harsh demands from the victor power, their most immediate concerns were the establishment of their policymaking authority and the revival of a war-shattered economy. And for that they felt compelled to rely on the business leaders and officialdom of Imperial Germany. The Hohenzollern monarchy was abolished, but key positions in the economy, the armed forces, the judiciary, and the public administration remained in the hands of supporters of the old regime. In that sense the so-called revolution of 1918 did not produce any basic changes, as the American and French revolutions did, nor did it mark the beginning of a gradual democratization, as did the English revolution of 1688.

The subsequent fourteen years of the Weimar era proved to be only a stormy interlude between two autocracies. The regime was often shaken by insurrections and assassinations directed against the democratic order and by politically destabilizing socioeconomic crises. In calmer times political stability rested on a fragile standoff between traditionalist and modernizing elements among a deeply divided people struggling along the road from a preindustrial to a full-blown industrial society. The complex constitutional arrangements for conflict management worked badly in a highly fragmented political system. The Weimar Constitution turned out to be an unsuccessful compromise between libertarian and egalitarian principles, between a unitary and a federal state, between a parliamentary and a presidential system, and between representative and direct democracy.

The formal system of checks and balances required an underlying popular consensus and, even more importantly, a basic willingness among the ruling groups to support the regime and to accept the legitimacy of its rules for the making and implementing of public policies. As it was, no generally acceptable political formula could be found that would overcome deep ideological divisions within the policymaking stratum and reconcile the divergent beliefs, values, and sentiments of encapsulated socioeconomic and religious subcultures.

The still extremely powerful remnants of the preindustrial aristocracy, entrenched in the army and civil service, sought overtly and covertly to restore princely particularism — especially in Bavaria — or the autocratic regime of the Hohenzollern Empire. Big business increasingly favored a nationalist autocracy that would suppress the trade unions of the industrial workers and promote German economic imperialism.

Leaders of feuding interest associations representing salaried employees, farmers, artisans, and small shopkeepers wanted a strong national government that would save their clientele from the socioeconomic effects of advancing industrialization.

Influential opinion makers — such as journalists, teachers, and clergymen — either were opposed to the Weimar regime from its inception or became alienated because it failed to live up to their perfectionist standards. Their frequently savage criticism implied or declared openly that another, more or less democratic regime could do a better job in meeting governmental responsibility for the welfare of the state, the nation, or the masses. The alleged neglect of such abstractions by Weimar governments was commonly advanced by the self-appointed spokesmen for the army, the judiciary, the public administration, and other governmental and nongovernmental groups to justify their opposition to the democratic constitutional order and their frequent defiance of the elected political leaders of the republic.

Party governments were unstable during the Weimar Republic and constantly shifting single-issue parliamentary coalitions proved to be brittle alignments. In fourteen years there were twenty-one national governments, most of which did not last more than six months, and eight national elections in which no party ever won an absolute parliamentary majority. The leaders of the large number of parliamentary parties were deeply divided over the proper scope, form, and functions of state and government and could not agree on enduring solutions to pressing policy problems.

Instead of producing compromise agreements on controversial issues, the Weimar regime intensified friction among socioeconomic, religious, and political factions. The liberal democratic alternative to an authoritarian system became increasingly discredited in the eyes of Germans who had learned to look to the state for authoritative guidance and expected its leaders to ensure order and harmony in society. The average citizen shunned the participant roles which were provided for him by the Weimar constitution, except when he was mobilized by political activists to exercise his voting rights in plebiscites and elections.

To an increasing extent these activists were radical opponents of the regime who used their constitutional liberties to
bring about its destruction. The Communists on the extreme
left promoted political instability in the hope that chaos
would lead to a "proletarian" dictatorship; the Nazis on the
extreme right pursued a similar strategy toward the establishment of a fascist dictatorship. In the last years of the Weimar
Republic these otherwise irreconcilable parties would occasionally join forces against the defenders of the liberal democratic regime, most notably the Social Democratic party. By
November 1932, 17 percent of the voters supported the Communists and 33 percent Hitler's National Socialists.

Perhaps, as some historians have maintained, more time
and fewer critical pressures might have allowed the development of more supportive political orientations. As it was, a
growing sense of fatalism undermined the determination of
the regime's defenders and played into the hands of its opponents. "We were at the mercy of events," the leaders of the
Social Democratic party argued when Hitler assumed power
in 1933.

Nazi Germany. A highly negative picture of Germany under
the dictatorship of Adolf Hitler has been employed by West
German opinion leaders to build support for the political system of the Federal Republic. The Nazi regime (1933–45) is
invoked as a standard for comparison between a frightful past
and a far more congenial present, and as a warning of what
may befall West Germans if they should fail to give firm
allegiance to the present political order. At most a fourth of
them are old enough to draw comparisons on the strength of
personal experiences under both regimes. For those who are
too young to have such firsthand knowledge of Nazi Germany
there is a vast literature of memoirs and historical studies that
demonstrate the evil consequences of blind faith in arbitrary
leadership.

Hitler, it now appears, had nothing but contempt for the
German people. But he successfully exploited mass feelings of
discontent and strong romantic, escapist sentiments produced
by the cumulative effects of military defeat in World War I

and subsequent socioeconomic crises in the Weimar era. He played on these emotions and integrated them by promising magical escape from national humiliation and distress; and an increasing number of Germans came to believe him. As a charismatic leader Hitler became the symbol of salvation for millions who were alienated from an increasingly urbanized and industrialized environment, particularly young people and impoverished small farmers, artisans, and shopkeepers. But though the head of the National Socialist German Labor Party publicly denounced the plutocratic enemies of "the German national community," he simultaneously sought and gained the covert support of big business leaders and other elite groups who wanted a more autocratic form of government than the Weimar regime.

Mass and elite dissatisfaction with the Weimar system finally came to a head in a severe economic crisis that caused mass unemployment, destitution, and desperation and paved the way for Hitler's "legal" accession in 1933. The prevailing climate of opinion allowed him to gain "temporary" dictatorial powers that he claimed he needed to provide full employment, stability, unity, and order. Hitler's confident cry "Give me four years time and you won't recognize Germany" held out the hope of satisfying very diverse values and inspired heterogeneous elements with the idea that Hitler's "new" Germany would correspond to their particular vision of what it should and would be like.

Very quickly, a leader who had never obtained the endorsement of a majority of the voters in a free election effected a dramatic shift in political opinion and gained the enthusiastic support of most Germans, primarily on the strength of negative memories of the Weimar regime and utopian expectations about the future. The Protestant Prussian aristocracy had visions of a return to the "glorious times" of the Hohenzollern Empire, while the leaders of the Roman Catholic church were encouraged to accept the Nazi regime by its treaty with the Vatican, granting their church privileges that they had sought in vain from Weimar governments. The paramilitary storm troopers who had fought Hitler's street battles expected to take control of the army, while the old military elite looked forward to building a new military establishment unencumbered by the "fetters" placed on German rearmament under the Weimar regime. Leading industrialists were cheered by the abolition of trade unions, while small businessmen and farmers expected that their interests would be served by the elimination of "Jewish capitalists" from German economic life. Nationalists were stirred by Hitler's spectacular successes in foreign policy, and anti-Communists applauded his destruction of the left-wing parties. Senior civil servants welcomed the elimination of parliamentary controls and the concentration of executive power in one hand, while young people looked to Hitler to realize their romantic dreams of a new German society released from the formalistic restraints of the past.

Hitler skillfully exploited this euphoric mood to consolidate his power. He destroyed the parties and interest associations of the Weimar Republic and transformed surviving formal structures into instruments of his personal rule. Respected governmental agencies like the public administration and the judiciary, as well as the "unofficial" terror and propaganda apparatus of the Nazi movement, were used to eliminate or gravely weaken competing groups, such as the churches and the aristocratic officer corps, which might deny the leader the absolute loyalty of his subjects. Big business was the notable exception in this process of "coordination" and was left pretty much unscathed to build Hitler's war machine.

As soon as Hitler took over he set out to establish a new political order built around the mythical notion of a German "people's community" from which Jews and other "inferior non-German races" were excluded. As Joseph Goebbels, the head of a newly created Ministry for Propaganda and People's Enlightenment, proclaimed in 1933: "The people shall begin to think uniformly, react uniformly, and put themselves at the disposal of the Government with full sympathy."[1] In the new autocratic "leader-state" all boundaries between state and society, and between political and nonpolitical roles, were to be

---

[1] Quoted in Marlis G. Steinert, *Hitlers Krieg und die Deutschen: Stimmung und Haltung der deutschen Bevölkerung im Zweiten Weltkrieg* (Düsseldorf-Vienna: Econ, 1970), p. 30.

eradicated. The new political system was to reflect solely the spirit of the national collectivity as articulated by its omnipotent leader. "Hitler is Germany and Germany is Hitler" was the slogan chanted in unison by the thousands at huge, carefully staged rallies and echoed all over the country from millions of loudspeakers. Belligerent nationalism, anti-Semitism, and radical romanticism were incorporated into a rather vague Nationalist Socialist ideology based on Hitler's speeches and writings and focused on the secular godhead.

For twelve years the political attitudes and emotions of the German masses were most effectively shaped by the agents of the Nazi regime. The political orientations taught in schools and in mass organizations, in the conscript army and labor service, in prisons and in concentration camps, established or reinforced hierarchical relationships of strict command and unquestioning obedience. The anti-Semitic image of the Jews, who were made the scapegoats for all ills, became a stereotype that was accepted readily and widely. Though Hitler did not publicize his "final solution of the Jewish problem," not many Germans worried about their Jewish neighbors' disappearance. A few abortive attempts to overthrow Hitler — most notably toward the end when he had lost World War II — did not involve more than a handful of conspirators.

The myth of the leader's unfailing intuition helped to sustain the regime until its destruction by foreign armies. Studies of German civilian and military morale during World War II show that even as bombing attacks were devastating the country and casualties were mounting into the millions, mass support for the Nazi regime and mass compliance with the commands of its leader maintained domestic stability. Criticism was directed against obviously false propaganda, and against secondary Nazi leaders who were blamed for unpopular actions ordered by Hitler. But until the day of his suicide in 1945, the Führer's personal image remained untarnished in the eyes of most of his subjects. Fervent believers in his magic gifts kept faith to the very end, trusting that their charismatic leader would somehow turn the tide by some miracle or wonder weapon.

After Hitler's fall, West Germans were informed, first by

foreign occupation powers and then by their new political leaders, that the supposed unity of the Nazi regime was a most costly illusion created by its monopolistic propaganda machine. They have been taught that the trust which subjects had placed in their autocratic leader was undeserved and that those who willingly danced to his tune ultimately had to pay dearly for it.

The overt totalitarian cohesion of Nazi Germany concealed the failure of its control apparatus to penetrate deeply and radically alter the underlying socioeconomic structure. Not only was the timespan too brief, but the man on the top did not establish the promised "new" Germany. From beginning to end Nazi policymaking contained pluralist features that limited Hitler's power. Even if he had wanted to, he could not have followed up the atomization of the pre-Nazi organization of political life with enduring new cultural and social patterns. Conflict management was personalized rather than institutionalized, and one-man rule accentuated rather than eliminated competition and conflict among leading members of various hierarchical segments of the Nazi system.

Essentially the Hitler dictatorship sought to manage Germany's continuing transition from a preindustrial to an advanced industrial society. But the Führer's erratic and intuitive style of government, as well as the organization of his leadership state, caused destabilizing tensions in Nazi Germany that became more pronounced as its fortunes declined. The one-sidedness of political communications in a system resting on command and obedience, and the dualism of governmental and Nazi party structures, led to widespread uncertainties about what kind of compliant behavior was expected, and to bitter jurisdictional disputes among the elites who were supposed to execute Hitler's orders faithfully.

In every sphere of public life, decision-making authority formally descended from the dictator, in his dual capacity as chief of state and leader of the Nazi movement, to thousands of subordinate Nazi potentates, military commanders, and public administrators. However, these official lines of command were deliberately obscured and often bypassed by Hitler who had the habit of unexpectedly reversing his previous decisions without explanation. The nature of his regime encouraged not only blind obedience, but "buck-passing." Although Hitler demanded and received the blind trust of the common people, he himself trusted only his dog and his mistress. Even his closest associates labored under the constant threat of sudden disgrace in a regime marked by arbitrary decisions affecting life, liberty, and status. The irrational, emotional, and antiformalist components of the Nazi system precluded the predictable, rational policy processes that are the requisite of a smoothly functioning political system in an industrialized society. "The revolution of nihilism" described by one perceptive observer at an early stage of Hitler's rule led eventually to anarchic conditions in the conduct of government and culminated in complete disintegration in 1945.[2]

The Occupation Regime. With the collapse of Hitler's regime in 1945 began the third attempt to establish a liberal democratic Germany. "The year zero," as it has come to be called, is now proclaimed as the start of an entirely new political beginning. It brought a great mass awakening from the dreams and nightmares of the Nazi regime, along with a sobering hangover. American, British, and French military governments assumed jurisdiction over what was to become, four years later, the Federal Republic and set out to teach a disillusioned, cynical people their versions of democracy.

The foreign occupation powers sought above all to remove what they took to be the principal elements of Nazi political and military power. Measures were taken to completely eradicate German authoritarian traditions and permanently eliminate from positions of status and influence individuals and groups believed to have been prominent in the Nazi regime or indirectly responsible for it. Not only surviving Nazi party leaders, but also civil and military officials, business managers, journalists, and educators considered members of the former ruling elites were purged.

The victors' authoritative decisions were based on a puni-

2 Hermann Rauschning, *The Revolution of Nihilism* (New York: Longman, Green, 1939).

tive policy toward a people held collectively responsible for the actions of the Nazi regime, and reflected an "enlightened despotism" aimed at preventing future German aggression. War crimes trials, denazification proceedings, educational reforms, dismantling of industrial plants for reparation payments, and the carefully controlled reconstruction of political structures were the means used by the three occupation powers to implement these policies.

At the same time, ostensible anti-Nazis and non-Nazis were encouraged to assume responsibility for the implementation of the military government directives and the gradual development of a Western-type liberal democracy under foreign tutelage. Such benevolent sponsorship, however, did not extend to Germans who had different notions about the best way to create a lasting democratic regime and who demanded more profound socioeconomic changes and a greater part in political reconstruction. The political duty assigned Germans during this period of imposed denazification and democratization was to obey commands, a duty they had become quite used to. Most of them had no difficulty in accepting the directives of their new rulers and adapting to foreign control.

As noted in the preceding chapter, economic recovery and social reorganization began about 1948 and developed rapidly in the following decade, along with the recovery of German political influence. As tensions between Western and Soviet leaders increased, foreign supervision and intervention in West German political affairs decreased. The establishment of the Federal Republic in 1949 terminated Western punitive and tutelary efforts, war crimes trials came to an end, and political decision making was gradually handed over entirely to German leaders. The new policy was to woo the West Germans into a voluntary and intimate partnership against the Soviet bloc by providing them with economic assistance and military protection, and by encouraging anti-Soviet opinion and behavior.

West Germans now learned that they could expect very tangible rewards — such as complete sovereignty, achieved in 1955 — in return for demonstrations of their reliability as anti-Communist partners of the West and of the stability of their new political system. Such lessons, combined with the effect of socioeconomic recovery, enormously strengthened the position of leaders who took over the direction of political reconstruction from the Western military governments — above all, Konrad Adenauer, chancellor of the Federal Republic from its inception until 1963. They rallied elite and mass opinion behind their efforts to institutionalize the new regime and give it legitimacy at home as well as abroad.

THE LEGACY OF THE PAST

What do West Germans make of their transmitted history and what have they learned from the object lessons presented by former regimes? Have they inherited not just their forebearers' land and language but also their political orientations? Do they look back in longing for "the good old days" when Germany was a powerful nation-state?

In probing for some answers we must bear in mind that the statements and actions of particular individuals at particular times do not necessarily reflect long-range developments. Articles in the press, parliamentary debates, opinion polls, and election results may merely indicate momentary reactions to temporary phenomena such as political scandals. A second point to remember is that expressions of opinion about a particular leader, party, or policy, may at best suggest rather than reveal more elusive and general patterns of underlying attitudes.

On the evidence of overt expressions of public sentiment, West Germans — and particularly young West Germans — appear to have made a conspicuous break with their autocratic past. Unpleasant memories of former regimes provide general support for the prevailing political order. At the level of mass as well as elite opinion its extremist critics are widely identified with the antidemocratic forces that destroyed the Weimar Republic. For most contemporary West Germans the changes advocated by such groups apparently do not represent desirable alternate arrangements.

Consider some trends in opinion polls. Since the establishment of the Federal Republic representative cross-sections of the adult population have periodically been asked to look back and compare present conditions with those in earlier times. To judge by the answers, ever larger proportions of West Germans have come to reject a return to previous autocratic regimes as the contemporary one has become institutionalized. In 1951, for example, 45 percent of the respondents still expressed the opinion that Germany fared best in this century under the peacetime Hohenzollern Empire; by 1970 only 5 percent did so, whereas an overwhelming 81 percent stated that Germany — meaning the Federal Republic — was best off "today." Those who openly favored another monarchy declined from one-third to one-tenth between 1951 and 1967, those supporting another dictatorship from one-half to one-third between 1955 and 1967. The positive images of the "great leaders" of earlier regimes have similarly declined. Bismarck's reputation as the man who had "done most for Germany" dropped from 35 to 21 percent between 1951 and 1971; Hitler's dropped from 10 to 3 percent.

According to opinion polls, West Germans have not only lost their taste for military ventures and their former esteem for the military profession, but have also increasingly come to consider Nazi Germany solely responsible for the start of World War II. In 1951 less than one out of three respondents felt that Germany was alone to blame; by 1967 it was two out of three. What is noteworthy here is not the "objective" validity of these views but that, in contrast to the Weimar era, war and defeat are now widely attributed to the previous regime and its leader, and not to pernicious internal traitors and external enemies or to uncontrollable events. Moreover, the number of respondents who believe that Germany will ever again be a great world power has sunk rapidly over the years and is by now a very tiny minority.

Most such comparisons are, however, based on increasingly vague and emotionally detached perceptions of the past, including the Nazi era. For better or for worse, West Germans have become gradually more relaxed and less defensive about what happened under Hitler's rule. As political wounds that still festered at home and abroad during the 1950s and 1960s have healed and ceased to cause pain and discomfort, they have also become less conspicuous scars on the body politic.

In part this is attributable to the passage of time and the disappearance of a generation whose members were directly involved in the Nazi regime as its victims, opponents, or supporters. What in the first two decades of the Federal Republic had been the problem of the "unresolved" Nazi past is thus being resolved by the natural course of events. In part, too, divisive sentiments have waned due to governmental policies designed to put to rest the Nazi legacy of persecution and aggression. The politicocultural restraints that this legacy had earlier imposed on the "normalization" of domestic and foreign relations have largely been lifted, and in the view of most West Germans the inherited moral debt has been more than paid off through generous restitution payments and territorial adjustments. Accordingly, they no longer think it necessary to make reparations on demand and to refrain from criticizing what they consider Nazi-like actions in other countries.

This growing sense of perceptual distance from the Nazi past may explain a seemingly contradictory phenomenon. In the early 1970s some West Germans and foreigners with still vivid recollections of Hitler's rise and rule were alarmed by a sudden outpouring of "insider" accounts of the Hitler years. The fact that these were avidly read in the Federal Republic suggested to them the danger of a Nazi revival built around a Führer cult, similar to the Bonapartist legend that allowed a second Napoleon to come to power in France thirty-five years after the fall of the first.

But rather than indicating widespread sentiment for a return to a glorious past, the popularity of such accounts appears to have reflected more a morbid curiosity about and horrid fascination with a man pictured as an evil genius by his erstwhile associates. The one-time leader of the Nazi youth movement, for example, described Hitler as "a fabulous monster" and the Führer's former architect wrote of his overpowering personal magnetism. For those West Germans who in their youth had blindly worshiped Hitler from afar these revelations by men once close to him may also have served to explain and excuse their own culpability to the younger generations. A German psychiatrist had earlier attributed the Nazi generation's failure to acknowledge its guilt for Hitler and his crimes to "an inability to mourn" and repent. New evidence that the "little people" in Nazi Germany could not have known then what is known now may have provided another mode of liberation from the spectres of the past.

For the post-Nazi generations, whose members have no reason to feel personally responsible for what happened, Hitler poses no such problems. Numerous studies have shown that insofar as they have any impressions of him, they tend to see him as a fallible leader who foolishly started a war he could not win, and to harbor neither strong negative nor positive sentiments about the Nazi regime. "The terror of it has to a certain extent become abstract to the younger generations," as Chancellor Willy Brandt told Israeli Jews in 1973. Himself once a militant anti-Nazi, Brandt said that he had to "learn again and again how hard it is after the passage of three decades to convey to others what is literally incomprehensible" for those who did not share his "burden of experience."

In general, only a few articulate West Germans invoke the past in commenting about current political developments. Some are aging former anti-Nazis, who are still haunted by their experiences in Weimar and Nazi Germany and warn that a major economic crisis could once again produce political turmoil and dictatorship. Others are old-line conservatives who call for a return to traditional civic virtues, such as patriotism. Proponents of the prevailing political order refer to conditions under earlier regimes in order to demonstrate that it has provided West Germans with unprecedented freedom and affluence. Radical social critics, on the other hand, cite history to show that changes in regimes have produced no appreciable changes in an inequitable distribution of power, benefits, and burdens.

These purported "lessons of history," however, are preached to a largely indifferent and uninformed public. For most West Germans today the Hitler era and earlier eras represent closed chapters in their collective past and offer few specific guidelines for their views of politics in the Federal Republic. In what is taken to be an entirely different policy environment, former conditions are ostensibly considered of little relevance to current problems, and evocations of the past seem more of a hindrance than a help in dealing with the "here and now." The question that concerns them, particularly the younger people, is not whether the present is better or worse than the past, but whether the future will be better or worse than the present. Contemporary West Germans appear to be an exceptionally ahistorical people unaware of elements of continuity in their socioeconomic and political systems. However, less explicit and conscious attitudes toward the state and its officials, and perceptions of the role of the ordinary citizen, indicate that although perceptual links to the past have frayed they have not been entirely broken.

THE INSTITUTIONALIZATION OF THE POLITICAL SYSTEM

We noted in the preceding section that attachments to former regimes have waned in West Germany as the present one has become more institutionalized. But what exactly do we mean here by institutionalization? It is essentially a process by which constitutional arrangements for the conduct of political affairs come to be valued for themselves and not just for what they are expected to produce. Above and beyond what people believe a particular government, official, or policy will do for them or to them, they will esteem public offices and procedures for what they are thought to represent, such as "the majesty of government," or "a democratic way of life," or "equal justice under law."

Such attitudes certainly did not prevail in West Germany when the Federal Republic was established in 1949. The new state and regime were superimposed on political orientations shaped by close to a century of mostly autocratic rule in a united Germany, and the outcome of this grafting operation was by no means certain. As we observed in the second chapter, the new political order was handed down by the foreign occupation powers and their German collaborators — ostensibly as a temporary arrangement pending the reunification of a divided country — and it was not submitted to the test of a popular referendum. The principles of a "democratic and social federal state" remained to be "bought" by the affected population, and prevailing political orientations gave no assurance that this would be the case.

The founders of the Federal Republic sought to establish a supportive consensus by legal engineering. They combined innovative with traditional organizational principles in the Basic Law and set forth constitutional norms which, they hoped, would in time lead to the institutionalization of the new regime. The Basic Law was thus designed to educate as well as regulate West Germans. By following its precepts faithfully they were expected in time to embrace the constitutional order wholeheartedly as the only conceivable way of dealing with public policy matters.

These efforts to reshape political orientations seem to have borne fruit after three decades of learning experiences. In striking contrast to the dissension that doomed the Weimar Republic, both leading and supporting players appear today to accept the legitimacy of the constitutional order not just in theory but in practice. The game of politics is played in the Federal Republic pretty much as the formal rules say it should be played. Expressions of dissatisfaction focus mostly on particular features of the political system rather than on the entire system. And it also seems that on the whole West German attitudes toward the legally constituted state and regime have come to transcend purely nominal commitments and to incorporate more enduring attachments.

POLITICAL COMMUNITY

A basic measure of the institutionalization of a state is its citizens' sense of a shared political identity. When the Federal Republic was carved out of the former German Reich, and for some time thereafter, most West Germans did not seem to consider themselves members of a new political community except in a purely formal sense. West Germany was perceived as a geographic expression or an economic system, and its status as a distinct political entity was widely believed to be only a temporary condition pending the reunification of the "German nation." An international opinion survey taken in 1959, ten years after the formation of the Federal Republic, found that the number of people expressing esteem for their political processes was a good deal smaller in West Germany than in the United States and England. Instead most West

German respondents took pride in nonpolitical characteristics they associated with the German people as a whole (e.g., cleanliness, diligence, efficiency, frugality), and the physical feature of "Germany."

More recent data indicate that over the years a subtle process of political acculturation has produced a greater identification with the Federal Republic. With the integration of the millions of refugees from Eastern Europe, the waning of prospects for reunification, and the absorption of new learning experiences, more and more West Germans have come to associate "Germany" with the Federal Republic rather than the territory of the former Reich. The "flawed sense of national identity," which in earlier years had seemed to many observers a decided obstacle to the institutionalization of the West German state appears to have given way to a national consciousness linked to the established polity. The "normalization" of domestic and foreign relations, particularly with respect to the Nazi past, reflected and accelerated this change in the climate of opinion. In 1972, the election posters of the ruling Social Democratic Party proclaimed "Germans: we can be proud of our country!" and the message was taken by the voters to refer to the West German people and the West German state.

Conspicuously absent from this emerging sense of political community is affective loyalty toward the Federal Republic, that is, love for the country that bears its name. West Germans may root for "our team" in international athletic competitions, but few of them think of the Federal Republic as their "fatherland." The intense patriotic attachments to a German nation-state that provided mass support for the Imperial and Nazi regimes have not been transferred to the rump that both the constitution and government pronouncements identify as but a part of the "German nation." Official efforts to promote West German communal sentiments through symbols of political integration tend to be either ignored or rejected, particularly by the younger generations. The black, red, and golden flag is recognized and accepted as the emblem of the Federal Republic, but its sight does not move people the way the black, red, and white of Imperial and Nazi Germany once did.

The new national holidays are not perceived as "holy" days, but as leisure days that are to be enjoyed rather than celebrated. On such occasions West Germans now prefer skiing in the mountains or basking at the beaches, to parading with fife and drum and listening to patriotic oratory and songs.

Thus far at least, the institutionalization of the Federal Republic has evidently not penetrated very deeply to the level of communal sentiments. In this respect East Germans may have developed stronger feelings of "belonging" to a political community. Refugees from the German Democratic Republic and West German visitors to "the other Germany" testify to a fraternal spirit there which they miss in the Federal Republic. Whereas in the West an emotional vacuum appears to have replaced the affective, integrative ties that had linked state and national community in the former Reich, in the East, patriotic, egalitarian, and anticapitalist sentiments seem to have been effectively fused into a new collective identity with the Communist state. Some West German commentators attribute the difference to a more drastic and widespread repudiation of the autocratic and nationalist patterns of the past in the Federal Republic and to a far greater emphasis on individual freedom and initiative in its society. In any event, developments in their respective political systems have increasingly drawn West and East Germans apart rather than together. Geography and official references to "intra-German ties" notwithstanding, on the perceptual map of most West Germans the Democratic Republic has become a distant, foreign land.

In sum, it appears then that neither the Federal Republic nor the image of a single German "nation" are today foci of mass sentiments of political community in West Germany. Some observers believe that this lack of national identity favors allegiances to a European political community. But the absence of one type of loyalty does not allow us to infer the presence of another. Rather vaguely perceived, European integration seems attractive to most West Germans and in principle receives massive support in both elite and mass opinion surveys. However, there is little evidence that these endorsements extend beyond purely pragmatic considerations, such as the perceived instrumental advantages of European economic cooperation. Emotional commitments to a truly supranational European community do not seem to exist, although there was a good deal of enthusiasm for such a community among idealistic young West Germans in the 1950s. It may be that the current lack of strong emotional attachments to a single German "nation" will someday make it easier for West Germans than for patriotic Englishmen and Frenchmen to join a European federation. However, the prospects for such a state appear rather remote. The affective integration of the West German polity alone, on the other hand, requires the development of national sentiments that both transcend regional loyalties and override allegiances to supranational ideologies.

CONCEPTIONS OF THE STATE

If a constitutional order is to work, its rules must be not only accepted, but interpreted in much the same manner by the people involved. That is, the people must agree on who should do what, and on how and why it should be done. Such understanding calls for a basic consensus on the nature and functions of the state and the proper relationship between public authorities and citizenry.

By all indications, the formal norms and role assignments of the present constitutional order have become imbedded in West German political orientations. At all levels of the polity they define today the legitimate organization and boundaries of policy processes in the state for governmental as well as nongovernmental actors. In a 1953 opinion poll only a little over half of a cross-section of West German adults opted for a democratic regime; close to three out of four did so in a 1967 survey. And whereas in a 1961 poll a majority accepted the regime rather apathetically as "one with which one can live," it was supported far more emphatically in a 1971 survey. Most of the respondents now saw the regime as generally well organized and efficient; 87 percent as democratic, 70 percent as tolerant, 68 percent as just, and 59 percent as dependable.

To a considerable extent the growth of such supportive orientations has been promoted not only by the coincidence of rising affluence and political institutionalization but by popular sentiments for law and order in West German society.

"Keeping order in the country," according to a 1970 opinion survey by the European Economic Community, mattered far more to West German adults than to respondents in France, Italy, and the Benelux countries, although the Federal Republic was perhaps the most tranquil country among the six. A concern for law and order is one of the distinctive elements of continuity in West German political attitudes, especially in prevailing views of the state.

Political reconstruction in the early years of the Federal Republic, like economic reconstruction, was not so much an entirely new beginning as a process of reorganization and, to some extent, restoration. As in the initial phase of the Weimar Republic, the new political leadership considered it above all necessary to provide for orderly legal procedures in the state. But this time the shattering of earlier authority patterns — begun by Hitler and carried forward by the occupation powers — as well as a more favorable climate of elite and mass opinion, made it easier to institute a new Rechtstaat, a state governed under law rather than by capricious rulers. In the German political tradition the rule of law over men was identified with legal principles that accentuated highly formalized and hierarchical authority relationships in the organization of the state, and explicit, as well as comprehensive codes of political conduct.

The incorporation of these notions into the constitutional theory and practice of the new political order appears to have greatly facilitated the acculturation of West Germans to its innovative features. The liberal democratic norms of the Basic Law deemphasize state control over the citizenry and call for public policies that are the product of peaceful bargaining and compromise among law-abiding members of a pluralist society. In this respect the state provides the organizational means for the adoption and enforcement of governmental decisions that flow from the resolution of legitimate conflict. At the same time the Basic Law accommodates the beliefs that the state is more than its parts and that its interests are broader and more enduring than those of particular parties, pressure groups, and politicians. In this sense public authorities are responsible for the collective welfare of present and future citizens of the Federal Republic, and must safeguard societal harmony and stability.

Over the years both concepts of the state have been accommodated in evolving political orientations. West Germans have learned to evaluate the operation of their governmental system in terms of the liberal democratic norms of the Basic Law. They have therefore come to see the choice of policies and policymakers as largely the outcome of an interplay among a plurality of elites, parties, interest associations, and voters. But West Germans still look beyond these groups to the authority of the state as the supreme guardian of law and order and ultimate arbiter of socioeconomic conflicts.

In current West German usage, "the state" has a rather different meaning than it has for Americans. When "the state" is said to do this, or is called on to do that, more often than not the association is with something more than the government and something different from the country. What the state "does" is rather vaguely perceived by most West Germans not so much as an expression of the will of the people but as the action of an abstract organizational entity. It is not an object of love or hate, of feelings of loyalty or alienation; it is something like a giant impersonal corporation with its managers (government), supervisory board of directors (parliament), and administrative staff (civil service). The average citizen appears in this view as a rather poorly informed small stockholder who may elect the directors but not control the management, who may or may not get efficient corporate services, and who gets whatever share of the profits the management considers his due. Members of the policymaking stratum are correspondingly perceived as large stockholders who know more and can do more about corporate policies and, therefore, who receive a disproportionate share of the profits and services. Policy processes are thus evaluated in essentially economic terms, the state distributing goods and services in exchange for payments rendered — such as taxes and other citizenship duties — with some people getting more and some paying more than others.

Though such orientations still retain elements of the traditional German idealization of the state as a guardian and provider, they have become increasingly business-like and pragmatic. The prevailing view of a state under law implies a contractual relationship between state and citizens based on reciprocal legal obligations. West Germans accept the constitutional principle of the supremacy of public over private interest, but in return they expect the state to provide for domestic harmony and stability, for their economic and social welfare, and for their physical security.

PERCEPTIONS OF POLITICAL AUTHORITY

In every political system the effective exercise of public authority rests on a mixture of coercive control by the governors and voluntary compliance on the part of the governed. As the ruled comply more readily and habitually with the decisions of their rulers those rulers will have less need for coercive measures.

In the Federal Republic constitutional and legal arrangements for the exercise of political authority by responsible elected and appointed public officials have over the years become imbedded in West German political orientations. Consequently the ruling elites of the policymaking stratum can today generally expect popular compliance with the decisions of the executive, legislative, and judicial agencies of the state.

Unlike their forebears, contemporary West Germans do not simply consider it their civic duty to be deferential, passive, and quiescent subjects. The days are past when German leaders could command popular obedience merely by virtue of holding positions of public authority. Younger West Germans feel particularly free to criticize public officials and to voice their objections to governmental laws and regulations they consider unfair or unreasonable. Agents of the state are expected to adhere to the rules of the constitutional order and to meet exacting popular standards of political propriety and efficient performance.

Governmental interference in matters that the Basic Law declares to be none of the business of the state and violations of the legal rights of West Germans by public officials have at times provoked strong and effective public protests. The dockets of the constitutional and administrative courts are always crowded with the complaints of ordinary citizens and private organizations who seek redress for wrongs allegedly committed by public officials. Investigative reporters are continually looking for cases of official malfeasance, and governmental authorities have learned to be very careful of what they do for fear of exposure in the public media. Elected officials have become much more aware of the voters' grievances, and members of the executive branches of the federal, state, and local governments have found it advisable to pay close heed to legislators voicing grievances on behalf of their constituents.

In the last analysis, however, most West Germans accept the legitimacy of the prevailing patterns of political authority. Normative standards for evaluating the political propriety and competence of the rulers have changed and continue to change, and they vary a good deal among different socioeconomic strata, age groups, and partisan alignments. However, the dynamics of change in political attitudes and shifting subcultural cleavages have not led to widespread popular disaffection from the regime and to mass civil disobedience. Quite to the contrary, the longer the regime has been in existence the more firmly have its basic organizational principles defined legitimate authority patterns for the general public.

Public opinion surveys indicate that West Germans quite realistically perceive authority relationships in the Federal Republic as rather rigidly dividing the rulers from the ruled. For example, in a 1971 poll, two out of three adults maintained that they had no personal influence over the conduct of public affairs. Democratic constitutional norms notwithstanding, most people believe that all major political decisions are made by a few powerful leaders and then handed down to the relatively impotent multitude through governmental channels. As noted earlier, most Germans place an exceptionally high premium on law and order. They therefore feel obligated to conform with legal arrangements for the formulation and implementation of public policy, which they may not always like but consider legitimate. But in return for their compliance they expect their policymakers to be equally law-abiding and accountable for their actions.

Public policymaking in the Federal Republic involves conflict, bargaining, and compromise among manifold leadership groups inside and outside governmental bodies. At that level,

as we shall see, the political system serves primarily to reconcile competing policy demands before the authoritative policymakers arrive at a final decision. But most of the people, who
are largely excluded from these processes, see the political system principally in terms of its effects — what it does for them
and to them. They therefore tend to evaluate the performance
of the system in general, and specific leaders in particular,
mostly by the consequences of authoritative policy decisions.
To the average citizen, the proper management of public
affairs seems an exceedingly complicated matter that requires
public officials who command exceptional knowledge and
skills. And here West Germans are more inclined to place
their trust in executive and judicial agents of the state than
in their legislative representatives.

Respect for the ability of legislators and the belief that they
are responsive to the wishes of their constituents have decidedly increased since the establishment of the present regime. But most West Germans tend to take a rather cynical
view of their elected deputies. To judge by opinion polls, they
see them not so much as "representatives of the whole people,
not bound by orders and subject only to their own conscience"
— as the Basic Law provides — but more as the creatures of
contentious party and pressure group elites. Younger people
seem to be less troubled by this notion of captive legislators
than older West Germans who still cling to the traditional
view that public officials should serve the general rather than
particularist interests.

West Germans do not face corruption in high places with
the same degree of equanimity as Americans. There have been
comparatively few instances of such misconduct among their
elected officials. But a few highly publicized cases of nefarious
deals involving prominent legislators have not exactly increased public esteem for parliamentary institutions. Civil
servants, on the other hand, have traditionally enjoyed far
greater public trust than in the United States. They are generally believed to be skilled and honest, though not always
fair and accommodating in their relations with ordinary citizens.

West Germans thus make a qualitative distinction between
functionaries of the state and those of political parties and in-

terest associations. The stereotyped roles of the statesman and governmental administrator are endowed with high prestige by virtue of their association with legitimate public authority. The roles of the politician and pressure group spokesman, in contrast, are widely associated with behavior that at best does little to advance the general interest and at worst injures it.

Such perceptions of the wielders of public authority impose cultural restraints on the conduct of West German political leaders. Elected and appointed officials seek to be known as statesmen and public servants and shun the labels of politicians and interest group representatives. In order to earn and maintain the confidence of the general public, and to give legitimacy to their actions, they try to show that they meet prevailing standards of political propriety and competence. Those who hold official positions as well as those who aspire to them want it to be known that they are qualified to exercise the authority of a public office efficiently and conscientiously.

However, because many of their activities are visible and can be evaluated by an attentive public, leading officials in the Federal Republic have some difficulty in projecting and sustaining such images at all times. The need to accommodate and reconcile many conflicting demands for domestic and foreign policy measures often threatens to tarnish their public posture as guardians of the commonweal. Political opponents are always ready to picture them as incompetent or opportunist characters who ought to be thrown out of office.

To extricate themselves from this dilemma and increase their freedom of action, governmental leaders have resorted to various devices. Some have appealed to traditional orientations of respect for legitimate public authority and paternalistic leadership. Others have sought to conceal their activities from public view and have accused prying critics of disruptive interference in the conduct of affairs of state. However, none of these measures have proven particularly effective in recent years and some have backfired, putting an end to rather spectacular political careers.

PERCEPTIONS OF THE CITIZEN'S ROLES

To most West Germans the formal rules of the political system today largely define the legitimate roles that an ordinary citizen can and should play in public affairs. In this regard cultural traditions stressing the need for law and order in state and society have been sustained by the patterns of socioeconomic stratification and the organization of political life in the Federal Republic. The average West German considers himself and his peers as "little men" who are entitled to the constitutional rights and benefits of German citizens and who are obligated to observe the law, but who have little or no real influence over the course of political developments.

As we observed earlier, the founders of the Federal Republic feared that too much popular participation could lead to political instability. Accordingly they formulated constitutional rules for a "representative" democracy in which citizens were to play only intermittent and indirect roles in the choice of governmental policies and policymakers. West Germans have by now learned to accept the legitimacy of these role assignments, though most of them also feel that they should have a greater voice in public affairs. In a 1973 poll, for example, two out of three adults wanted more "direct" democracy than provided for by the Basic Law. Significantly, the higher the educational level of the respondents, the more content were they with prevailing arrangements. In other words, those most favored by present patterns of socioeconomic stratification were also most inclined to leave well enough alone.

For most West Germans, but especially for older persons, women, and people living outside the urban centers, their rather formalistic perceptions of the state and its authority relationships inform their sense of political involvement and efficacy. They see little reason to engage in sustained political activities since they believe that they are essentially consumers rather than producers of governmental policies.

Nonetheless, West Germans seem on the whole to be exceptionally interested in politics according to various crossnational attitude surveys — more so than Americans, Englishmen, and Italians, for instance. Why this should be so in light of their sense of political impotence is at first glance a bit puzzling. West German politics have been singularly devoid of the intense ideological conflicts and mass turmoil that are often associated with a high degree of political interest. According to any number of political theories the fact that most contemporary West Germans have received less formal education than Americans should make them less rather than more interested in politics than Americans.

Part of the reason for the apparent gap between a large, politically attentive public and a small, politically active public in the Federal Republic may be the exceptionally high political content of the mass communications media. Extensive coverage of public affairs in the press, radio, and television has made politics something of a spectator sport in West Germany.

But there seem to be more basic reasons. Ordinary citizens may today be poorly motivated to enter the political fray but they want to be seen as attentive to politics. German cultural values have long stressed the possession of knowledge and, over the past three decades increasingly, of political knowledge. Particularly younger people who grew up under the present regime have had it impressed on them by civic educators that mass political ignorance led to mass political impotence under former regimes and that a democratically "competent" citizen is a politically informed citizen. To judge by their responses in opinion polls, West Germans have learned this lesson rather well. Whereas, for example, only one in four adults in a 1952 poll professed to be "generally" interested in politics, one out of two did so in a 1973 survey.

A closer examination of such polls indicates, however, that most West Germans are in fact no better informed than most Americans about particular aspects of their political order and find it no less difficult to comprehend the intricacies of public policy processes. As in other representative democracies, the further removed people feel from the centers of decision making, and the less they consider their personal interests to be involved in policy outcomes, the greater is their propensity to be bored by everyday politics. Furthermore, it seems that when West Germans tell a pollster that they are "generally" interested in politics, their responses are more often than not expressions of conformity with what they take to be the norms of democratic citizenship rather than of a belief that they know enough to play the game of politics.

Public authority in the Federal Republic emanates in the

last analysis from the people, according to the Basic Law, and is to be periodically delegated by them to their representatives in elections. Compared to other regimes that provide such opportunities for popular control through entirely voluntary electoral participation the turnout in West Germany has been exceptionally high over the years. Whereas in the United States, for example, only about half of the eligible voters cast their ballots in national elections, in the Federal Republic federal elections have consistently brought practically all qualified voters to the polls. The exercise of the franchise then, would seem to indicate a singularly high sense of popular involvement independent of changing issues and candidates. But here too we find a gap between formal adherence to the constitutional norms of democratic citizenship and perceptions of political efficacy in the way most West Germans perceive their participant roles.

The turnout for federal elections has been even higher than in the turbulent national elections of the last years of the Weimar Republic. But whereas then a high rate of participation was attributable to the mobilization of voters by radical parties opposed to the regime, the reasons and consequences now appear to be entirely different. West German election studies have shown that the campaign rhetoric of contending parties and candidates usually leaves the voters rather cold and that most of them do not believe that casting their ballots matters very much over the long run. The major parties, naturally enough, seek maximum mass support by making every election appear to be crucial, but with few exceptions West German voters have not considered electoral outcomes truly crucial for their own or the country's future. In effect the large turnout in federal elections has enhanced rather than weakened the combined strength of the parties supporting the present regime and thereby has promoted its institutionalization.

On the whole it appears that the turnout has been high not so much because West Germans believe that their votes determine governmental policies but because they consider it their civic duty to go to the polls. Although social pressure to exercise one's franchise is rather high — particularly in smaller communities where abstentions are more noticeable — the cost is not. Since elections always come on Sundays a voter can spare the time and will not suffer a loss of income. And as legal residence and age automatically entitle every citizen to cast a ballot, there is no need to register, pay a poll tax, or take a qualifying test.

In sum, an electorate which believes that voting has no decisive effect on the way political issues are dealt with by the ruling elites has been extensively but not intensively involved in elections. Popular dissatisfaction with some political leaders may produce some shifts in electoral support for the major parties; but usually such shifts have until now reflected comparatively mild protest votes directed against particular actors rather than against the regime and the operation of the political system.

THE INCOMING GENERATION

Almost half of the adults in a 1971 West German opinion survey asserted that the preservation of law and order required strong governmental leadership. However, only one out of three young people between fifteen and twenty shared this view. Furthermore, most of the adults but only a minority of the young people thought that the government and opposition parties in the Federal Parliament should work together rather than stress their differences. And close to half of the young persons believed that more than small changes were needed to modernize "antiquated" socioeconomic and political structures in their country.

Polls and election returns indicate notable generational differences in West German political opinions. In the 1970s, traditional, parochial, and law-and-order orientations were most prevalent among the oldest age groups. The middle aged tended to be less steeped in the past and less orthodox than their seniors but more conservative than their juniors. Young people, who were born and raised in the Federal Republic, were on the whole more strongly committed to the principles of the present constitutional order than their elders. Many of them were, however, critical of what they took to be its shortcomings. In their view, the Federal Republic was a "democratic and social" state more in constitutional form than in actual fact. Far-reaching reforms and more direct democracy were said to be needed to make the political system more egalitarian and more responsive to the needs of ordinary people.

Rather different learning experiences distinguish this incoming generation of West German adults from that of their parents and, even more, from that of their grandparents. Its members grew up in an era without war and bitter domestic conflicts, an era that witnessed a pronounced decline in paternalistic authority patterns in state and society and rapidly rising standards of living in all socioeconomic strata. These young West Germans have become accustomed to material affluence in a mass-consumption society and to extensive associations with peoples of other countries. And they have been the objects of massive civic education efforts by governmental and nongovernmental agencies designed to teach them the "legitimate" rights and responsibilities of citizenship under the constitution of the Federal Republic.

According to recent studies West German adolescents and young adults are today a good deal more self-assertive and less conformist than were equivalent age groups in previous years. They are more likely to question the justification for particular rules and regulations, they are less ready to accept prevailing hierarchical structures, and they tend to be more independent in forming their political opinions. They are also prone to be more tolerant of political dissent and more in favor of mass participation in major policy decisions than their elders. However, most of them are just as disinclined to join a political party or civic association, though they usually feel more competent to participate in politics.

Young people in contemporary West Germany are far more individualistic — or self-centered, if you will — than their forebears. They have no use for collectivist ideologies of the past, such as romantic nationalism, and they are not disposed to put the interest of the state above their personal interests. Compulsory military service, for example, is seen as an unwelcome burden rather than as a patriotic duty as it once was. The young expect the state to provide for their personal welfare.

They are usually more concerned with what they consider to be their private affairs than with what their political leaders and would-be leaders call the public interests, except where the two appear to them to coincide.

Some international studies suggest that differences in the political orientations of younger and older citizens of the Federal Republic cannot simply be attributed to the young West Germans' more emphatic break with the legacy of a specifically German past. Similar generational differences have been noted in Britain, France, Italy, and the United States. They may be due to the normal propensity of young people to question, if not reject the "old-fashioned" notions of their elders. In West Germany, at least, they have thus far not given rise to a general conflict of generations. In fact, political orientations that distinguish the young have tended to be overshadowed by cleavages based on differences in socioeconomic background and education.

According to a 1973 international opinion survey, young West Germans were less likely to consider their elders conservative than their age peers in other advanced industrial countries with liberal democratic regimes (see Table IV.2). They were more prone to believe that family background determined a person's future station in life, but at the same time they were exceptionally satisfied with the way they were governed. In short, notwithstanding the inequalities in socioeconomic and political opportunities in the Federal Republic, most young West Germans were decidedly not alienated from their political system.

Members of the incoming generation of adult citizens may be more outspoken in their criticism of certain features of the system than their elders and more vocal in demanding reforms. However, they generally share the view that the average person normally has little or no control over public policy decisions. Among younger as among older West Germans a sense of actual or potential political influence increases with the level of schooling. This is not surprising; it seems rather realistic in the light of the prevailing close relationship between educational achievements and socioeconomic status. Attitude

TABLE IV.2. *Sociopolitical Views of Young Adults Aged 18–24*
in Major Non-Communist Industrial Countries, 1973
(in percentages)

Question	G.F.R.	U.S.	U.K.	France	Japan
Does the government protect the rights and welfare of the people?					
Yes, fully	22	7	4	4	1
Yes, more or less fully	62	44	39	27	10
Subtotal satisfied	84	51	43	31	11
No, not fully	10	39	40	28	67
No, not at all	2	9	14	18	22
Subtotal dissatisfied	12	48	54	46	89
No answer/no opinion	4	1	3	23	—
The government is placing too much emphasis on the benefits of the nation as a whole at the cost of individuals.					
True	44	74	68	68	88
False	49	25	28	13	11
No answer/no opinion	7	1	4	19	1
The government sometimes goes in the opposite directions from those in which the people really want to go.					
True	56	87	90	76	85
False	38	12	8	9	13
No answer/no opinion	6	1	2	15	2
Man's future is often virtually determined by his parents' profession and his family background.					
True	72	48	42	38	48
False	23	51	57	53	51
No answer/no opinion	5	1	1	9	1
Older men think too highly of maintaining things without change.					
True	68	79	76	78	74
False	26	21	21	13	24
No answer/no opinion	6	—	3	9	2

Source: *Gallup Opinion Index*, report no. 100 (October 1973), pp. 28–29.

surveys among secondary school students have found that those in the vocational schools are far more likely to have a low sense of future political efficacy than those in the university preparatory schools attended by children from the middle and top social strata.

Intragenerational distinctions attributable to differences in social background and education are especially evident in the political orientations of university students. The institutions of higher learning, as we have noted, act as the recruiting ground for the policymakers and the teachers and opinion makers of future years. For that reason the supposed political "restlessness" and discontent of university students in the early 1970s pleased some and alarmed more of their elders. The former welcomed what they took as evidence of the emergence of a particularly democratic and idealistic generation of West German leaders; the latter believed that the universities were the breeding grounds for a new generation of politically alienated, antidemocratic radicals who were determined to overthrow the present regime.

Both interpretations appeared in the latter 1970s to rest on a rather distorted image of young West Germans in general and university students in particular. In the first place, the demands for drastic socioeconomic and political changes came only from a small and highly fractionalized minority concentrated in a few disciplines and at few universities. It consisted mostly of students of the social sciences and these, again, were divided into feuding factions belonging to the youth organizations of the Social Democratic party, a very small Communist party, and various minuscule left-wing extremist groups. Most university students were far more conservative in political outlook, far more passive in political behavior, and far more willing to become integrated into the prevailing political order.

Second, although some young Germans showed greater tolerance toward these dissident groups than their elders, and agreed with some of their demands, most were far more moderate in their desire for reforms. The efforts of left-wing radicals to mobilize the support of young workers from lower socioeconomic strata appeared to be singularly unsuccessful. In time, university radicalism may trickle down to students in the secondary schools. But it is also conceivable that a conservative reaction will occur among the incoming generation, lending greater strength to right-wing elements.

POLITICAL INSTITUTIONALIZATION AND CHANGE

Policymakers in the West German state have to deal with environmental factors over which they have at best only limited control. More often than not significant changes in domestic and international conditions cannot be anticipated by the decision makers. These problems exist in all states, but they are particularly prominent in a complex modern industrial society and in a country that is as intimately involved in international affairs as the Federal Republic.

The efforts of West German policymakers to achieve their objectives under uncertain environmental conditions depend on a stable climate of supportive mass opinion. Their ability to deal with unanticipated developments will be enhanced if they can rely on ready compliance with their decisions by the public officials who have to implement them and by the citizens who are affected by them. In this regard the authority of the governors and the viability of the regime are strengthened by a close correspondence between the formal rules and the actual operation of the political system. This calls for sufficient popular appreciation of the value of basic organizational arrangements to ensure their continuity. It also requires a style of political intercourse that is flexible enough to accommodate political change and the adaption of rules to style and style to rules. Over time governmental performance and policy processes have influenced and been influenced by the patterns of continuity and change in the political orientations and relationships of rulers and ruled in West Germany.

On the whole West German political attitudes have thus far been marked by domestic peace and harmony. Over the years opinion surveys and election returns have reflected a generally low level of political conflict and a strikingly prosaic climate of opinion. Various coalitions of policymaking elites have rather easily achieved agreement on what have usually been fairly mundane issues without involving a largely indifferent mass·public. The occasional intense disputes in the policymaking stratum — such as the controversy over the new Eastern foreign policy of the 1970s — have therefore appeared all the more exceptional.

Compared to the destabilizing political divisions that once rocked the Weimar Republic and that now prevail in many other countries, the political order in the Federal Republic appears to rest today on a broad popular and elite consensus that sustains stable political relationships. In contrast to former times, the political orientations of most citizens are not tied to divisive ideologies or to exclusive national and subnational collectivities. Socioeconomic distinctions and disparities have not surfaced in the form of bitter conflicts between employers and employees and the richer and poorer members of an affluent society. A strong sense of class consciousness, of belonging to and sharing the policy interests of a privileged few or underprivileged many, is far less evident in present-day West Germany than, for example, in England, France, and Italy.

The constitutional order for the organization of political life is endorsed by most West Germans principally on the basis of instrumental standards rather than emotional loyalties. The major parties accordingly compete for the voters' favor by promising above all efficient governmental performance. Political leaders present themselves as agents of stability as well as of progress. Organized interest groups and public officials vie with each other in advertising their skills in satisfying the policy demands of different types of clients.

Such activities reflect and reinforce the prevalent view that the political system is much like the economic system: services must be provided for payments rendered, and contractual obligations between active and passive actors in the system must be honored. They are furthermore sustained by the prevalent belief that the interests of particular groups and individuals will be best served if everyone adheres to the rules of the constitutional order.

The incorporation of these rules into West German political orientations has two major consequences for the operation of the political system. (1) Key participant roles in public policy-making are today exercised by the occupants of a few top elite

positions — above all the leaders of the major parties and interest associations, key governmental officials, and opinion
leaders in control of the principal media of mass communication. (2) In pursuing their objectives, the members of this
policymaking stratum are relatively unencumbered by mass
pressures for the satisfaction of irreconcilable policy demands
and find it correspondingly easier to reconcile their own differences. The ruling groups have not only been far more
united on basic principles than under the Weimar Republic
but they have also been far less exposed to the buffeting winds
of an unstable climate of mass opinion.

As we have noted, most West Germans have acted only as
political spectators on the grounds that ordinary citizens are
essentially consumers rather than producers of public policies.
Political stability over successive governments has therefore
been sustained not only by the fact that West Germans have
manifestly desired it, but by a more subtle process that is
called "audience flow" in American broadcasting circles. Here
the sponsors and producers of television and radio programs
have found that they inherit much of their mass audience
from preceding shows, because viewing and listening habits
are controlled more by inertia than by the exercise of free
choice. Like a river that continues to flow in the same direction unless it is diverted, program consumers are therefore expected to stay tuned in as long as they do not have a strong
reason to switch to another program. West German policy producers have in a like fashion proceeded on the assumption
that law-abiding policy consumers are likely to buy their output — even when they do not like particular aspects — as long
as they are generally content with the performance of the system.

The institutionalization of the political system has thus
been furthered by the fact that West Germans have come to
accept the system on the strength of its performance and by
force of habit. But though the regime's chances of survival appear to have increased over the years, they seem by no means
assured. Like older and more solidly established liberal democratic regimes, the Federal Republic faces domestic and international problems that may exceed the capacity of such systems

and discredit their modes of government unless they find ways to adapt themselves to new contingencies.

In the Federal Republic a decided slowdown in economic growth coupled with rapidly rising living costs in the 1970s indicated an end to the constantly increasing affluence that had produced great popular satisfaction with the performance of the political system. And the very institutionalization of once innovative political arrangements led critical observers to pose the question whether the system, as constituted, was flexible enough to cope with emerging policy issues in a dynamic world. If it was not, they maintained, continuing changes in political attitudes and environmental conditions were likely to overtake, antiquate, and ultimately put an end to the principles of a federal and representative West German parliamentary democracy.

The ambivalence and paradoxes in contemporary West German political attitudes appear to be not so much the products of deliberate equivocation as the reflection of unresolved contradictions and tensions in a changing society. The inclination to saddle the state and public authorities with responsibility for the collective welfare seems largely to be an attempt to escape the uncertainties of a policy environment that appears incomprehensible and even frightening to many West Germans. A good deal of mutual distrust and preoccupation with what are seen as private matters provide few incentives for collective political action. At the same time new, emotionally satisfying political ideals and reference symbols have not developed to take the place of the discredited nationalism and charismatic leader-mass relationship of the Third Reich. The average West German is torn between his desire for personal freedom in an increasingly complex and bureaucratized society and his wish for protection against material deprivation and physical destruction. In the contemporary version of this well-known conflict between liberty and welfare the new sense of freedom from authoritarian controls clashes with the demand for peace, domestic harmony, and economic security.

Although the elites who largely "run" the political system enjoy a good deal of latitude in what they can do, they need to be highly sensitive to changes in the climate of mass opinion. The rulers thus have a difficult task: they must try to anticipate and satisfy diverse and not always obvious demands from the mass public while remaining keenly aware of mass values and emotions that might be mobilized against them by antiregime groups. However, they also have strong motives for molding mass opinion and curbing dissident elements who would radically alter the system.

The present leaders of the Federal Republic are essentially united in their determination to maintain the basic components of the prevailing socioeconomic system. They want West Germans to stick with the present constitutional program and to keep them from switching to another program by supporting proponents of radical revolutionary change. They differ, however, on how much, and in what manner, the ongoing program needs to be adjusted if it is to retain its mass audience.

The more conservative members of the policymaking stratum believe that necessary political authority in the state is in danger of being seriously undermined by an excessive emphasis on individual rights and by the loss of communal solidarity. In their view the preservation of political stability and social harmony in the years ahead is threatened by the waning of traditional civic virtues. Young people seem to them too hedonistic, too preoccupied with their personal well-being, and too little concerned about the public interest. West Germans should assume greater responsibility toward the state, Deputy Federal Chancellor Hans-Dietrich Genscher said in May 1973, and stick to the "old fashioned ideals" of simplicity, thrift, and achievement. Other leaders, in like fashion, have called for a return to such traditional moral values as the work ethic, religious faith, collective discipline, and patriotic self-negation for the "public good."

More reform-minded leaders agree with the conservatives that excessive popular expectations of satisfactory policy outputs combined with low emotional attachments to community, state, and regime provide a rather weak basis for the maintenance of the system in the event of a major economic or foreign policy crisis. However, they hold that this possibility points to the need for "progressive" policies that will accommodate and anticipate changing West German political values. In their view it is better to take the wind out of the sails of the system's radical critics than to resort to punitive measures that may silence dissenters but not terminate popular demands for more socioeconomic and political democracy.

CHAPTER V

Politicization and Participation

WHO PARTICIPATES WHEN, where, how, and why in West German politics is a matter partly of structured opportunities, partly of personal motivation. The two are closely related. The organization and rules of the West German political system offer several opportunities for legitimate participation. But the perceptions of such opportunities and the inclinations to use them vary.

Relatively few West Germans are constantly involved in public affairs because they need to be or choose to be. Government officials and functionaries of political parties and pressure groups cannot help but be involved, but for most people active participation is the exception rather than the rule. Those who say "I could if I would" lack motivation; they believe they have the competence and the freedom to participate but usually see no reason for doing so. Those who say "I would if I could" consider themselves most, if not all of the time, in no position to take effective political action; the political system, as they see it, does not give them the opportunity. Consequently most full-time political activists in the Federal Republic, as in other countries, are first of all exceptionally motivated by ambition, ideology, and other personal values to assume participant roles. Second, they usually have a particularly high sense of potential or actual political efficacy. They believe themselves sufficiently well situated in the system to realize some, if not all of their objectives in the public arena.

In short, a West German's participation in politics depends not only on his position but his disposition. Differences in the prevailing patterns of participation are in this regard both a source and product of variations in perceived opportunities and motivation.

In the first sections of this chapter we will examine some key factors in the development of participant orientations and, we will see more generally what public policy processes West Germans feel they can demand and should support. We will then turn to the present structure of participation, particularly at the policymaking level.

INFORMATION AND LEARNING

Political man is primarily a child of nurture rather than nature. Similarities and differences in attitudes affecting political behavior patterns within and across countries are conditioned by the interplay between what people learn about contemporary developments and what they learned previously. And here variations in the mixture of current information and prior experiences, and in their respective effects on political orientations, give rise to differences in the way public affairs are perceived and evaluated. Political man in his various contemporary West German versions is in this respect a product of both his informational environment and his socialization.

From what he personally observes, and from what others tell him, a West German derives today an image of his political environment, a sense of his place in that environment, and certain ideas about what he likes or dislikes about it. He learns and may relearn to link his political self-perception with his perception of other political actors, to relate his views of proper political roles and desirable goals to theirs, and to rank his policy preferences. And he learns to formulate and express his views in terms of an acquired language of political intercourse. All of this knowledge leads him to attach a positive or negative meaning — or perhaps none at all — to such concepts as private property rights and to give political importance to some interpersonal communications and associations and not to others.

Here socialization experiences, particularly political socialization, provide the West German with a basic frame of reference for his underlying orientation. They may, and generally do, establish the seeding ground for informational cues that can politicize social and cultural attitudes and activate as well as deactivate behavioral dispositions.

Through continuous and cumulative learning experiences from childhood onward, all West Germans acquire beliefs, values, and sentiments about their social environment and how it affects them. Political socialization focuses these on public policy processes, such as authority relationships in the state. This socialization is usually diffuse and implicit early in life, becoming more concrete and explicit later on. What a West German has learned about political relationships is most likely to influence his political behavior as his private affairs become intertwined with public affairs and his personal concerns with the political activities of collectivities, such as governmental bodies, parties, and interest associations.

New learning experiences may reinforce, weaken, or alter an individual's political orientations. As a rule, the more stable and homogeneous a West German's informational environment, and the more congruent it is with his established views, the less likely he is to change his fundamental political outlook. This does not mean that even then his perceptions, expectations, and preferences will always be consistent with and attributable to his socialization. What it does imply is that the responses of most West German adults to current information about specific political events and actors — say their votes in an election — are apt to be influenced by salient earlier learning experiences and that efforts to structure mass opinion need to take this influence into account.

The socialization and occasional resocialization of individuals can be a source of continuity or change in collective political attitude patterns and can serve to maintain or alter habitual patterns of political behavior. As we saw, the elite-controlled resocialization of West Germans to the precepts of a new constitutional order promoted its cultural institutionalization. Initially they were, so to speak, simply rebaptized by their leaders with a mixture of political wines from bottles bearing both old and new semantic labels and issued a new set of political birth certificates declaring them to be members of a "democratic and social" German state. Effective mass conversion followed more gradually as West Germans were slowly inducted into new political roles and taught a new terminology of political communications. They learned to discard or attach negative connotations to terms like Nazi and nationalism, and positive ones to such concepts as representative government, civil liberty, and the rule of law. More importantly, they learned to associate valued goals, such as social and economic security, with the organization and smooth operation of the constituted political system and to identify the proper distribution of political roles with the established order. Learned behavior thus became habitual behavior.

In contemporary West Germany both the proponents and the critics of prevailing political arrangements believe that political socialization will determine whether these arrangements will endure. But whereas those who are well satisfied with the present political system want socialization to provide mass support for its continuity, those who are not want it to produce mass demands for political change. Who should learn what about politics, and from whom and how, has therefore been and promises to remain a major policy issue in the Federal Republic.

What is essentially at stake here is the basic problem of the nature and scope of democratic politics in an advanced industrial society. According to West German conservatives political socialization should above all provide for popular orientations that will ensure the preservation of social harmony and political stability. In their view this requires that present and incoming citizens realize that effective representative government calls for a hierarchical distribution of political roles which allows a competent few to make public policy for the benefit of the less competent many. Correspondingly, conservatives stress the need for governmental measures designed to imbue West Germans with respect for law, order, and authority, and a strong sense of civic duty.

According to liberal reformers the inadequate political education of West Germans is largely to blame if the present system is not as much of a participatory democracy as it should be under the terms of the Basic Law. They do not share the conservatives' distrust of mass democracy and believe that radical criticism of the regime may do more good than harm as it teaches West Germans to be more than passive political spectators. Political socialization, as they see it, should be directed toward providing the nonelites with a stronger sense of involvement in policymaking and give them greater incentives and qualifications for participation. Here the liberal reformers have stressed participation at the grassroots level. They have, for instance, supported governmental measures to give students more of a voice in the operation of their schools and universities and workers more of a say in the management of their factories.

Left-wing radicals — a small but highly vocal minority — assert that such reforms are at best inadequate and at worst merely symbolic gestures on the part of the ruling elites. In their view conservatives and liberals are essentially united in their determination to perpetuate socioeconomic and political relations that must be changed fundamentally if West Germany is to become a genuine democracy. As they see it, the "real" interests of ordinary West Germans require that the masses be alienated from, rather than integrated into a system that serves only the interests of ruling groups who control the principal agents of socialization and information. Accordingly radicals endeavor to socialize young people and resocialize adults into an awareness of the allegedly pseudodemocratic character and terminology of the present system. The more militant radicals have sought to achieve this objective through illegal actions designed to provoke official countermeasures. In this way they hope to show to the masses the allegedly oppressive and exploitive nature of the contemporary regime.

Any group that hopes to give a particular direction to the course of political socialization must contend with the fact that socialization is an extremely complex process. The transmission of political orientations over several generations has been complicated by sharp discontinuities in the socialization experiences of different age cohorts. Political socialization today also involves a large variety of agents, all sorts of manifestly political and ostensibly nonpolitical relationships, and a far more dynamic informational environment than in former times. Finally, relevant learning processes in a comparatively open and pluralist society cannot be coordinated to the same degree as under such authoritarian systems as those of Nazi Germany and Communist East Germany.

PREADULT SOCIALIZATION

A citizen of the Federal Republic gets his first formal opportunity to influence the course of political developments when he turns eighteen and may vote as well as run for an elective public office. At that stage in life a West German's preadult socialization experiences are apt to have a more immediate effect on his political outlook and behavior than in later years. They are not only more recent, but normally less complex than subsequent socialization experiences. A young person in contemporary West Germany usually grows in a subcultural environment that provides him with closely intertwined social relationships and with fewer and simpler behavior cues. He is therefore likely to come to his adult political roles with deeply ingrained social beliefs and values which will influence his participant orientations and partisan dispositions early on and, possibly, for the rest of his life.

Home Environment. Socialization begins at home, but there is very little hard evidence of the family's influence on West German political orientations. There is some indication that in the Federal Republic, as in other advanced industrial countries, the formative influence of the family is waning. It is evidently no longer as profound as it was in the postwar era of social dislocation. However, the evidence also suggests that family background and home environment may still have some importance for political socialization and differentiation, particularly during the impressionable years of childhood and early adolescence.

To begin with, the form and content of family socialization may have a political spillover effect. That is, ostensibly nonpolitical social roles and standards of behavior taught in the home can shape political orientations. It seems, for instance, that in the absence of stronger new socializing experiences, what a West German child generally learns about authority relationships in the family is likely to affect his subsequent attitudes toward governmental authorities; sex-role differentiations acquired in the family appear to have a significant bearing on the fact that West German women are less inclined than men to become involved in politics; and perceptions of social status differences passed on from parent to child evidently relate to corresponding distinctions between elites and nonelites in West German politics.

West German parents, like parents elsewhere, want their offspring to embrace precepts they themselves hold dear and to learn what they consider proper norms for social conduct. To judge by the structured responses to mass opinion polls, such standards have been changing. As indicated in Table V.1, adults continue to consider it important that children be taught to be orderly and diligent. However, far more adults now emphasize the need to teach self-reliance, independence, and tolerance and far fewer stress the preparation for obedience, conformity, and religious devotion in adult life. Such survey data also suggest that these shifts are largely attributable to generational changes and are particularly pronounced among well-educated members of the higher social strata.[1]

The influence of the West German family on explicitly political preadult socialization and differentiation evidently also varies a good deal with the social milieu of the home. The home environment appears to have the strongest effect on the acquisition of participant orientations and partisan identifications in ideologically cohesive families.

According to a number of studies, West German children

[1] The results of a 1973 representative survey are illuminating here. It asked West Germans over eighteen years of age how they felt about an "antiauthoritarian education" for children, a rather new notion propounded especially by radical reformers. Practically all had some idea of what it meant, though not necessarily the same one. Only eight percent favored it without reservations and 38 percent rejected it categorically, but as many as 43 percent considered it at least in some respects not a bad idea. And the younger a respondent and the more extensive his schooling the more he favored some antiauthoritarian education for his children.

Table V.1. *Adults' Norms for Preadult Socialization*
(Mass opinion data in rounded percentages)

Question 1: Which of the qualities listed here should be particularly
stressed in children's education?

	1951	1969
Independence and self-reliance	28	45
Obedience and subordination	25	19
Orderliness and diligence	41	45
Other qualities	5	2
Don't know, no answer	1	5
Total	100	116[a]

Question 2: Which of the following traits listed here do you consider
particularly important for the way children should be
trained at home for adult life?

	1967	1972
Good manners	85	74
Tolerance	59	63
Social conformity	61	51
Interest in and understanding of politics	30	34
Firm faith, firm religious ties	39	28
Total	274[a]	250[a]

[a]Total exceeds 100 percent because multiple choices were permitted. Absolute numbers are not available.

Sources: Question 1: EMNID Institute, *Informationen*, no. 42 (1964), no. 1 (1970). Question 2: Elisabeth Noelle-Neumann and Erich Peter Neumann, *Jahrbuch der oeffentlichen Meinung 1968–1973* (Allensbach: Verlag fuer Demoskopie, 1974).

are most likely to develop an interest in politics — and expectations that they will participate in public affairs when they grow up — in homes where political issues are frequently and openly discussed. And, as these studies also show, such discussions are most prevalent in families of the higher social strata and have the greatest learning effect on the children of parents who are well educated and display a high degree of political knowledge and competence.

Continuity in a family's partisan identification over several generations is today not nearly as common in the Federal Republic as in England and the United States. The sharp political discontinuities of the past and a widespread blandness of contemporary partisan allegiances have militated against the development of strong family loyalties to a particular political party. Some recent investigations indicate that the effective transfer of partisan attachments from parents to children is strongest in those West German homes where father and mother support the same party. They also suggest that this phenomenon is linked to more general factors of family socialization. One such study, for example, has hinted that school children who favor conservative parties tend to come from religiously devout and generally "conservative" families, whereas those who favor reformist parties are likely to come from less religious and more "liberal" home environments.[2]

The Schools. The primary focus of current controversies over preadult political socialization is the educational system. One of the disputed issues pertains to the implicit political consequences of what West German children generally learn at school; another concerns the scope, content, and effect of explicit political training, especially at the secondary level.

Here conservatives, liberals, and radicals share two underlying assumptions. The first is that the formal instruction and social training West Germans receive in school will have a profound effect on their political dispositions in adulthood. From this follows the second assumption that public policies in this area are crucial for the development of regime-supportive attitudes and participant orientations among the incoming generations.

When a West German child starts to go to nursery and primary school his or her political socialization takes on a new

[2] Kendall L. Baker and Thomas N. Long, "The Acquisition of Partisanship in Germany," an unpublished study based on a 1967 questionnaire survey of fourteen- to sixteen-year-old youngsters in Cologne.

dimension. The child passes from the more exclusive, private sphere of family socialization and is exposed to new learning experiences shaped by public authorities. For the most part these are authorities in the various states of the Federal Republic, above all in the state governments. Teachers are civil servants of the states and the states' educational ministries tell them what to teach. Furthermore, both state and federal governments heavily subsidize nongovernmental organizations — youth groups of the major churches, parties, and trade unions — which are considered to make constructive contributions to the political education of young West Germans.

Preadult political socialization in the West German schools is in this respect less diversified than in the United States, but more so than in countries with a more highly centralized educational system, such as France and Britain. There are no popularly elected school boards, and local educational authorities have little autonomy. The state governments cooperate to a certain extent in deciding what should be taught by whom and to whom. In the early 1970s, for example, they agreed that radical opponents of the present regime should not be permitted to teach any subject. The quality and quantity of political education vary considerably from state to state and school to school. The political complexion of different state governments, the party affiliations and personal preferences of their ministers of culture and educational administrators, the strength of regional traditions, and the relative power of various nongovernmental groups that endeavor to influence educational policies, make for considerable heterogeneity.

Studies on the effect of direct and indirect governmental control over preadult political socialization in the Federal Republic have been limited and rather inconclusive. In particular it is by no means clear how much influence the methods and content of formal instruction have on the development of participant orientations. For example, contemporary West German school children have greater opportunities to participate in classroom discussions and to question their teachers' views than their forebears. But how much of a difference this will make when they grow up remains an open question.

What is most clearly indicated is that home and school socialization interact to varying degrees and with varying effects. Because the present educational system segregates children early, largely on the basis of their family background, their social environments inside and outside school are likely to be quite similar. And both tend to combine in promoting significant distinctions in the way West German children are trained for their future participant roles in the political system.

Schooling appears in this regard to have a multiplicator effect. Children from the upper social strata tend to go to academic high school, which gives them the formal training necessary to enter higher social status positions (see pages 52–55). Then, their interpersonal contacts are apt to be largely confined to teachers and peers from a similar social background. Both factors usually interact with continuing family socialization to provide them with communications skills that enhance their opportunities for playing preeminent participant roles when they reach adulthood. Children from lower social strata, on the other hand, are mainly restricted to primary social relations with their own kind inside as well as outside the prevocational and vocational schools. Especially in the case of girls raised in a rural area or in an urban working-class environment, family and school socialization evidently combine to limit their opportunities, their capacities, and their inclinations for active political participation when they grow up.

By the time a West German reaches voting age he is also likely to have received some form of explicit political training on the rights and duties of adult citizenship. But the vast majority of young people whose formal education ends when they are fifteen or sixteen receive a far more elementary civic education than those who graduate from academic high schools.

According to any number of official and semiofficial declarations, the purpose of civic education is to produce "democratically competent" citizens who can understand and cope with political reality in terms of the precepts of the established constitutional order. In the words of a report of the federal government, it is to promote the "integration" of West German youths into the political system by "creating, securing, and reinforcing" identification with the Federal Republic and its regime, and the principles on which they rest.[3] Here the institutionalization of the present system and the emergence of a new generation of political leaders and educators have gradually led to far-reaching changes in the nature of such explicit political socialization in the different states.

During the era of political transition in the 1950s and 1960s, "education for democracy" was essentially indoctrinational and conformed rather closely to traditional concepts of the state as the supreme source of political authority. The state, as a leading political scientist put it, imposed "on children and youths a duty to be instructed" about legitimate political role relationships and proper standards of behavior for its citizens.[4] Such instruction was designed in those years to forge a popular consensus of support for the new regime and its allocation of political roles among the incoming generation. It emphasized the acquisition of formal knowledge about the organization of the constitutional order and stressed that the interest of all West Germans called for authoritative rules which provided for necessary harmony in state and society. Anti-Nazism and anti-Communism were employed to impress on young people the superiority of a libertarian democratic system and to imbue them with the idea that responsible government, resting on the consent of the governed, required citizens who voluntarily subordinated their private interests to the public interest.

By the late 1960s it became apparent to West German policymakers that civic education in the schools was not a particularly effective training for democratic citizenship. They were alarmed by a brief but dramatic upsurge in right- and left-wing radicalism. Especially the latter seemed to them to find all too much resonance among just those youths who were particularly interested in politics and who were supposed to get the best political education — the students in the university preparatory high schools for the future elites and opinion leaders.

[3] Bundesminister fuer innerdeutsche Beziehungen, *Bericht der Bundesregierung zur Lage der Nation 1971* (Bonn: [government publication], February 1971), pp. 217–18.

[4] Theodor Eschenburg, *Staat und Gesellschaft in Deutschland,* 5th ed. (Stuttgart: Curt E. Schwab, 1965), p. 452.

Although this upsurge in radicalism accelerated the movement for reform, other factors entered into it. One was an emerging youth subculture among West German adolescents that was primarily peer-oriented and politically informed more by the mass media than by explicit instruction in the classroom. Another factor was the growing distance from the Nazi past. Along with the waning of Cold War tensions, it decreased the West German leaders' reliance on anti-Nazi and anti-Communist indoctrination. Finally, studies on the effects of on-going civic instruction showed that although it reinforced the participant dispositions that some young people acquired at home, it could not counteract political apathy and indifference. For most West German youth, what they were taught about politics in school seemed too abstract and remote from their personal concerns to have much meaning for their future roles in public affairs. At best it led them to believe that they had the competence and opportunity to become involved in politics, that they could if they would. But it evidently did not provide them with motivation and a sense of potential efficacy.

All this led to adaptive policy changes which West German political leaders and educators hoped would enhance the formative effect of civic education. Heretofore largely an elective subject, it was now required for ninth- or tenth-grade students in most of the states. Less emphasis was to be placed on teaching them the need for social and political harmony and more on a critical examination of individual and group conflicts and their resolution; less on the acquisition of descriptive knowledge and more on learning analytical skills that were to enable them to comprehend and cope with their political environment as adults.

What effect these changes will have on the preadult political socialization of the incoming generation of political actors remains to be seen. Social research suggests that in open, pluralist, and industrially advanced countries civic training in school is not a sufficient and, possibly, not even a necessary condition for the development of regime-supportive or, for that matter, regime-opposing attitudes. Other preadult socializing experience and subsequent learning in adulthood appear to be far more important than those who strive to control the scope and content of West German civic education tend to assume.

POLITICAL LEARNING IN ADULTHOOD

As West Germans near and then enter into adulthood the sources of their political learning proliferate and current information becomes more decisive in shaping their political outlook. Thereafter, the nature and extent of continuing socialization for participant roles vary a good deal with age, social background and environment, and political engagement.

Young adults are on the whole more open to new political learning experiences than older ones. For example, they are likely to adopt a wait-and-see attitude before committing themselves to a political party, especially if they come from homes where public affairs were rarely or never discussed and partisan attachments weak.[5] Highly educated members of the upper social strata are likely to be better politically informed and to be correspondingly more open to new learning than the more poorly educated members of the lower strata. And differences in the character and stability of their social environment provide West German adults with extensive and intensive resocializing contacts after their preadult socialization. Travel and geographic mobility, for example, tend to broaden the political mind, as do occupational and social mobility. West Germans who marry within their social strata, who reside and work for most of their lives in the same place, and who are generally rooted in a particular subcultural setting, are also likely to be most constant in their political outlook.

West Germans who make it their business to acquire new knowledge for effective participation are apt to be exposed to a particularly large variety of political communications and relationships — formal as well as informal — and to be especially sensitive to implications of political developments. This has been particularly notable in the careers of elected public

[5] A 1968 survey of West German party members found that the more apolitical their home environment had been the later they became interested in politics.

officials, such as the self-proclaimed pragmatists who have in recent years assumed leading participant roles — men like Chancellor Helmut Schmidt and members of his cabinet. In the course of making their way to the top in governmental and party hierarchies, they have shown themselves highly adaptable to changing environments. Among the present policymakers, in fact, are quite a few former radicals who were integrated into the prevailing political order as they learned to adjust to its structured opportunities in order to realize political ambitions.

In the Federal Republic, as in the United States, the better informed and more attentive political public is a small but influential minority. Most adults feel they have neither the need nor the ability to stay constantly abreast of political developments and are more likely to tune out than tune in when confronted with information that goes beyond their immediate experiences and concerns. Like most people in other advanced industrial societies, they find it difficult to understand complex domestic and international policy issues. Moreover, in West Germany, as elsewhere, various political groupings use a special language for political communications that in effect excludes outsiders. The esoteric terminology of left-wing radicals, for example, has been largely incomprehensible to the workers they have sought to resocialize. And access to and membership in the West German policymaking stratum require familiarity with a particular form of elite communications. In both instances those on the outside have not only the problem of understanding the in group's language, but the problem of articulating their own values and emotions in a way that will be understood by its members. Poll-takers may try to take the political pulse of the masses, and votes at election time may give some indications of popular political views, but by and large the voice of the ordinary people is heard through those who claim to be their spokesmen.

The conditions of a modern industrial society and the present system's principles of political participation enhance the role of elite opinion makers in shaping the political orientations of the average West German through the mass media.

Mass political communications and relations are in this respect essentially structured by formal governmental and nongovernmental organizations. If an average citizen is at all interested in public affairs, he usually relies on information and interpretations provided by trusted and respected sources — notably eminent journalists, civic leaders, professors, and high public officials.

At the mass level of West German politics informal contacts in primary groups that might supplement or by-pass such channels are less important. Frank exchanges of political views between family members, friends, neighbors, and co-workers are uncommon. Except in some small towns and villages, few people still go to their neighborhood taverns after work for leisurely political discussions with old acquaintances; most stay at home watching television or listening to the radio. Various studies have shown that the more urbanized an ordinary West German's social environment, the more likely he is to keep his view to himself.

The Mass Media. Political events and actors assume prominence in the eyes of the general public largely on the strength of their exposure by the mass media. The organizers of pressure group demonstrations, for example, have sought to obtain the largest possible media coverage in order to gain mass support for their objectives. The strategic role of the mass media in shaping the informational environment of West Germans — and consequently their perceptions of and reactions to political developments — is beyond dispute. However, for that very reason, who does and should control the media — and for what purpose and to what effect — has been a matter of considerable controversy among leaders and would-be leaders who seek to shape mass opinion in the Federal Republic.

To begin with, all of them see the mass media as a key communication link between the politically engaged minority of West German and the vast majority of peripheral participants. Furthermore, implicit and explicit political messages transmitted through the media are taken to have a long-term, cumulative effect on beliefs, values, and sentiments. That is, leaders as well as led, governors as well as governed learn to adapt their outlook and consequent behavior to "political reality" on the basis of information provided through the mass media. And it is generally assumed that those who manage the media can influence adult political socialization directly and preadult socialization indirectly. They may act as "gatekeepers" and interpreters of the news they consider fit to be seen, heard, and printed; they may also act as powerful partisan advocates and adversaries in the realm of public policy.

The extent of the particular and long-range influence of diverse media on the development of mass political orientations in West Germany is, however, by no means self-evident. Here, too, existing social research studies offer indications rather than conclusive answers. They suggest first of all that the media are indeed preeminent agents in the structured flow of socializing political communications. Secondly, although the effect of information varies with different media, circumstances, and audiences, it seems on the whole to be greater than ever before. Finally, it appears that such current information as ordinary West Germans take from favored media and consider salient is more likely to reinforce than alter their prior political dispositions, including their inclination and sense of opportunity for political participation.

In this regard we need to distinguish between the public and private mass media; they evidently differ considerably in their effectiveness. In the 1970s just about every West German home had a television set and at least one radio; in fact, there were more of these per capita than in any other country outside the United States. The Federal Republic, like the United States, has no truly national press (in contrast to France and Britain); there, as here, surveys have shown that radio and television are for most people the most frequently used and most trusted sources of political information (see Table V.2). But in West Germany broadcasting stations and networks are not even partially private enterprises. All are organized as "nonpartisan" public corporations that are formally under the exclusive jurisdiction of the states and supervised by boards appointed by their governments to represent the major politi-

Table V.2. *Public and Private Mass Media as Sources of*
Political Information, 1970 (adult mass opinion data
in rounded percentages)

1. Principal sources of information
   a. Public media
Television newscasts	81
Television reports on particular developments	53
Radio reports on particular developments	23
Subtotal public media	157[a]
   b. Private media
A single newspaper	57
Several newspapers	37
Weeklies and political periodicals	29
Subtotal private media	123[a]
   c. No time to keep informed, none of the above — 19
      Total — 299[a]
2. Frequency and mix of information
   a. Listen to newscasts on radio and/or television every day but do not read about politics in daily papers — 45
   b. Read about politics in a daily paper but do not listen to newscasts every day — 3
   c. Listen to daily newscasts *and* read about politics in a daily paper — 31
   d. Do not follow political developments on a daily basis — 21
      Total — 100
3. Preferred source if only one should be available
   a. Radio or television
All respondents	65
Women	69
Skilled and unskilled workers	70
   b. Newspaper
All respondents	33
Men	40
High-ranking white-collar employees	47
Graduates of academic high schools (Gymnasium)	60

[a] Add up to more than 100% since several sources could be given.

Source: E. Noelle-Neumann and E. P. Neumann, *Jahrbuch der oeffentlichen Meinung 1968–1973* (Allensbach: Verlag fuer Demoskopie, 1974), pp. 180–81.

cal parties, religious associations, and socioeconomic interest groups.[6]

6 The Federal Government has jurisdiction over broadcasts to foreign countries and "intra-German" programs beamed to the German Democratic Republic.

As in most other areas of public policy, the manifest object of these formal organizational arrangements is to accommodate the polycentric and pluralist elements in West German society within a federalist and representative democratic order. Attempts by the Federal Government to obtain a share of the public broadcasting media have been blocked by the Federal Constitutional Court; private enterpreneurs attempting to break the states' monopoly have thus far not been able to overcome the prevailing view that their efforts are not in the public interest.

The public media are more than passive agents of political communications, as the Federal Constitutional Court has pointed out. The charters of the public broadcasting corporations stipulate that news reports be accurate and objective and clearly distinguished from interpretive news commentaries. But they also provide that their presentations should not only conform with constitutional and ordinary law, but actively promote mass support for the basic principles of the established regime. Broadcasting stations are for instance specifically directed to emphasize the need for peace, freedom, and international understanding in their programs. And although the representatives of "legitimate" nongovernmental groups — such as legal political parties — have free access to the public media, views that are considered "subversive" by the controlling authorities may not be aired.

Within these limitations, the West German radio and television stations offer their mass audience an exceptionally rich and variegated fare of political information. Opposing viewpoints on key political issues are presented in frequent panel discussions, and many programs present a critical and, often, highly controversial examination of particular aspects of the present political system.

In comparison with the public media, the socializing effect of privately owned publications on mass political attitudes appears today to be neither as great as some observers wish it would be nor as powerful as others fear it is. In the early 1970s West Germany had some 500 newspapers and 48 weeklies with a combined sale of more than 22 million copies; according to survey data 83 percent of West Germans over sixteen read at least one daily paper. What these figures do not show is that the number of independent publications has grown ever smaller, that there has been increasingly less variety in political publications, that the press serves more to entertain than to politicize West Germans, and that the political content of most newspapers focuses on local and regional rather than national and international developments.

Freedom of the press and expression are fundamental citizenship rights under the Basic Law; public authorities are enjoined from monopolizing the mass media and manifestly they control not a single newspaper and only a few small periodicals. In light of the great influence of the German press in the past the framers of the constitution expected that an independent and pluralist "fourth estate" would play a major part in the future development of mass political attitudes.

Initially there was indeed a great blossoming forth of publications that offered their readers a wide variety of political information. But this proved to be a temporary phenomenon. Economic exigencies forced many to fold and others to be absorbed into a few publishing empires. In 1954 West Germany had 225 newspapers with independent political editorial policies and staffs; twenty years later it had only 120. More than half of the press was owned by only fifteen publishing houses and more than half of its total circulation was controlled by just 3 percent of all independent publishers.

The largest of these is today Axel Springer, a conservative or, as some would have it, nationalist publisher. Springer puts out virtually all of the Sunday papers, and one out of four West Germans over sixteen reads his *Bild Zeitung,* the only popular daily with a nationwide readership (see Table V.3). Springer's commercial preeminence has led his critics to ascribe to him a great deal of political influence over mass opinion; but there has been little solid evidence to support this belief. The *Bild Zeitung* is a tabloid which gives little space to political matters unless they are sensational, and by all indications most of its readers do not depend on it for political guidance.

Most West German newspapers and periodicals are today

Table V.3. *Leading Publications with Political Content (1972–73)*

Type of publication	Political orientation	Copies sold (in thousands)	Readers as percentage of population over 16	Nature of readership
All dailies	misc.	21,867	83	misc.
Local and regional	misc.	16,765	65	misc.
National	misc.	5,111	35	misc.
Bild Zeitung[a]	conservative	3,510	26	mass public
Welt[a]	conservative	230	3	political public
Frankfurter Allgemeine	conservative	268	3	political public
Sueddeutsche	liberal	282	n.a.	political public
Frankfurter Rundschau	liberal	160	n.a.	political public
Weeklies				
Bild am Sonntag[a]	conservative	2,191	24	mass public
Quick	conservative	1,307	n.a.	mass public
Stern	liberal	1,610	n.a.	mass public
Der Spiegel	liberal	881	n.a.	political public
Welt am Sonntag[a]	conservative	354	7	political public
Die Zeit	liberal	333	n.a.	political public

[a] Indicates Springer publications.

Sources: Institut fuer Demoskopie, *Allensbach Inter-Media,* 1972; Inter Nationes, *Kulturbrief,* October 1972; *Die Zeit,* August 17, 1973; *Stamm Leitfaden fuer Presse und Werbung,* 26th ed. (Essen: Stamm Verlag, 1973).

primarily commercial enterprises and feature items intended to attract a wide range of readers in local and regional advertising markets. About three-fourths of the dailies are local editions of regional newspapers that account for approximately four-fifths of the total circulation and two-thirds of the newspaper readers. As in the United States, independent local dailies have been disappearing, and particularly in rural areas there may only be a single paper, if any. In any event local papers provide their readers with little political information and primarily contain reports about social affairs, sports news, and lots of advertising. Regional dailies carry more political material, especially about politics in the various states; but here, too, the public broadcasting media are for most readers the primary sources for news that interests them.

Journals devoted primarily to political subjects do not have a mass readership, but more than three-fourths of West German adults read one or more of the illustrated weeklies containing political material. The most popular of these — *Quick, Stern,* and *Revue* — are, like the *Bild Zeitung,* commercial enterprises designed to attract as many customers as possible for their advertisers. Since competition between them is intense, they seek to scoop each other with sensational political items that will boost their circulation. Along with sex, sports, and gossip about prominent personalities, they feature titillating political revelations, interviews, and commentaries that focus on alleged shortcomings of the political system — such as factional fights and bribery scandals — rather than on its more mundane aspects. Consequently, these periodicals often present a rather negative picture of the system, which does not encourage their readers to participate in public affairs. Opinion surveys indicate, however, that most adults do not consider the illustrated weeklies important sources of political information.

On the whole, then, the average West German derives his image of political development and political actors primarily through the public broadcasting media. Opinion leaders who endeavor to shape his political attitudes and influence his partisan preferences rely to a corresponding extent on these media to get their messages to the general public. Insofar as they succeed, they structure political learning processes by drawing the attention to some political developments and not to others, and by emphasizing adherence to a particular political outlook and behavior. This applies particularly to leading public officials who command exceptional opinion-making authority by virtue of their formal positions.

The orientations of the politically more engaged public, on the other hand, are informed far more extensively through various printed media in the private sector, through books as well as newspapers and periodicals. Only one in three adult West Germans reads about politics in a daily paper, and the better educated they are and the higher their occupational status, the more likely West Germans are to prefer printed news over that presented by the broadcasting media (see Table V.2). At most one in ten consistently reads one or more of the few supraregional dailies that specifically address themselves to a politically attentive and involved public: the *Frankfurter Allgemeine,* the *Welt,* the *Sueddeutsche Zeitung,* and the *Frankfurter Rundschau* (see Table V.3). The first two are more conservative than the others, but all firmly support the present political order. These papers are read by the most influential participants in public affairs and provide a forum for interelite political communications and for airing elite controversies over policy issues. Along with two weeklies, *Die Zeit* and *Der Spiegel,* they both mold and express the views of top West German opinion leaders and policymakers in adversary as well as collaborative relationships.

POLITICAL PARTICIPATION

As we move from political orientations to political behavior let us recall that by our definition politics within countries revolve around the choice of public policies and their implementation. Political participation is in this respect identified with active, though not necessarily successful behavior on the part of individuals and groups directed toward the satisfaction of their values in the realm of public policy. The political efficacy of participating actors is measured correspondingly by their ability to realize their objectives through the promotion, modification, or prevention of governmental policy decisions.

Disparities in the extent of political participation and influence exist in every country. But their specific forms in contemporary West Germany reflect a particular mixture of socioeconomic, cultural, and organizational patterns. Changes in these patterns under the present regime have reduced, but not eliminated the inequitable distribution of participant roles and political power that prevailed under earlier, less democratic German regimes. As in other democratic countries, political stratification in the Federal Republic is based on qualitative differences that modify the egalitarian principles of the constitutional order.

Formally structured distinctions in the opportunities for effective participation in effect reinforce the differences we have noted in the participant orientations of children and adults from higher and lower socioeconomic strata. As a result we have a rather sharp division between a mass public that is for the most part only peripherally involved in policy-making and a small political public of active and influential participants. Insofar as ordinary West Germans have the opportunity to participate, they confine themselves largely to a single role, that of the voter (see Table V.4). Leading mem-

Table V.4. *Involvement in Politics*

Political stratum	Percentage of citizenry	Degree of participation and influence on policy
Political public		
Top-level participants (national elites)	0.001	high
State and federal legislators	0.03	medium-high
Members of local and district councils	0.4	medium
Functionaries of organizations in politics	0.5	medium
Active party members	1.0	medium
Inactive party members	3.0	medium-low
Members of organizations in politics	10.0	medium-low
General public		
Voters in local elections	50.0	low
Voters in state elections	55.0	low
Voters in federal elections	65.0	low
Eligible voters	70.0	—

Source: Calculated from survey data, membership data, election statistics, and various studies on political participation and influence.

bers of the political public, on the other hand, frequently hold several organizational positions in the political system, allowing them to play several participant roles simultaneously. A federal minister, for example, is not only a voter, a deputy, the chief of a government department, and a cabinet member; he also usually occupies leading positions in his party and other nongovernmental organizations.

The political public is for its part further stratified. At the top are the policymakers who may on occasion sharply disagree on particular policy issues but share a common understanding of the "proper" rules of the game of politics. Such rules define the limits of intraelite conflicts and provide for processes of conflict management that largely bypass the general public. The ruling elites are in turn recruited from and supported by second-string participants in governmental bodies and nongovernmental organizations.

In short, though the West German political system encompasses a large variety of participant roles these are played by few actors. Leaders and led agree on the whole that policymaking is best left to "experts." The prevalent view is that the political arena is no place for amateurs or for actors who will not play by the rules. In effect, the premium placed on the need for political "know-how" and legitimate forms of participation has both enhanced the authority of the incumbents and inhibited the development of grassroots support for nonprofessional civic action groups, particularly when these are identified with radical opposition to the present regime.

The Electorate. In three out of every four years regular local, state, and federal elections offer practically all adult West Germans formal opportunities for intermittent and peripheral participation in politics. Though the ostensible object is usually the choice of local and regional legislators, even nonfederal elections tend, in fact, to have a nationwide import. There are no by-elections for offices that fall vacant, as in the United States and Britain, or referenda, as in France. Proposals to increase mass participation through American-type primaries and presidential elections have gotten nowhere.

Periodic local and regional elections are therefore considered of correspondingly greater significance as interim tests of the popularity of national parties and their leaders than in the United States. National party leaders are apt to devote a great deal more effort to winning them and the mass media are likely to attribute greater weight to their outcome than the actual importance of the offices at stake seems to justify.

Although casting their votes gives West Germans a chance to express their preference for policies and policymakers, this form of political participation has limited significance for the recruitment of governmental leaders. Particularly in state and federal elections the electorate has only an indirect and not necessarily decisive voice in the selection process. In the first place election laws provide that half — in some states all — of the parliamentary deputies are to be chosen through a system of proportional representation that compels a voter to cast his ballot for a party list rather than a particular candidate. Thus, in federal elections for the lower house of parliament, every voter may cast two ballots, one for a local constituency candidate and one for a party. Accordingly, only half the federal deputies owe their seats to a direct choice of the voters in single-member districts, as in the United States, Britain, and France. The rest owe them to having been placed high enough on their party's state list by its leaders to be elected by a system of proportional representation that equitably apportions seats among these lists in accordance with the results of the nationwide vote for a party.

A further restriction on the realization of electoral preferences is the so-called five percent clause. The West German system of proportional representation does not discriminate against electoral minorities to the same extent as the winner-take-all procedures in countries with a pure single-member plurality system. However, parties that fail to secure 5 percent of the votes in federal and most state elections obtain no seat at all, and all those who voted for those parties thus have no voice whatever in deciding who is to govern. Finally, under the prevailing parliamentary form of government, the ultimate choice of the legislative and executive leadership rests nominally with the elected deputies, but in fact usually with the leaders of the dominant majorities.[7]

[7] The direct popular election of mayors in Bavaria and Baden-Württemberg is an exception to this practice.

As various West German voting studies have indicated, the consistently high rate of participation in federal elections provides two important elements for the stable operation of the political system. First, there is no sizable reservoir of qualified electors who ordinarily do not vote but might be activated by dramatic events or leaders, as in the last years of the Weimar regime. Beyond the limited and gradual influx of eligible new voters, the present turnout of 91 percent of the electorate precludes the possibility of sudden political changes produced by a substantial increase in electoral participation. Though the direction of voters' preferences may change, the extent of participation lends stability to the political system.

Second, present attitudinal and voting patterns suggest that electoral participation is a function of neither intense political engagement nor socioeconomic distinctions. Under earlier German regimes and in other countries increase in turnout has reflected greater public involvement in election outcomes. However, most West Germans evidently participate today not so much because they expect their vote to have a significant effect on public policy decisions but because they have learned to see voting as a civic duty. Ordinarily, people with pressing policy demands rely more heavily on other formal structures of interest articulation, such as pressure groups with direct access to governmental authorities. And whereas turnout in other countries with voluntary electoral participation tends to vary a good deal with socioeconomic background — particularly age, sex, education, income, and place of residence — in the contemporary Federal Republic this factor influences electoral participation hardly at all.

Public participant orientations and organizational structures thus interact to produce a self-fulfilling prophecy. According to the prevailing view, "those on top" largely can and will do what they deem best. Most West Germans, as we have seen, have a low sense of political efficacy and see little point in extending their participation in politics beyond discharging their civic responsibilities as voters. Casting their ballots represents for them a very low commitment to political participation, and electoral arrangements tend to confirm their belief that the average citizen may have some say in the selection of policymakers, but little influence over the choice of specific policy measures. The general public thus has limited opportunities for participation under rules of a representative democracy and is not very highly motivated to make the most of such opportunities or to seek their expansion. Consequently, the ruling elites in the Federal Republic do indeed enjoy a good deal of policymaking autonomy, and those who owe their positions to the voters usually interpret their electoral mandates pretty freely.

Middle-Range Participants. Middle-range participants in local, regional, and national politics link the general West German public to the top policymaking stratum, primarily through the media and formal organizations. They constitute about one-tenth of the citizenry and a good part of the well-informed and attentive political public. Middle-range participants include the leaders and members of radical student movements who want to change the present political system as well as the ad hoc civic action groups that have lately sprung up in West Germany. But most such middle-range participants are only intermittently recruited into active political roles on specific policy issues through their occupational positions or organizational affiliations.

In contrast to the situation in Britain, France, and other European countries, only a very small percentage of the citizens of the Federal Republic belong to a political party (see Table V.4). By far the largest proportion of middle-range participants are dues-paying members of compulsory or voluntary interest associations organized primarily for nonpolitical purposes but sporadically involved in pressure group activities. Most of these are occupational associations, and middle-range participants are thus recruited largely from the most extensively organized occupational groups — businessmen, farmers, skilled industrial workers, and professional people such as doctors, lawyers, and teachers. They are almost always men, preponderantly middle-aged, and, except for trade unionists, are usually among the better educated, higher income white-collar workers.

Such middle-range participants exert little direct influence on public policymaking. They mainly represent the reserve forces of the political parties and interest associations; occasionally they are mobilized by the leaders of their organizations to lend quantitative support to their policy demands. Rank-and-file party members will be called on at election time to help solicit votes and funds. Labor leaders may summon trade union members to demonstrate their political strength and solidarity in mass demonstrations, and those of farm, religious, and business associations every so often ask their members to press legislators to support or oppose a particular bill.

A small minority of upper middle-range participants plays more active and, sometimes, more influential roles in public affairs. These mid-elites usually are in governmental and nongovernmental positions that involve them in the articulation or aggregation of policy demands or in the recruitment of top decision makers. They may be party officials or civil servants whose occupational tasks include such activities, but they may also be interest group functionaries, clergymen, or journalists who devote themselves primarily to nonpolitical matters.

Like the rank and file of middle-range participants, but to a more significant extent, these actors perform a strategic function in the West German political system. They are the links between leaders and followers, governors and governed, and they help balance demands from below with control above. Insofar as they facilitate two-way political communications between the bottom and top of the political participation pyramid, they help to maintain congruence between claims and supports within the system, and within its political subsystems. A clergyman or journalist, for example, may not only justify and explain the policymakers' actions to a mass audience, but may also address the top leadership on behalf of inarticulate "public opinion." Similarly, a middle-range party or government official or interest group functionary may not only serve as an instrument of leadership control, but communicate "upstairs" attitudes gathered from his contacts with the general citizenry.

All told, middle-range participants are only intermittently involved in public policy processes. With the notable exception of activists within the political parties — a matter we shall consider in the next chapter — they are usually content to let their formal leaders run the system. Participation by the rank-and-file members of the numerous organizations in the pluralist West German society is mostly sporadic, and usually does not provide a particularly strong emotional bond between leaders and followers, or much control from below. Upper middle-range participants may be more continuously and profoundly engaged in politics, but highly formalized and hierarchic organizational structures severely restrict their opportunities for influence on public policy decisions.

These patterns, too, allow elite policymakers a large degree of autonomy in everyday public affairs; but they also point to a source of potential weakness in the present regime. Responsible and responsive leadership requires open channels of communications not only to the political public but to the general public. Elections and public opinion surveys provide only limited opportunities for the articulation of mass concerns and demands. That is to say, they allow an ordinary West German to express his views and interests only in response to, and in terms of, the questions that are put before him, such as whether he prefers this or that party, policy, or leader.

For these reasons upper middle-range participants are strategically important in the day-to-day operation of the West German political system. Although few in number, they carry a heavy load as they intervene between organized and unorganized citizens and the elites. Cultural patterns and organizational forms tend to assign control rather than representative functions to upper middle-range participants; but democratic procedures require that these people be free to speak as well as to listen and that they be sensitive to demands from below as well as from above. This process of interaction seems to be more extensive today than in earlier years of the Federal Republic. But it still appears to be inadequately appreciated and understood not only by the general public and its leaders, but by many of the upper middle-range participants themselves.

Leading Participants. A few thousand elected and appointed, coopted and anointed leaders form the top layer in the political influence and participation hierarchy. As national and subnational decision makers in various areas of public life they not only know a great deal more about the specific operation of the political system than other citizens do, but they can do a great deal more to shape popular demands and support, as well as policy outcomes. Some wield political power on the basis of formal governmental positions, others on the strength of special skills, financial resources, or mass support. Some are widely known; others are active behind the scenes.

The policymaking elite can be divided into two groups. The *manifest political leaders* occupy influential positions that involve continuous participation in public policy processes. The *latent political leaders* hold positions in the system that call for only intermittent participation but involve considerable potential influence.

Manifest political leaders belong to the policymaking stratum on the strength of their key constitutional and paraconstitutional positions of authority under the terms of the Basic Law. Most obviously they comprise the leaders of the federal and state governments and the Federal Diet. But they also include top administrative officials, military officers, and judges who influence policymaking in an official advisory or direct rule capacity.

In West Germany the top functionaries of the major parties are formally manifest political leaders by virtue of their paraconstitutional positions in public affairs. Under Article 21 of the Basic Law, legitimate parties "participate in the formation of the political will of the people." This constitutional provision invests the leaders of both the principal governing and opposition parties with key participant roles even when they do not hold public offices.

Latent political leaders are less obviously and less constantly involved in public affairs. They may use their prominent positions in ostensibly nonpolitical sectors of West German society to influence major policy decisions, but they enter the various policymaking arenas only intermittently. Mass support, financial resources, professional expertise, or a generally recognized status of moral or intellectual authority provide them with access to the manifest leaders, and with the means for exerting influence when a policy decision touches on their particular concerns.

The political power of latent leaders is far more balanced today than under previous German regimes, and their policy interests are more diversified. Industrialists and bankers, employers and labor leaders, and the spokesmen for religious, agricultural, and professional associations often press conflicting demands on government and party officials. Mass media leaders and prominent, politically engaged intellectuals may play influential but also competing roles as they interpret ongoing policy developments for other members of the political public and for the general public.

Only about a thousand of these manifest and latent political leaders have key roles in federal policymaking. Because of the polycentric character of the Federal Republic, its national leadership is geographically more dispersed than that of most other advanced industrial countries. But excellent communications facilities and strong associational ties give the national policymakers easy access to each other and to their respective clienteles, and allow them to participate in nationwide affairs as effectively as if they were all concentrated in a single capital city. Even more important, the development of political life since the establishment of the Federal Republic has focused increasing attention on national policymaking and consequently has drawn key participants deeper into federal politics.

Indirectly the preeminence of federal politics is largely attributable to progressive consolidation of the informational media and the economic system. It is a by-product of the concentration of the mass media as well as of the economic dominance of a few industrial, commercial, and banking empires and competing interest associations. More directly, two explicitly political factors have promoted the significance of membership in the national elites.

Our earlier discussion of the policy environment emphasized the Federal Republic's intense involvement in international affairs and the significance of extrasocietal factors in West German politics. More than in the United States, almost all major questions of domestic policy touch on foreign issues.

Leading participants in the political system are compelled to contend with such national problems as the dependency of the Federal Republic on foreign trade and military allies. The recognition that international relations have a significance bearing on a broad range of domestic problems has therefore led diverse elite members to seek national political roles involving participation in foreign policymaking.

A second reason for the nationalization of elite political participation is that public benefits and obligations are distributed primarily by agents of the Federal Government. Increasingly, the mobilization, allocation, and control of West German human and physical resources have — in fact if not in form — been placed in the hands of national officeholders; consequently, key participants either occupy such offices or seek access to them. Ambitious politicians, for example, have been willing to forego secure and influential offices in state and local governments for even secondary positions in the Federal Government and Diet. The appropriation of vast federal funds for social welfare services and subsidies to various economic groups have focused the efforts of interest group leaders on appropriate national executive and legislative organs. Federal legislation regulating wages and hours concern business and labor leaders. Roman Catholic and Protestant religious leaders take a keen interest in federal regulations of family life and public morals, such as divorce and abortion laws, and university administrators lobby for federal aid to higher education. In short, in domestic as in foreign policy, influence on decision making requires political participation in prominent national roles.

WHO GETS TO THE TOP AND HOW

The processes of leadership recruitment confirm the average West German's belief that it takes a good deal more than a sense of competence to play an influential political role. Although the Basic Law declares for instance that "every German shall be equally eligible for any public office" it qualifies this right by stipulating that he must also have the necessary "aptitude, qualifications, and professional achievements." When it comes to the selection of manifest as well as latent top political leaders, such generally restrictive criteria are translated into rather exclusive standards governing admission to the policymaking stratum.

In the Federal Republic, as in other countries, the structured opportunities for getting to the top first of all favor university-educated males from the highest social classes. As shown in Table V.5, in the early 1970s more than 80 percent of a sample of West German leaders had a higher education, compared to only 5 percent of the entire adult population. Except for the labor leaders, few of them were the children of manual workers, many had fathers who had gone to a university, and most were the offspring of civil servants, businessmen, and professional people (such as doctors, lawyers, and engineers). As in the United States and other Western democracies, elected officials and party leaders in the Federal Republic are somewhat more representative of the general citizenry than the occupants of top positions in other sectors in public life; they include, for example, more Roman Catholics and persons from the lower social strata. However, here too we find few women. Some are elected to the Federal Diet, but not many; in 1977, only 7 percent of its members were women.

Also as in other countries, the structure of opportunities discriminates against young people. Even more than in the United States, and as much as in England, France, and Japan, they must as a rule bide their time if they want to make it to the top. As indicated in Table V.5, West German leaders are usually in their late forties and early fifties when they get there and are then likely to stay put for a decade or more. To get ahead in government and politics today, as in other careers leading into policymaking, one must be highly motivated and have a great deal of patience and endurance. Unless mandatory retirement rules, illness, or electoral defeat compel their withdrawal from elite positions, senior West German leaders are no more disposed than their counterparts in other countries to give way to younger men. They are equally apt to believe that wisdom and sobriety are essential leadership qualities and that these increase with age and experience.

Leading participants in the West German political system usually insist that those who aspire to join or succeed them

Table V.5. *Profile of West German Leaders (1972)*

	Organizational sector of leadership position									
Characteristics	*Federal/ State cabinets*	*Federal Diet*	*Political parties*	*Federal administration*	*Military*	*Industry*	*Finance/ insurance*	*Trade union*	*Mass media*	*All sectors*
Age										
Average age [a]	50	52	45	53	55	54	52	52	47	51
Percentage under 45 years	21	20	53	17	—	14	18	11	44	23
Percentage 45–60 years	62	62	31	53	98	56	47	79	41	53
Percentage over 60 years	17	18	16	30	2	30	35	11	15	24
Social Background (in percentages)										
University educated	73	66	69	98	54	77	78	26	77	81
Father, univ. educated	35	25	31	46	38	55	38	11	37	42
Father, civil servant	25	25	27	42	44	23	24	18	25	35
Father, businessman	14	20	18	20	12	36	25	13	27	23
Father, manual worker	14	19	8	6	—	7	9	38	7	9

Career										
Average no. years from first to present position	21	21	11	20	30	21	20	23	17	20
Average no. years in present position	4	7	6	4	2	8	8	7	7	6
Previously held a high leadership position (in percentages)	50	42	33	22	88	40	43	50	35	42
Began career in another sector (in percentages)	98	92	83	64	15	37	44	44	27	55
Religious identification (in percentages)										
Protestant	57	47	46	56	68	59	49	40	48	57
Roman Catholic	20	44	42	37	24	25	32	32	27	30
Other/none	23	9	12	7	7	16	19	28	24	13

[a] Percentages are rounded off, averages are arithmetic means.

Source: A 1972 survey of 1825 West German leaders (excluding the judiciary). Data in Ursula Lange-Hoffmann et al., *Westdeutsche Führungsschicht* (Universities Kiel and Mannheim, unpublished, 1973).

first pass through a socializing apprenticeship in various middle-range organizational positions. The data on age and career patterns in Table V.5 show that most of these leaders of the early 1970s entered the policymaking stratum by this route. Some followed political career lines in governmental and party hierarchies that culminated in a key position, others became leading political participants after they had made their way to the top in some nonpolitical occupation.

The accumulation of experience has become more important as room at the top has opened up more slowly. Ambitious but inexperienced young men were able to advance rather quickly in the years of socioeconomic and political disorganization and reorganization immediately preceding and following the establishment of the Federal Republic. For example, Franz Josef Strauss, one of the most prominent of today's senior leaders, began his political career immediately after the fall of the Nazi regime when he was thirty; within four years he had become a major party leader and within nine a federal minister. Self-made business tycoons and mass media leaders, such as Axel Springer, made a similar rapid ascent.

The chances for zooming to the top have been far more limited in recent times. The stable and increasingly institutionalized structures of leadership recruitment have stayed the political ambitions of younger men. In this respect the youthfulness of the party leaders of the early 1970s may well prove to be a temporary phenomenon caused by the long-delayed retirement of the postwar generation of senior politicians.

Becoming a leading participant calls finally for occupational skills and organizational ties. Lateral movements between manifest and latent political positions have been the exception and ascent through a series of lesser positions the rule for entry into the policymaking stratum. A national leader is likely to have switched to politics as a vocation before rather than after reaching the top of some nonpolitical hierarchy.

Generally speaking, the more sharply defined the functions of a leading position the more difficult it is for someone who lacks the required skill and expertise to attain it. Note that almost all of the West German military leaders in Table V.5 — the most highly professionalized elite in the sample — began their careers as military men and moved to the top from other high military posts. Elective political offices, on the other hand, demand less professional expertise and more all-around skills and permit a greater transfer of knowledge and experience from other organizational positions. Practically all of the government, parliamentary, and party leaders in Table V.5 started in another sector; in 1974 one-third of the federal ministers came from trade unions and one-third of the federal deputies from the civil service. Business and mass media leaders are, however, less likely to go into politics than in the United States.

In contrast to the general public, leading participants are always members of at least one and usually several nongovernmental organizations involved in policymaking, some of them manifestly political and partisan and others ostensibly nonpolitical and nonpartisan. These leaders usually belong to a political party and, more often than not, to an occupational association and several civic organizations. In the tightly structured West German political system, the aspiring leader with few specific technical skills for getting to the top and staying there requires the popular or elite support provided by such formal associational ties. His ascent and influence are measured by the size of such political capital. He may be able to do without popular support — particularly if he holds a nonelective position — but rare indeed is the leader who makes it to the top of the political pyramid without some benevolent sponsorship from members of the organizational elites.

Organizational bonds are most important in the recruitment of key public officials, particularly ties to a major party. Since the establishment of the Federal Republic, political parties have increasingly replaced other structures as routes to manifest political leadership. Party membership — rather than specific occupational skills — has become a chief criterion for ministerial posts and, frequently, for key administrative positions. Federal ministers are now almost always members of the ruling parties and their delegations in the Federal Diet, although membership is not required by law. Between 1949 and 1977 only three federal ministers were members of neither and received their appointments as experts in their field; one was subsequently elected to the Diet and the other two did not remain in office for long. Ministers in the state governments are more often recruited from outside parliament, but they, too, usually belong to the ruling parties.

Sex, education, experience, skill, and organizational affiliation are thus the principal sources of upward political mobility in contemporary West Germany. By and large, the opportunities for getting into the policymaking stratum are considerably less restricted than under earlier German regimes and in many other countries. Consider, for instance, that Willy Brandt — the illegitimate son of a salesgirl — could rise to become the chancellor of the Federal Republic in 1969. Leading participants are no longer recruited from aristocratic families and a military caste, as in the Hohenzollern Empire, nor must they fit standards of "racial" and ideological purity, as in Nazi Germany. They are neither the graduates of a few elite universities — as is still very much the case in Britain and France — nor do they belong to tight cliques based on informal social bonds and shared socialization experiences. And in West Germany wealth is not nearly as much a valuable resource for gaining entry into the policymaking stratum as it is in the United States.

ELITE HOMOGENEITY AND HETEROGENEITY

The most profound differences between the political system of the Federal Republic and those of earlier German regimes are to be found at the top layer of active participants. They go beyond formal changes and extend to the style of political relationships among West German leaders. The deep elite cleavages of the past have certainly not entirely disappeared, but elite relations are marked today by an unprecedented degree of mutual trust and cooperation.

Leadership groups that formerly were alienated from the prevailing political systems — for example, labor leaders in Imperial Germany and military leaders in Weimar Germany — now identify themselves with the regime and its preservation. No influential group of participants rejects the contemporary constitutional order. It expresses and reinforces broad elite support for political arrangements that generally suit the present leaders and conform to their perceptions of the proper distribution of role assignments in state and society.

Every major leadership group today has a share in policy-making, and the elite political culture allows all key actors some influence as long as they observe the rules of the game. The spokesmen for organized labor are no longer excluded from the ruling establishment. High civil servants and military leaders can no longer ignore or bypass the authority of elected officials but must reconcile their policy demands with those of the representatives of the voters. The federal structure of government prevents national officials from riding rough-shod over regional interests — as they once did — and compels them to negotiate with the state governments on most matters of domestic policy. These more inclusive patterns of leadership participation have in turn led various elites to value arrangements that regulate adversary relationships among them without involving the general public.

In this regard the radical critics of these arrangements are essentially correct when they hold that the Federal Republic is ruled by leaders who are united in their commitment to the prevailing system. But the radicals overstate their case in claiming that elite pluralism is simply a useful democratic myth concocted by an ideologically homogeneous ruling class whose members manipulate mass opinion strictly for their own benefit.

Contemporary elite attitudes and relations do reflect a basic, if diffuse, leadership consensus on the legitimacy of a representative system of government and operative rules that provide the top leaders with considerable policymaking autonomy. Fundamental agreement on the proper modes of political conduct and patterns of participation transcends ideological and partisan differences and disagreements on particular policy issues among West German leaders. On the whole, present policymakers give the established political order high marks on its adaptability to changing environmental conditions and its ability to maintain societal harmony by processing diverse policy demands smoothly and efficiently. Incumbent

West German leaders are basically attached to the regime and do not want a strongman at the helm dictating what they may or may not do.

At the same time this does not mean that all leaders are unreservedly enthusiastic about every aspect of the workings of the political system. Far from it. As we have noted, liberal reformers maintain that the system should produce more socioeconomic democracy, whereas conservatives demand that it provide more law and order. Business elites complain that labor leaders have too much influence over public policy and labor complains about the excessive influence of business leaders. Civil service elites object to the "partisan meddling" of party leaders in their sector and these in turn lash out against the narrow-minded bureaucrats. Federal leaders insist that leaders in the states have too much political power; state leaders insist that they have too little. Such complaints are all too familiar to Americans — the others always seem to wield more influence in public affairs than is their due — but they are not expressions of bitter hostility toward the regime.

In contrast to the authoritarian rule of a single political elite in Nazi Germany and the Communist German Democratic Republic, a fairly balanced pluralism among different sectorial elites prevails today in the Federal Republic. Formally, governmental and legislative elites possess the ultimate authority to determine the course of public policy and to mediate conflicts among other leadership groups, such as employers and trade union leaders or the heads of various hierarchies in the public administration and the military. But by law they may not, and for practical reasons they cannot, ignore other key participants whose interests are likely to be affected by their policy decisions. No matter how great their support among the voters, the responsible governing leaders must seek the consent of other involved key actors in order to assure the effective implementation of their policies. In effect this means that they are unlikely to slight the wishes of influential veto groups among the latent political leaders and will usually try to accommodate them in formulating governmental laws and regulations.

In the West German political system the effectiveness of a

governmental leader thus depends largely on his bargaining skills. The great political power of Konrad Adenauer, the long-time chancellor of the Federal Republic, was ostensibly based on his rather autocratic use of his formal position; but equally important was his immense skill in balancing counter-vailing elite demands and preventing the formation of strong leadership alignments hostile to him.

The patterns of elite interaction in the realm of public policy are today structured by institutionalized organizational arrangements for delegated authority and limited popular participation. Formal governmental decisions are normally the products of complex, but orderly and stable bargaining pro-cesses among diverse groups of key participants. At the local, state, and federal levels, these groups negotiate with each other on the distribution of public benefits and obligations. Policy outputs are usually compromises worked out according to the issues involved, the alignment and strength of contending forces, and the feasible options. Legislative and elective policy choices thus flow as a rule from interelite negotiations among politicians, civil servants, and interest group functionaries.

This balanced interdependence among the elites is pro-moted by an elaborate network of formal and informal rela-tionships. In large part these relationships are regulated by law, as we shall see in subsequent chapters. But they are facili-tated by interelite communications through the newspapers and periodicals for the political public, as well as by direct personal contacts among West German leaders (see Table V.6). Above all, there is a network of organizational ties and offices among and within elite sectors, linking governmental and non-governmental leadership groups and, through them, respective subordinates and clienteles.

For the country as a whole this organizational network cen-ters on the manifest national political elites; apart from the federal legislature, it encompasses an enormous number of formal policy planning, coordinating, and advisory bodies of the federal executive. Functionally specific deliberative bodies exist in practically every sphere of public policy — for instance, the Educational Council *(Bildungsrat)* and the "Concerted Action" for economic affairs that periodically brings together

Table V.6.   *Direct Contacts Among German Leaders (1967)*

	Percentage
Leaders personally acquainted with	
A high official of a business association	96
One or more deputies of Federal Parliament	94
A high official of a federal ministry	93
A leading scholar	92
A deputy of state parliament	91
Leading journalists	90
A high trade union official	84
A leading member of the clergy	79
Federal deputy in own constituency	70
A high-ranking military officer	68

Source: Interview data from a study of a representative cross-section of German leaders, reported in Erwin Scheuch, "Sichtbare und unsichtbare Macht," *Die Zeit*, November 28, 1967, p. 3.

key ministers and civil servants with leaders of the major economic interest associations.

Table V.7 provides some indications of the nature and extent of interlocking and overlapping elite positions and of the chief points of contacts between policymaking sectors. Notice that in 1972 more than seven out of ten West German leaders held at least one other leadership office in addition to their principal one, and that most leaders holding multiple office were manifest political leaders of the government, legislatures, and parties or latent political leaders in business organizations and the trade unions. Observe, too, that the executive branch of the central government — especially the chancellor's office — was a particular focus of interelite contacts, pointing to the dominant role of the federal executive and its leader in West German policy processes.

THE INCOMING LEADERSHIP AND CHANGE

Some observers of contemporary West German politics believe that a conflict of generations is developing that will eventually shatter the present patterns of elite collaboration. They see a new generation of political activists coming to the fore that places less emphasis on the need for social harmony and political stability than the present leadership and is more deeply committed to divisive ideologies.

What is the basis for such prognostications? We noted in the preceding chapter some differences in the beliefs and values of West Germans who grew up before and after the establishment of the Federal Republic. But we also observed that by and large age distinctions have evidently not given rise to major political cleavages between older and younger people and have been far less pronounced than under earlier German regimes and in other countries. There seems to be little indication here of the type of generational conflict that contributed to the collapse of the Weimar Republic. Hitler's rise to power was then promoted by his ability to exploit the anticapitalist, romantic sentiments of young idealists who were alienated from what they considered the overly materialistic values of their elders and who longed for a less mundane "new order." By comparison, most young people in the Federal Republic appear to accept the prevailing order.

But what seems to hold for the youthful mass public appears to be not as valid in the case of the political public. Particularly in recent years the politically most interested and engaged young people in the universities and the major parties — the pool for the leadership of the 1980s and 1990s — have served notice on their elders that they are not prepared simply to follow in their footsteps and that they have rather different ideas about the purposes and responsibilities of political leadership. And although left-wing radicals have been most vocal on this score, young liberals and conservatives also appear unwilling to carry on as the present top leaders believe best.

The men who now rule the Federal Republic were born roughly between 1915 and 1930 and belong for the most part to what a German sociologist termed some years ago the "sceptical generation" of the post-Nazi era. The older leaders — such as Helmut Schmidt, the Federal Chancellor of the mid-1970s — grew to adulthood under the Nazi regime, usually served in its armed forces, and launched their careers soon after its fall. Those who were once attached to the Nazi creed are now apt to consider it a youthful folly; those who were not are all the more determined to keep young West Germans

Table V.7. *The West German Leadership Network (1972)*

	Organizational sector of principal leadership position									
	Federal/ State cabinets	*Federal Diet*	*Political parties*	*Federal administration*	*Military*	*Industry*	*Finance/ insurance*	*Trade union*	*Mass media*	*All sectors*
Organizational ties—additional leadership positions										
None	7[a]	9	18	49	80	8	9	8	59	28
One more	16	13	21	20	14	7	2	8	17	14
2–4 more	36	40	39	19	—	23	20	32	17	27
Over 4 more	24	25	15	4	—	35	36	36	3	18
Unknown	18	14	8	7	7	27	33	16	4	13
Total	101	101	101	99	101	100	100	100	100	100
Type of organization										
Economic enterprise	31	14	20	18	2	73	79	57	7	30
Business association	10	11	8	5	—	48	39	37	14	24
Trade unions	—	3	—	1	—	1	—	42	2	2
Political party	56	47	54	5	—	2	4	21	1	16
General political organization	36	67	20	8	2	2	2	18	1	13

Regional/local administration	11	10	20	3	—	2	2	5	1	6
Public administration	14	2	4	5	2	8	2	24	—	7
Mass media	17	8	11	4	2	3	4	8	20	9
Scientific/educational organization	23	11	13	17	—	30	12	34	11	14
Religious organization	14	6	7	2	2	2	5	5	3	5
Sustained contact with										
Federal chancellor's office	52	60	36	82	22	10	9	53	62	n.a.
Federal ministries	95	98	81	99	95	78	61	97	77	n.a.
Federal Diet committees	81	92	57	90	59	30	38	73	45	n.a.
Federal Diet parties	92	93	95	63	32	21	37	86	69	n.a.
Frequent contacts with										
Federal executive	38	48	28	84	71	26	15	71	37	n.a.
Federal legislature	24	74	43	38	22	4	4	45	22	n.a.
Political parties	56	37	55	4	2	4	2	31	44	n.a.
Public administration	13	2	3	5	2	2	2	5	3	n.a.

[a]Numbers are rounded percentages.
Source: Same at Table V.5

from succumbing to a new perverted romanticism. The younger policymakers — such as Hans Apel, the Federal Finance Minister of the mid-1970s and the Federal Minister of Economics, Hans Friedrich — were still children in the Nazi era. Their political views are therefore not as much the products of learning experiences under the Hitler regime as they are the consequences of resocialization in the postwar period of socioeconomic and political reconstruction.

These leaders see themselves as rational policymakers who have no use for 'woolly romanticism' and doctrinaire ideologies. They are suave, but tough and highly skilled organizational managers who prefer to focus their attention and energies on immediate rather than long-range problems. Though they may belong to different sectors of the elites, today's leading participants share what they consider a hard-nosed, pragmatic approach to public policy issues and inter-elite bargaining in domestic and foreign affairs. They place a high premium on achievement and efficient performance, on "inside information" and expert knowledge, and on the need for negotiations and compromise. Although they may not agree on what should be done and who should do it, these leaders essentially understand each other.

Partisan differences notwithstanding, most contemporary key actors basically agree that the preservation of fundamental political harmony and stability demands that government policymaking be guided by a sense of moderation and caution. The dominant policymakers hold that what has been achieved must be preserved and what does not seem feasible should not be tried. Unavoidable adjustments to changing circumstances are to be made as gradually as possible to avoid unsettling the basic patterns of West German domestic and foreign relations.

But will the elite consensus supporting the present regime outlast these leaders? The ruling elites have certainly sought to ensure its continuity by grooming as their successors men who essentially share their attachment to the prevailing political system. At the same time they have endeavored to block the ascent of young political activists who seem to them doctrinaire ideologues and radical extremists. Whether such measures will in the long run suffice to overcome frictions between members of the present and the incoming leadership generations remains to be seen.

POLITICAL PARTICIPATION AND POLITICAL STABILITY

The theme of this chapter has been that different forms and degrees of political activism in the Federal Republic depend on personal motivation and structured opportunities. As we have seen, variations in motivation are largely the products of past socialization and current information; opportunities for participation vary for the most part with different positions in state and society.

Patterns of differential participation seemed in the mid-1970s well embedded in the West German political system. Close to three decades of elite-controlled institutionalization had yielded orderly, unspectacular relationships between the rulers and ruled under a representative, liberal democratic form of government. Most of the people were willing to leave the running of the system to policymakers who claimed to know what needed to be done and how to do it. The elites, protected as well as controlled by their agreement on the basic rules of the game, enjoyed a corresponding degree of autonomy in pursuing their various objectives and in overcoming policy conflicts over particular issues. As the principal agents connecting the tops of different functional sectors of a pluralist society to its political structures, policymakers explicitly and implicitly provided the nonelites with norms legitimating and supporting the existing order, and managed a balance between political continuity and change.

Contemporary politization and recruitment patterns suggest that the distribution of participant roles is unlikely to undergo major changes in the foreseeable future. Whether it will continue to conform to the formal framework of a liberal democratic regime is another question. The exceptional emphasis that West German leaders have placed on legal rules governing interelite and elite-popular relationships, and their expressed concern about the durability of present arrangements, seem to reflect their belief that the present regime needs to be even more solidly anchored in the West German political culture, especially in the elite subculture.

As we have noted, the lopsided participation structure rests on role perceptions and assignments that leave a wide gap between the political and general publics. If deteriorating economic conditions or other developments were to cause popular and elite interests and values to diverge more sharply than they do now, key participants identified with the present regime might find popular opinion turning against them and lending support to leaders intent on its abolition or drastic transformation. This does not mean that such a challenge would succeed. There is abundant evidence demonstrating that even considerable mass disaffection need not menace a political order as long as the dominant groups are essentially united in its support.

The Federal Republic has not yet experienced a severe test of its political system. If that system should be tested, the crucial question would be whether the unity and determination of the West German elites would be great enough to preserve the existing regime. And this leads to a second question: Can the present elite consensus on basic rules and policy objectives be maintained? Given the prevailing mix in the political attitudes, and the pluralism of functionally specific elites in an advanced industrial society, this consensus appears to depend principally on three conditions. First, the rules of the game must be flexible enough to accommodate the values and interests of diverse elites and their clienteles. Second, the rules must be adaptable to dynamic conditions in domestic and international policy. And since the making and changing of these rules are essentially functions of governmental leadership, the preservation of the system calls for political leaders who are responsive to the demands of other elites and recognized by them as the ultimate agents of legitimate and binding policy decisions. Last, the rules must be acceptable to the incoming leadership generation to maintain basic political agreement among future policymakers.

Thus far, political and economic circumstances have favored elite cooperation, and organizational structures have functioned extremely well in facilitating elite integration. But though the present recruitment and participation patterns have seemed well able to maintain political tranquillity they include a conservative bias that has excluded from the top stratum individuals and groups who significantly differ in their experiences and attitudes from those now dominant. Elites essentially committed to the preservation of the status quo are usually not especially receptive to major innovations, or to aspiring leaders who sharply deviate from their own beliefs and values. In the years to come, however, the dynamics of intrasocietal and extrasocietal developments may confront West German policymakers with the need for decisions that might strain elite consensus. Ideological cleavages and recruitment processes that bar ambitious political activists from leading positions because they lack the "proper" qualifications and outlook might alienate key groups. The regime needs the support of the incoming generation if it is to survive without fundamental structural changes.

CHAPTER VI

Political Parties

REPRESENTATIVE DEMOCRACY in the Federal Republic rests today on a competitive party system, and party government provides West Germans with the measure of its effectiveness.[1] Approvingly or not, they conceive of the present regime as a state controlled by political parties (*Parteienstaat*) and, more particularly, by the leaders of the major parties. The regime of the Hohenzollern Empire, in contrast, is remembered as an autocratic "administrative state" (*Verwaltungstaat*) run by government bureaucrats, that of the Weimar Republic as a state dominated by interest associations (*Verbändestaat*), and that of Nazi Germany as a dictatorial "leadership state" (*Führerstaat*).

The constitutional rules of the present regime call merely for governments that are the products of free and open parliamentary elections and ultimately accountable to the voters.

---

[1] A competitive party system depends, first, on regular free and open elections that give the voters periodic opportunities to express their preferences for various parties and their candidates for public office. Second, it requires generally accepted, orderly procedures that (1) allow a legislative majority to assume control over authoritative policymaking structures and (2) assure the opposition inside and outside the legislature that it will continue to have adequate opportunities to obtain such control in the future. In this sense, a party system is not competitive if opposition parties are barred from coming to power by legitimate means and parties are not competitive unless they can participate in elections with reasonable expectations of achieving at least some control over public policymaking.

But in fact governments are formed and led by party elites commanding a majority in West German legislatures and dependent on support within their respective parties.

The preeminent role of political parties in contemporary West German public affairs is based on (1) the organization of the regime, (2) the patterns of competition and collaboration among pluralist party elites wedded to the regime, and (3) the effect of different types of party government and different forms of interaction between governing leaders and their parties. Formal regulations and the actual style of political intercourse have in this respect combined to shape the relationship between the parties and other components of the Federal Republic's political system — notably the electorate, interest associations, and governmental agencies — as well as relationships among and within the parties. All of these relationships are interdependent; they have been molded by continuous reciprocal adaptation and by patterns of continuity and change in the domestic and international environment for West German politics.

DEVELOPMENT OF THE PARTY SYSTEM

In such older democracies as the United States and Britain the regime came before the party system and the uninterrupted evolution of governmental structures decided the course of party development. In West Germany, on the other hand, the sharp discontinuities between the present and the Nazi regime reversed the process. The party system was formed before the establishment of the Federal Republic and its constitutional order and party elites therefore had greater influence on the development of new patterns of politics and government.

The leaders of parties licensed by the allied military governments after the collapse of the Third Reich were the principal architects of political reconstruction in West Germany. Summoned by the foreign occupation powers to fill the vacuum left by the elimination of the Nazi leadership, they very quickly became preeminent in public affairs. The remnants of the former elites were for the most part prevented from assuming leading roles by socioeconomic dislocation and allied regulations. Thus, party leaders with little past involvement in Hitler's totalitarian regime could lay the foundations for a new political order before the creation of the Federal Republic in 1949. By the time the occupation authorities asked them to devise a constitution for a West German state, the leaders had become sufficiently entrenched to forge a regime designed to institutionalize party control over the political system.

The party leaders who wrote the West German constitution incorporated a competitive party system into their design for stable as well as representative government in a pluralist society. The conditions needed for a well-functioning, democratic party system had been lacking under past German regimes; West Germany did not have the strong historical roots that had long sustained the operation of such a system in the United States and Britain. The authors of the Basic Law and subsequent implementing legislation considered it accordingly all the more essential to give firm legal underpinnings to the party system. Competing "legitimate" parties were by law to be the principal instruments for the expression and representation of partisan cleavages in West German society, and a regime-supportive party system was to be the organizational framework for electoral processes and the interplay between party government and opposition inside and outside the legislative chambers.

Contemporary West German politics reflect the structural consequences of this design. To an extent unprecedented in German history, political parties now control the recruitment of elected as well as appointed key public officials and coordinate diverse policy preferences among the political and general publics. In contrast to the situation in former times and in other countries, political parties in the Federal Republic are today not the instruments of particularistic cultural and socioeconomic interest associations, but rather more general linkage structures between state and society. The present patterns of party government and opposition restrict the role of pressure groups and administrative agencies in policymaking, and they also limit as well as shape the role of the electorate. As broadly based electoral organizations, the major parties have served to legitimate regime principles that call for responsive and

responsible democratic government; as more narrowly constituted membership organizations, they serve to integrate partisan activists into the political system.

In the light of the numerous and deep political divisions of
the past, many of the founding fathers of the regime expected
— and many contemporary observers feared — a revival of the
highly unstable, multiparty system of the Weimar Republic.[2]
As it turned out, the parties that were the largest from the
outset obtained between them an increasingly larger proportion of the popular vote and elective offices. The so-called
"union parties" — the Christian Democratic Union (CDU)
and its Bavarian affiliate, the Christian Social Union (CSU) —
only barely outdistanced the Social Democratic party of Germany (SPD) in the first federal election of 1949. Thereafter
the CDU/CSU took a commanding lead; in 1953 it became the
first party in German history to win an absolute parliamentary
majority and in 1957 the first to win a majority of the popular
votes as well. The SPD managed to obtain majorities in subnational elections but advanced more gradually in federal
elections and did not score a popular plurality until 1972.

By the mid-1970s the West German party system had become
essentially bifurcated; there were two major parties, controlled
by elites who supported the regime and furnished its principal
policymakers. Parliamentary government at the federal, state,
and local level meant party governments that consisted mostly
or entirely of Christian Democrats or Social Democrats. The
combined popular vote for the CDU/CSU and SPD in federal
elections went from 60 percent in 1949 to 91 percent in 1976
and their share of the seats in the Federal Diet, from 67 to 92 *Bundestag*
percent (see Figures VI.1 and VI.2). Of the seven other parties
in the first Diet only one, the Free Democratic party (FDP),
remained — rather precariously — represented in federal and

2 The new electoral system provided for a more restricted form of proportional representation, but its critics held that it was still likely to
produce legislatures divided into many, deeply antagonistic parties and
the sort of governmental instability that had led to the breakdown of the
Weimar regime. In their view the democratic representation of partisan
differences should have been tempered even more by the adoption of a
straightforward "first past the post" constituency system, which they
identified with stable party governments in the United States and Britain.

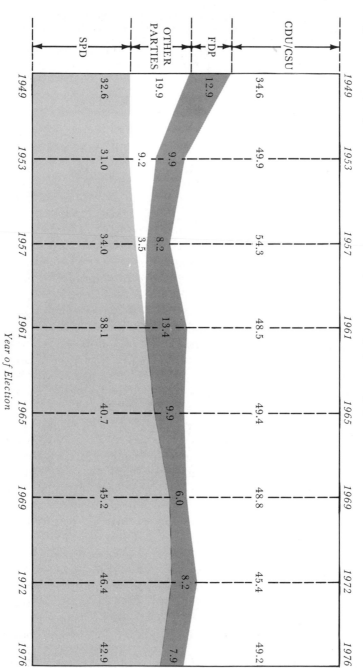

Figure VI.1. *Party Representation in the Federal Diet, 1949–1976 (in percentages)*

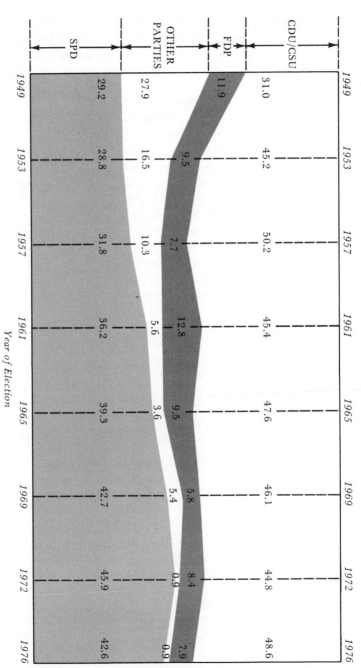

Figure VI.2: *Elections for the Federal Diet, 1949-1976: Popular Vote (in percentages)*

Year of Election

state legislatures by 1977. All the others — such as a party claiming to represent the special interests of refugees from Eastern Europe and a sectional Bavarian party — had failed to stay in the competition; various new parties that sought elective offices — such as the right-wing National Democratic party (NDP) and the German Communist party (DKP) — had been unable to cut into the strength of the major parties. At the local level of government, the once fairly significant "city hall parties" and "nonpartisan" alignments had all but disappeared from municipal and county councils.

"TO THEM THAT HAVE SHALL BE GIVEN"

The Christian and Social Democratic party elites have over the years been able to expand and consolidate their paraconstitutional position in West German politics on the basis of Article 21 of the Basic Law. As we noted earlier, this provision holds that political parties are essential intermediaries between the voters and their government in a democratic polity, but it limits that function to parties supporting the present regime. In effect, this formal modification of the classical principles of direct as well as representative democracy has first of all enabled the leaders of the major parties to make these parties the primary foci for electoral choice. Secondly, it has allowed them to restrict alternative opportunities for political participation and the expression of policy demands.

The specific legal implications of Article 21 and related constitutional provisions have been set forth in numerous laws, administrative regulations, and judicial decisions. In the early 1950s, for example, the Federal Constitutional Court sustained the contention of a government led by Christian Democrats that a right-wing party and an earlier version of the present Communist Party should be outlawed as "antidemocratic" organizations. These rulings served to warn other groups critical of the regime that they risked a similar fate if they overstepped the boundaries of "legitimate" opposition. Laws sponsored jointly by the Christian and Social Democratic elites in the late 1960s have imposed severe restrictions on the formation and survival of new parties. These parties must have "democratic" objectives and structure and must publicly account for their activities and major sources of income; new parties also lose their legal status if they do not participate in any federal or state election in the space of six years. The political activities of interest associations and civic action groups have been similarly limited by laws that restrict their ability to influence governmental policymaking by penetrating or bypassing the major parties.

Beyond these restrictive rules, Article 21 has enabled the CDU/CSU and SPD elites to derive tangible benefits from their preeminent position in the party system. As the leaders of the principal governing parties, they have been able to exercise the power of patronage, most significantly at the very top of the public administration. For, other than in Britain, key West German civil servants are "political officials" subject to appointment and removal by their ministers and entitled to a pension. And unlike civil servants in the United States, those in the Federal Republic need not resign to run for and serve in an elective office; they may take a temporary leave as did more than a third of the federal deputies elected in 1976. Leading civil servants in the federal, state, and local governments have become much more politicized than in former times and many are openly and closely identified with one or the other major party.[3]

A second advantage enjoyed by the major party elites is that they have far greater access to the public and private media of mass communications than the leaders of other political organizations. As spokesmen for the government or major opposition party, they make frequent appearances on television and, as representatives of the major parties, they receive more of the free time allocated to the parties during election campaigns.

A third advantage is financial. West German parties get most of their income from membership dues, private contribu-

[3] At that, the penetration of the civil service by deserving party members was in 1974 still considered far from sufficient by the chairman of the SPD, former Chancellor Willy Brandt. For an analysis of the trend toward the politicization of the civil service elite from a comparative perspective, see Robert D. Putnam, "The Political Attitudes of Senior Civil Servants in Western Europe," *British Journal of Political Science* 3 (1973): 257–90.

tions, and public funds. The major parties get most of this income, allowing them to support organizational and promotional activities that are beyond the means of the smaller parties. For example, the latter simply cannot afford the expensive services of public relations firms and polling organizations, which have become ever more important in West German electoral campaigns.

For the SPD, the party with the largest membership, dues are the biggest source of income (see Figure VI.3). The CDU/CSU depends more heavily on private donations, mostly from businessmen and business organizations, and the small FDP would find it difficult to carry on without them. The major parties receive further substantial funds from the public treasury for their "civic education" activities as legitimate political organizations.

Under the West German Campaign Finance Law, parties — rather than candidates — draw funds from the public treasury for some of their campaign expenses if they receive more than 0.5 percent of the vote in federal elections. Such subsidies are advanced before an election on the basis of a party's votes in the previous election. If it gains votes the party will get more money after the election, but if it loses votes it must repay an appropriate amount to the public treasury. New and minor parties find it correspondingly more difficult than the large, established parties to borrow money before an election, and the smaller their competitive chances the greater the rate of interest on such high risk loans is likely to be.

By current estimates, as much as a quarter of the income of the principal parties is today derived from public funds. The growth of such income has made the major parties and their leaders less dependent on private contributions, membership dues, and the free services of dedicated volunteers. And, since public funds are paid into the organizational treasuries of the parties, this increased income has strengthened the leading party officials' control over the internal allocation of money to various activities and candidates.

Regulations affecting the nomination and election of parliamentary candidates have provided the major parties with another competitive advantage. Sponsored by the CDU/CSU

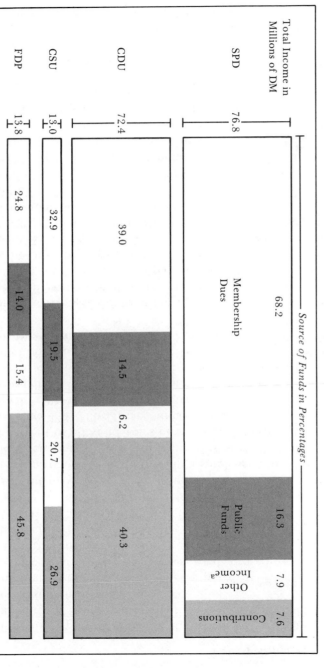

Figure VI.3. *The Financing of the Major Political Parties in the Federal Republic (1973)*

a E.g., loans and interest on investments.
Source: "Parteien in der Bundesrepublik Deutschland," *Inter Nationes*, SO 1-75 (January 1975), p. 6.

and SPD elites, they have made it increasingly difficult for independent and minor party candidates to win seats in the federal and state legislatures.

A candidate must first of all be nominated by a legitimate political party according to proper legal procedures. This stipulation prevents persons who are not sponsored by such a party from entering the race. Under the prevailing system for federal elections, an individual may then run as a constituency candidate, or as a candidate on a party list in the states, or both. As you may recall, a constituency candidate who captures a plurality on the first ballot in a single-member district will, however, not get the seat unless his party has won at least 5 percent of all valid votes or two additional constituencies (see page 143). The list candidates of a party that meets these qualifications will not be elected unless they are placed high enough on its list in the state to benefit from the ultimate proportional allocation of seats on the basis of second-ballot votes for the various parties. Either way the candidates of small parties face greater hurdles than those of the major ones.

In short, when it comes to minor parties, there are limits to the system of proportional representation in federal and state legislatures. These limits, in effect, restrain electors from voting for the constituency candidates and the lists of parties that appear unlikely to gain representation; at the same time they enhance the representation of the major parties, because votes for parties that do not make the race are not counted in the distribution of legislative seats.

A fifth advantage enjoyed by the major parties and, more particularly, their leaders has stemmed from the rules of legislative organization and procedures in various West German parliaments. Under the standing orders of the Federal Diet all key legislative posts and all committee assignments are reserved for members of properly constituted parliamentary parties (*Fraktionen*) and distributed by the leaders in proportion to their party's strength in the chamber. A deputy will thus be excluded from the most important policy processes in the legislature if his party's delegation constitutes less than 5 percent of its membership or if the leaders blackball him.

Such arrangements discourage interest associations from supporting minor or independent candidates and strengthen discipline and cohesion within the parliamentary parties. A deputy can resign from his parliamentary party but retain his seat; when several did so in 1972, it produced a deadlock in the Federal Diet and that led to new elections. But, in the absence of a situation where every vote is crucial, a deputy who quits his parliamentary party and does not join another will have little or no influence in the chamber and is unlikely to be reelected. It is therefore not surprising that on the few occasions when deputies left their parliamentary party they switched sides rather than choose splendid isolation and probable electoral defeat as independent members.

PARTIES AND VOTERS

Earlier we examined West German electoral processes in terms of general political orientation and participation patterns; now let us take a closer look at the specific relationship between parties and voters. Voter turnout has consistently been much higher than in other representative democracies such as Britain. But in the Federal Republic, as in Britain, voting as such has been more the product of a sense of civic obligation than of a deep concern with the outcome of elections. Under these conditions the West German parties have not so much needed to get their supporters to go to the polls — like American parties — but to translate a propensity to vote into ballots for their candidates.

The electoral choices of West German voters have largely been shaped by three interdependent factors: (1) the organization of representative government in the Federal Republic; (2) the partisan dispositions of the voters; and (3) the strategy and tactics employed by the parties to gain new votes without losing those of past supporters. Together these elements have over the years interacted with gradual, unspectacular changes in the environment for West German politics to produce fairly stable voting patterns.

The operative rules of the political system structure and limit the opportunities of West German voters to elect whom they please when they please. Elections ordinarily are held at regular intervals determined by the lawmakers; but they may come before their appointed time if a parliament is dissolved, as the Federal Diet was in 1972. Except in some local elections, the voters cannot choose their governmental leaders directly; they can only opt for or against the parliamentary candidates of legitimate political parties. Votes for minor parties are likely to be wasted on unsuccessful candidates. The electorate has furthermore no immediate influence on nominating processes; in the absence of open primaries, it can only accept or reject as its deputies party candidates designated by a small number of active party members and functionaries.

A choice between the major competitive parties has offered West German voters only rather general and limited alternatives among governmental policies and policymakers. Both the CDU/CSU and the SPD today are above all electoral organizations for the broadest possible alignment of partisan supporters; their rival campaign appeals have accordingly been pitched to what their leaders take to be the lowest common denominator of political differences and preferences of the moment in a pluralist society.

In that respect, minor parties that have no chance to become governing parties may provide unorganized interest groups — such as most West German consumers — with a means for articulating policy demands that they feel are ignored or opposed by the major parties and organized pressure groups. It is often overlooked that votes for radical parties may, in fact, provide the prevailing political system with a safety valve against major explosions and its ruling elites with a reading of the temperature of mass opinion. Support for such parties need not be, or become, an expression of outright opposition to the regime; it may furnish ordinary West Germans with a legitimate outlet for protests against policy bargains struck without their approval. Take, for instance, the period of the Grand Coalition between the Christian and Social Democrats of the latter 1960s. The two parties controlled more than two-thirds of the votes in both houses of the federal parliament and pushed through a number of highly unpopular "emergency" measures with the close collaboration of the major interest group elites. Public support increased not only for the "extraparliamentary opposition" of the radical left but for the National Democratic party of the radical right. After the break-up of the Grand Coalition, the SPD absorbed most of the votes of the former and the CDU/CSU those of the latter.

The partisan dispositions the parties seek to tap and mold are conditioned by a voter's beliefs, sentiments, and values; the more consistent these are with the voter's image of a party, the more likely it is that he or she will support it. In large part such congruence appears to be a matter of a voter's socialization experiences and informational environment. Studies of West German electoral behavior have found that attachment to a particular party is significantly related to homogeneity in a voter's past and current social relationships. Firm party identification tends to be strongest when it ties in with the political values voters have derived from their parents, from their religious faith and organizational affiliations, and from their most immediate interpersonal relationships. Party loyalty is usually weaker when it is not reinforced by highly valued social contacts and cultural norms, and is particularly weak when it conflicts with them.

The most loyal supporters of the major parties are today middle-aged and older voters who were raised in a distinctive "proletarian" or "Christian" setting and now live and work in a corresponding encapsulated subcultural environment. The SPD has thus been most consistently supported by skilled industrial workers in its so-called red strongholds, mostly urban areas of the northern and central parts of the country. Many of the workers were brought up in a politically "leftist" home, most belong to a trade union, and their closest associates are usually people who share their "working-class" background, life-style, and organizational ties. For these voters the SPD has traditionally been the only democratic party for the German workers. More often than not, such voters are nominal, anti-clerical Protestants who consider the CDU/CSU a reactionary party tied closely to the Roman Catholic Church as well as to big business; they are also likely to be strongly anti-Communist and emphatic in their rejection of all radical Marxist groups opposed to the SPD.

The most consistent supporters of the more conservative

and emphatically "Christian" CDU/CSU, on the other hand, look on the SPD as almost as much of a "red" menace to all they hold dear as the radical groups to the left of it. They may be devout Protestants and owners of large business enterprises; most often they are devout Roman Catholics who own shops and farms in the predominantly Catholic small towns and rural areas of the southern states, especially Bavaria. In these so-called black strongholds, a Social Democratic candidate has as little chance to be elected as a Christian Democratic one in a solidly working-class neighborhood and a SPD partisan is as much of a deviant here as a CDU/CSU supporter is there. In both cases a voter is likely to be subject to all sorts of social and pyschological pressures for conformity with the preponderant climate of political opinion in the immediate environment.

Voting habits are not necessarily the only, or even the principal, bases of party constancy. The most consistent supporters of the major West German parties are also apt to be their most faithful supporters. That is, they are voters who implicitly trust the party of their choice to do what is right and necessary according to their beliefs, feelings and values. They vote for their party — rather than against another — because they are strongly attached to it for ideological and sentimental reasons. For these staunch loyalists, the strength of a symbolic attachment to the party and its leaders may override any dissatisfaction with the party's performance in and out of government.

In past years the Christian and Social Democrats could count on the votes of party loyalists for most of their support, but such constant voters have lately constituted an ever smaller proportion of the electorate. As in other Western democracies, there are more independent voters who vote now for one party and then for another and who in West Germany may split their ballots between the constituency candidates and electoral lists of different parties. Competition between the parties has come to focus to a corresponding extent on winning the independents' support.

The partisan preferences of these floating voters are more closely linked to current political issues than those of party loyalists and are accordingly more sensitive to short-term changes in the policy environment. Their choice of party is largely determined by their personal involvement in political developments and their corresponding perception and evaluation of what different party governments can and should do about them. The Christian Democrats, for example, have been especially identified with the preservation of law and order and military security; when these issues are preeminent for independent voters, they tend to favor the CDU/CSU. The Social Democrats, on the other hand, have been more closely associated with social welfare measures, educational reforms, and income redistribution; when these actions coincide with the wishes of independent voters, such voters are apt to prefer the SPD. West German electoral campaigns are therefore largely pitched to the prevailing mood of such floating voters — as they are in the United States — with parties endeavoring to capitalize on partisan dispositions that are to their advantage and to play down, or overcome, those that are not.

Independent voters in the Federal Republic are likely to be younger than constant voters, to have had more variegated socializing experiences, and to live and work in more heterogeneous sociocultural settings. They are usually geographically and socially mobile persons who have worked at various jobs. Many commute between factories or offices in urban centers where they associate with fellow employees and take orders from their bosses, and suburban homes where they relax with their families. When it comes to choice of party, such voters are therefore more likely to be subject to a larger variety of incongruent, if not conflicting, pressures than those exposed to a more homogeneous social environment, and to be less firm in their partisan allegiances.

Significantly, shifting party preferences and ticket splitting have become particularly pronounced with highly educated, middle-income, salaried white-collar employees in the major metropolitan centers; in other words, the same sort of people who are also disproportionately represented among what we termed the political public. From about the mid-1950s onward, their votes floated increasingly to the SPD and, to a lesser extent, the FDP and proved decisive for the victory of

the reformist Social-Liberal Coalition in the 1969 and 1972
federal elections. Subsequently, the direction of these floating
votes was reversed and moved toward the CDU/CSU, largely
because of deteriorating economic conditions and a more conservative climate of political opinion. But in any event, as an
analysis of West German voting patterns concluded after the
1972 elections, "No party . . . has a firm hold on this metropolitan; middle-class segment. It is a swing group that can
apparently support any of the three parties at any given time;
its flexibility may well make for more frequent alternations
between government and opposition." [4]

With the gradual arrival of a new generation of West German voters, partisan differences based on traditional sex and
religious distinctions have waned. Most of the women's vote
used to go to the Christian Democrats, but it no longer does.
The significance of religious affiliation in an electorate composed of roughly an equal number of Protestants and Roman
Catholics is still greater than in most other European countries and the United States. But although Catholics have continued to vote preponderantly for the Christian Democrats,
and Protestants against them, this pattern has become decidedly less pronounced, particularly among organized industrial workers who are only nominal members of the Roman
Catholic church. The bid of the CDU/CSU for the support of
all Christans, whatever their occupation and income, has met
with the strongest response among the devout members of
both major churches (see Table VI.1).

During the era of general and growing affluence, socioeconomic distinctions became less important in West German
elections than in former times and in other European countries — notably Italy, France, and Britain. In the 1972 federal
election, for example, the votes of unorganized workers were
divided pretty much as those of the electorate in general (see
Table VI.1). Organized workers have heavily favored the SPD,
but then only about a third of West German employees are

4 David P. Conradt and Dwight Lambert, "Party System, Social Structure, and Competitive Party Politics in West Germany: An Ecological
Analysis of the 1972 Election," *Comparative Politics* 4, no. 1 (October
1974): 81.

Table VI.1. *Vote for Major Parties, 1972 Federal Election*
(*in percentages*)

	CDU/CSU	SPD	Minor parties	Total
Vote for party lists	45	46	9	100
Protestants	38	55	7	100
Devout[a]	51	37	12	100
Catholics	60	35	5	100
Devout[a]	87	11	2	100
Unorganized workers	43	47	10	100
Organized workers	26	68	6	100

[a]Indicates regular church attendance.

Source: Postelection mass opinion survey reported in Elisabeth Noelle-Neumann and Friedrich Tennstädt, *Rückblick auf die Bundestagwahlen 1972* (Allensbach: Institut fuer Demoskopie, 1972), hectographed.

trade union members. Subsequent developments suggested, however, that this pattern of diminishing socioeconomic distinctions in elections might not hold under less favorable conditions for political consensus in a mass-consumption society. In the mid-1970s rising inflation and unemployment, along with governmental tax policies designed to boost a lagging economy through capital investments by the rich, combined to sharpen socioeconomic cleavages in the West German electorate. Lower-income voters resented the more pronounced differences in purchasing power, and interest conflicts between rival claimants for the largest possible share in a diminishing national product became more intense.

As the two major parties have become closely balanced in their electoral strength, their tactics for winning new and floating votes — without losing those of past supporters — have assumed increasing importance. A small shift in votes may decide which of them will have the parliamentary votes to form a government, whether they can rule alone or have to win the support of a coalition partner, and whether the party or parties that dominate the popularly elected Federal Diet, the lower house of the Federal Parliament, will also control the upper house, the Federal Council. The latter, as you may recall, represents state governments, which may be the products of electoral outcomes and coalition arrangements that provide the opposition in the Diet with an absolute or suspensive veto over legislation in the Federal Council. It is therefore not surprising that competition among the principal parties in federal as well as state elections has recently become less polarized in some respects and more so in others. Convergence has been most marked in their campaign platforms. Phrased in the most general of terms, platforms now resemble each other so closely that independent voters find it difficult to discover any significant differences in the programs of the CDU/CSU, SPD, and FDP. Each party has claimed to stand for such popular policy objectives as military security through the NATO alliance, economic security through the welfare state, and social progress through reform legislation; and each has asserted that it could do what the others could — only better.

The more indifferent voters have been to such appeals, the greater has been the inclination of party campaigners to rely on divisive slogans and rhetoric to overcome their apathy. Christian and Social Democrats have thus sought to engage the values and sentiments of independent voters by claiming that which party won would be crucial for their country's and their own well-being. Divergence among the major parties has been most pronounced when closely fought elections have involved heated disputes over ideological issues and the fitness of particular candidates to hold public office. On such occasions Christian Democrats have, for example, tried to invoke a "red scare" and turn anti-Communist sentiments against the Social Democrats; the SPD, for its part, has endeavored to mobilize anti-Nazi sentiments by denouncing its opponents as cryptofascists. Conservative Christian Democratic leaders, such as Franz Josef Strauss, have presented themselves as guardians of law and order against Social Democratic radicals; Social Democrats, in turn, have pictured these men as dangerous reactionary nationalists.

The problem that such divisive efforts to arouse the emotions of independent voters poses for moderate party leaders is that they may transcend the heat of electoral campaigns and endanger the basic elite agreement on the form and rules of the political system. At the policymaking level, bitter opponents in elections have thus far managed to collaborate quite smoothly between elections; however, this turnabout has not only produced a good deal of cynicism among the voters and criticism from intransigent party militants, but may prove to be a great deal more difficult, even impossible, to accomplish if socioeconomic developments should lead to more intense interparty conflicts. Firebrands among the Christian and Social Democrats are willing to take that risk; in fact, many maintain that a more sharply defined competitive party system would enhance democratic processes by providing the voters with more meaningful and therefore more effective choices and influence over public policy. Moderate leaders, on the other hand, want above all to preserve the consensual basis of representative government by party elites.

GOVERNMENT BY PARTY ELITES

Policymaking has been more of a "positive sum" than a "zero sum" game among West German party leaders. That is, key participants have not normally ended up as outright winners or losers, but have tended to derive at least some benefits from interparty and intraparty bargaining processes. One reason is that the party system as a whole has not been sharply polarized into incompatible camps; this has permitted Christian, Social, and Free Democrats to join together in various mutually beneficial combinations at the federal, state, and local levels of government. A second reason is that party government has as a rule not only meant coalitions among different parties, but elite coalitions within the major parties. A third reason is that policymaking activities are not as centralized under the prevailing constitutional order as they are in such unitary states as Britain and France.

In contrast to the present British system, the outcome of a single parliamentary election has not allowed national West German party governments to determine policies for the entire country. The division of public powers between the executive and legislature and between the central and state governments provides the leaders of a strong and united opposition party with extensive opportunities for influencing national policies.

Thus, when one of the major parties has controlled the executive branch of the Federal Government, the other has been
able to modify if not block legislation on the strength of a
large representation in the Federal Diet, or control of a majority of the votes of the state governments in the Federal
Council, or both. And much as in the American two-party
system, regional party leaders who are not members of the
national executive and legislature have frequently played key
roles in the formulation of national policies.

At election time the major party elites have fought against
each other and accentuated their differences; between elections, their joint desire to make the present system work under
conditions dictated by the policy environment has impelled
them to seek parliamentary compromise solutions to partisan
conflicts. This desire has been especially notable with respect
to constitutional amendments to the Basic Law — requiring a
two-thirds majority in both houses of the Federal Parliament
— but it has also applied to a good deal of bargaining over
ordinary legislation. Many of the laws passed by federal as
well as state parliaments have been the product of informal
"behind-the-scenes" agreements among leaders of nominally
opposing parties. Such forms of conflict resolution have been
all the more important when public opinion and governing
coalition parties have been sharply divided on policy issues;
for instance, the 1965 law extending the statute of limitations
on the prosecution of Nazi crimes could not have been passed
without a de facto coalition between the governing CDU/CSU
and the opposition SPD.

In the light of this customary pattern, astute observers of
West German politics were all the more surprised when a
parliamentary deadlock over the 1972 treaty with the Communist German Democratic Republic could not be resolved and
the government had to appeal to the electorate to break it.
For the first time in almost a quarter of a century the voters
were asked to settle what their representatives could not decide for them; and decide they did by providing the governing
SPD and FDP with more than enough votes to get the treaty
through the Diet.

In federal and subnational politics, party government has

been shaped by two rather different types of relationships between the head of the government and the governing party elites. One is characterized by the autonomous and authoritative leader of an executive-centered elite coalition who dominates his party and considers it his instrument. In the other, the formal chief of government is, in fact, the chairman of a team of more or less coequal party leaders, and party elites inside and outside the legislature may play a much greater role in fashioning government policy. At different times and in different settings, the prevailing relationship has been determined by the personality and style of performance of the governing leader, and by the power alignments among and within the political parties. Variations on both types are exemplified by party government under the first five chancellors of the Federal Republic.

A Christian Democrat, Konrad Adenauer (1949–63), employed a highly personal and rather arbitrary style of leadership during his long tenure in office. At the time, the proponents of a more liberal parliamentary system considered his "chancellor democracy" too autocratic and arbitrary; it now appears that Adenauer's highly popular leadership made a significant contribution to the institutionalization of party government. Chancellor democracy was congruent with cultural traditions of strong executive authority in the state and served to integrate West Germans into their new political system during a difficult period of socioeconomic and political reconstruction.

In the Adenauer era the CDU/CSU attained a position of hegemony in the West German party system, and its fortunes were closely tied to the popularity of the chancellor. Adenauer managed to establish and generally to maintain a tight reign over the Christian Democrats by skillfully combining his roles as chief of the federal government, chairman of the party, and leader of an interparty parliamentary coalition. Formally distinct, these roles — along with those of Adenauer's subordinates — became in practice all but indistinguishable. Major policy decisions were often made by Adenauer alone, or in consultation with the members of a small "kitchen cabinet" of trusted ministers, key civil servants, and party lieutenants; on such occasions the regular cabinet, Diet deputies, and national CDU organs ratified rather than determined governmental policy. As the supreme arbitrator between legislative and administrative elites between party and interest group leaders, Adenauer relied primarily on his assistants in the Chancellor's Office to see to it that his objectives were realized.

Under the next three chancellors, party government became less personalized and more collegial. A Christian Democrat, Ludwig Erhard (1963–66) presided over a brittle coalition with the Free Democrats, and his style of party government proved unsuited to the evolving patterns of partisan alignments inside and outside his party. Erhard had been Adenauer's minister of economics since the establishment of the Federal Republic and was by training and experience a better economist but a much poorer and less astute politician. He could not give West Germans in general, and the Christian Democrats in particular, the strong, authoritative leadership that they had come to expect after fourteen years of chancellor democracy under Adenauer. He did not have the prestige and skill that had allowed Adenauer to resist or vitiate competing policy demands and control factional disputes, and he permitted contending interests far greater autonomy and himself less. This turned out to be his undoing.

Erhard sought to apply his strong faith in economic laissez-faire processes to transactions in the political marketplace and relied far more heavily than Adenauer on the spontaneous evolution of a supportive consensus. However, his style of leadership was much more passive; he had much less control over the CDU/CSU, and decision-making power in the still dominant governing party shifted to its leaders in the states and the Federal Parliament.

In some respects Erhard's style as chancellor resembled that of American presidents who defer to their party's leaders in congress and the states; in others, it was closer to that adopted by the leaders of unstable and fractionalized parliamentary governments. His attempt to play the part of a plebiscitary "people's chancellor" above partisan strife helped the Christian Democrats to win the 1965 federal election, but his popularity proved to be fleeting and he was unable to check increasing factionalism in the CDU/CSU elite. Erhard was publicly criticized as an inept and weak chancellor by leaders of his own party, especially by Adenauer whom he characteristically allowed to remain as national chairman for some time before reluctantly assuming the position himself. The still immense prestige of the former chancellor helped to seal Erhard's fate after he completely lost control over the Christian Democratic elite; it decided, against his wishes, to form a Grand Coalition with the principal opposition party, the SPD.

Collective government by collaborating party elites shaped the political style of Kurt Kiesinger, the Christian Democratic Chancellor of the Grand Coalition (1966–69). It was an executive-centered coalition — but one without a dominant chief of government — which brought together the principal leaders of the two major parties in the name of maximum political stability and harmony in a time of economic crisis. In contrast to the Erhard government, the Grand Coalition made party authority identical with governmental authority. For all practical purposes, there was no longer an opposition in the federal parliament; the Free Democratic party, with only 8 percent of the remaining seats in the Federal Diet and no veto power in the Federal Council, could do little to influence policymaking. Many West German and foreign observers therefore believed the Grand Coalition to have seriously delayed, if not blocked, the institutionalization of a truly competitive party system.

In fact, this unprecedented form of collaboration between the major party elites was a temporary marriage of convenience. The Christian Democratic leaders hoped that as a result they would win either an absolute parliamentary majority in the next federal election or, at least, a large enough plurality to dominate the next government. The Social Democratic leaders overrode protests in their party with the argument that they had at long last gained an opportunity to eradicate the popular image of the SPD as a permanent opposition party in national affairs; it would now be able to establish its legitimacy and capacity to govern the country.

The partners in the Grand Coalition were bound together by a carefully drawn coalition contract which balanced their formal authority and responsibilities and provided for informal arrangements to iron out differences over government policy. For example, the chancellorship went to the party chairman of the Christian Democrats, Kiesinger, but the chairman of the Social Democrats, Willy Brandt, became deputy chancellor and foreign minister; other posts were similarly apportioned between the two parties. Government measures were decided on by interministerial consultations within or, more often, outside the cabinet, and legislative strategies were worked out in frequent meetings with the governing parties' parliamentary leaders.

In these circumstances Chancellor Kiesinger was, in effect, something like a board chairman who is at most first among equals. He was severely restrained in using the preeminent formal powers that were his under the Basic Law and did not enjoy Adenauer's autonomy in the choice of his ministers and the determination of governmental policy. The composition of the government as well as its actions had to satisfy the need for balance and collegial unity in a heterogeneous coalition of independently powerful party leaders. These, in turn, had to contend with party opponents who charged them with putting "opportunistic" considerations ahead of party principles. And although neither the Christian Democrats nor the Social Democrats could govern alone, both parties were strong enough to form an alternative coalition with the Free Democrats if their policy differences proved irreconcilable.

Kiesinger was thus a weaker leader of his government and party than was Adenauer, but he was also a more astute politician than Erhard. As chancellor, he acted primarily as a discreet mediator among his colleagues in the government; as the chairman of his party, he sought to use his personal charm and considerable political skills to mollify Christian Democratic critics of the Grand Coalition. He did both rather well, but evidently at the cost of muting his "chancellor effect" on the electorate's choice of party.

The prestige attached to the incumbent chancellor had contributed to electoral victories of the CDU/CSU in the days of Adenauer and Erhard, but it was not enough of a magnet in 1969 to give the party the parliamentary majority it had sought. The SPD still came in only second best, though with more votes than ever before. The Grand Coalition had, however, done its intended service for the Social Democratic leaders;[5] they were unwilling to continue as the junior partners, and found the Free Democrats eager to join them in an alternative "Social-Liberal" Coalition. For the first time in the twenty years since the establishment of the Federal Republic, the SPD became the principal governing party and the CDU/CSU the opposition party in the federal parliament. The precedent of the Grand Coalition survived as a model for future "crisis" governments by party elites.

The Social-Liberal Coalition was once again a marriage of convenience, though a more enduring one than the Grand Coalition. It was confirmed and strengthened by the 1972 federal election, which gave the Social Democrats for the first time a parliamentary plurality but not a majority. Subsequent gains by the Christian Democrats in state elections accentuated the interdependence of the coalition parties. The SPD needed the FDP to remain the senior governing party and the FDP needed the SPD to stem the apparent trend toward a two-party system. These considerations strongly influenced the collaborative association among leaders of the two parties in the federal as well as various state governments; and they entered into the relationship between these leaders and the functionaries and members of their respective parties. In both cases the basic theme was that the Social Democrats and Free Democrats had to swim together lest they sink together in turbulent political waters and that their common predicament called for mutual assistance in elections and reciprocal concessions on policy differences.

During the chancellorship of Willy Brandt (1969–74), foreign policy issues were in the forefront, making collaboration

[5] Interviews with a representative sample of Diet deputies in 1969 indicated general agreement among party elites that the Grand Coalition had (1) reduced the distinction between CDU/CSU and SPD in the eyes of the public, (2) established the SPD as a competent governing party, and (3) produced interparty consensus necessary for the passage of important "emergency" legislation and other key laws. See Fredrick C. Engelman, "Perception of the Great Coalition in West Germany, 1966–1969," *Canadian Journal of Political Science* 5, no. 1 (March 1972): 28–54.

fairly easy. The SPD and FDP elites were both determined to "normalize" the relationship between the Federal Republic and the Communist countries of Eastern Europe, above all the German Democratic Republic, and fought together to overcome the opposition of the CDU/CSU. As long as foreign policy was preeminent in West Germany, Brandt was in his element. He drew on his worldwide prestige as a statesman to play the role of a conciliator in domestic and foreign affairs and left more mundane party problems to other Social Democratic leaders. He took pride in his rather easygoing style of leadership, which worked well enough in international and coalition politics, but was less effective in dealing with growing intraparty conflicts in the SPD. Brandt kept rather loose reigns on the party in his capacity as its chairman and maintained a tolerant view toward young militants who wanted to transform the party into a more radical "vanguard of the working class." More moderate Social Democratic leaders vainly sought to induce Brandt to keep the radical wing in line and to curb activities they considered harmful to the party and its reformist program.

Brandt, like Adenauer and Erhard, was more or less eased out of the chancellorship by fellow party leaders, rather than being deposed by an election or a "positive" vote of no confidence in the Diet. He resigned in 1974 when one of his closest assistants was arrested as an East German agent. But by all accounts key members of the Social Democratic elites made no move to stop him and were not particularly distressed to see him go. In their view Brandt had ceased to be an asset to the party in its electoral battles with the CDU/CSU. They believed that he was unable to deal forcefully with increasingly pressing domestic economic issues; off the record, some of Brandt's most bitter critics in the SPD held that he was too much of a moralizer to be a good politician and that he had turned himself into a living monument to the foreign policy achievements that had won him the Nobel Peace Prize. In any event, Brandt was not considered an indispensable chancellor, not least because a successor was readily at hand in the person of Helmut Schmidt.

As the new SPD chancellor of the Social-Liberal Coalition, Schmidt evidently took Adenauer for his model. His political style marked him as a highly pragmatic and, if need be, ruthless man of action. In the government and the Federal Diet he sought to establish himself as the dominant personality of an executive-centered coalition; in the Social Democratic party he assumed a hard line toward the radical left wing and insisted that it accept his more conservative position in socioeconomic matters. Although Brandt remained the SPD chairman, Chancellor Schmidt quickly became its leading figure in the eyes of the electorate. In fact, his personal popularity came to exceed that of his party.

But Schmidt was caught up in a sudden downturn of the West German economy that weakened his popular support and almost cost him his office in 1976. In the federal election of that year the SPD lost its previous plurality to the CDU/CSU, the combined forces of the Social Liberal Coalition barely scraped through, and Schmidt was reelected chancellor by only a one-vote margin in the Federal Diet. His personal authority in the government, the parliament, and the Social Democratic party was consequently greatly reduced. However, the survival of the Social Liberal Coalition and the accomplishment of its legislative program depended largely on Schmidt's ability to control the restive left-wingers in his own party and, at the same time, maintain the support of the leaders and all of the deputies of the pivotal FDP.

INTRAPARTY RELATIONS

Relations among West German elites — and especially those among the party elites — shape and are shaped by relationships within the major parties. As in other countries, intraparty relationships involve of course many elements — from the momentary effects of particular issues, and the personalities and associations of particular individuals, to the more general and enduring patterns of the political system and policy environment. Two interdependent factors are however exceptionally important.

The first is a party's proximity to the levers of public authority in the Federal Republic. Do its leaders have a great deal of influence over policymaking, or only some influence, or none at all? Is the party represented in legislative bodies and, if so, is it a governing or opposition party? If it is a governing party, at what level do its leaders wield public authority, and how firmly and in what form? For example, do they command majorities in only one or both houses of the Federal Parliament? Are they out of power in national politics but in control of strategic state governments? Are they able to rule alone or do they depend on the cooperation of coalition partners? If they depend on cooperation, how solid is the alliance? And what are a party's chances for retaining or obtaining government power in the next election? A strong governing party may be able to manipulate public policy on behalf of its electoral strategy whereas a weak one is more apt to provide opposition parties with opportunities to score electoral gains. On the whole, the greater the present or prospective influence of particular party leaders on public policymaking the greater, too, is likely to be their influence within their party.

The second major factor is the dual character of the major West German parties. Like American parties, they are electoral organizations for directly or indirectly recruiting leading public officials; but they are also mass organizations of dues-paying party members, like most European parties. As electoral organizations the principal West German parties are integral parts of the political order and jointly link the representative components of the state to the pluralist components of an advanced industrial society. As mass membership organizations, however, they stand apart and are associated with opposing partisan viewpoints and philosophies. As competing electoral parties the CDU/CSU, SPD, and FDP try to appeal to a wide range of values, sentiments, and policy demands and to unite behind their banners the largest possible alignment of voters. In this respect, their activities are aimed outward to gain the support of diverse interest groups and to project a favorable image to a broad and heterogeneous electoral public. But as membership parties, they are committed to particularistic ideologies and programs that may not necessarily appeal to outsiders. In this respect the major West German parties are internally oriented and their character is defined by intraparty relationships among leaders, middle-range activists, and rank-and-file members.

The role of the electoral party is measured numerically in terms of votes gained or lost; that of the membership party qualitatively in terms of its effect on the selection and actions of political leaders. Here we need to notice first of all that though party membership has increased in recent years it still does not include more than 5 percent of West German voters. Second, the ratio of party members to voters varies a good deal among parties, but in any event is very large (see Table VI.2). Third, there are many more nominal than active members; these may have been drawn into the party by their families or friends, or joined it to obtain or retain a job, but beyond paying their dues they will do little more than sporadically participate in grassroots electoral campaigns.

Table VI.2. *Party Members and Voters*

	SPD	*CDU*	*CSU*	*FDP*	*Total*
1974 membership (in thousands)	1,000	500	120	63	1,683
1972 votes (in thousands)[a]	17,167	13,187	3,610	3,129	37,093
Ratio of members to voters	1:17	1:26	1:30	1:48	1:22

[a]Second-ballot votes in federal election.
Source: Calculated from official election statistics and membership figures provided by the parties.

For most of the time and in places where its influence is most telling, the membership party consists in effect of an even smaller minority of party activists. They, however, tend to be politically far more engaged and committed partisans than most West German voters. To the extent that they have been united on their party's principles and objectives they have given strength to its leadership; insofar as they have been deeply divided on this score they have weakened it. To some degree all of the party elites have had to contend with intraparty tensions arising from conflicts between their party's internal and external relations, and from efforts to reconcile the purposes of an ideologically diffuse electoral party with those of a programmatically cohesive membership party. Generally they have managed to deal with such problems, through compromise where necessary and party discipline where possible. Both forms of conflict resolution are facilitated by the organizational rules of West German parties.

Party Organization. The "democratic" framework for intraparty relations is defined by public law and derivative party statutes and corresponds to the federal and representative structure of the state. The regular party organizations are composed of interlocking local, regional, state, and national components; in addition there are special sections for young members, women, and occupational groups. The affiliated union parties, the Christian Democratic Union and the Bavarian Christian Social Union, maintain separate party establishments all the way up into the Federal Parliament; both include federated suborganizations representing particular interest groups, such as the major churches, agricultural and business associations, and organized labor.

Representative leadership rests nominally on authority delegated from below, but in fact largely on oligarchic control by party elites. Federal party organs are formally supreme, but they depend on autonomous parliamentary parties and regional organizations to implement their decisions. And although the tasks of various party units and officials are formally divided along horizontal and vertical lines, they are generally connected through a hierarchic network of party functionaries who occupy several positions simultaneously.

Executive committees elected at periodic party meetings essentially run the regular organization at different levels. As a rule, local party chapters provide the ordinary members with their only opportunity to participate directly in party deliberations because all higher party organs are representative bodies. By law local organizations must be small enough to permit such grassroots participation, but frequently the membership is too dispersed or too small to warrant a local chapter.[6] Local party meetings are furthermore usually poorly attended and dominated by a few active party members. Most

---

[6] In 1969 the SPD, with by far the largest membership, had 8700 local organizations with an average of eighty-seven members. Other parties did not publish such information, but presumably had fewer local chapters.

of these leaders will be local government officials and sea-
soned, nonsalaried party functionaries who place each other
on the local executive committee, and represent the party in
communal elections and the local membership on higher party
bodies.

Beyond nominating constituency candidates for state and
national elections local leaders play on the whole only minor
roles in wider party affairs. For party activists in state and
federal politics the local chapters are principally a source of
grassroots support; for the party organization they are the
reservoir for unpaid campaign workers at election time; for
ordinary party members they offer a means of access to public
officeholders of their party who may intercede on their behalf
with governmental agencies.

Regional party organs, in contrast to the local chapters, are
key arenas for intraparty relations. They vary in size but
normally include several state and federal electoral districts
and a hundred or more local units. Delegates to regional party
conventions elect the regional party chairman and executive
committee and regional representatives to state and national
party congresses.

It is at the regional level that the functions of the electoral
party and the membership party intersect most significantly
and middle-range activists become particularly important.
This is the level at which intraparty alignments, and the influence of affiliated and outside interest groups, primarily enter
into the choice of candidates and platforms for the electoral
party and into crucial deliberations on ideological programs
for the membership party. It is also the key organizational
level for the conduct of the most intense personal campaign
activities in state and federal elections — canvassing, mass
meetings, and the like. Lastly, it is the level at which incumbent party leaders maintain — and aspiring leaders seek to
obtain — a strong power base for prominent roles in state and
federal politics. Members and likely members of the top party
elites usually command the support of one or more large regional organizations.

The stepwise contraction of membership representation by
leading party activists continues upward through the state to

the national level. At conventions of the state party, delegates from the regional organizations elect the state chairman and executive committee, select and rank the pary's list candidates for state and federal elections, and designate their choice for chief of the state government. These proceedings are normally controlled by the regional party elites, though they may occasionally involve a good deal of conflict and bargaining among party factions and spokesmen for socioeconomic interest groups. The designated head of the state government is usually the incumbent government leader or the chairman of the state party and should the party win the next state election, the choice of the party convention is customarily binding on its state Diet deputies, though constitutionally they are free to elect whom they please. Should the chief of a governing state party resign between elections his successor will be chosen by the leader of the parliamentary party with the advice and consent of the state executive committee. The strength of the ties between these two party organs will vary with differences in the nature of intra- and interparty relations in various states; since there is usually a large overlap in membership, serious conflicts between the leadership of the parliamentary party and of the party organization on the outside are unlikely unless they are controlled by opposing party factions.

The national organization of the Social Democrats is formally more centralized and integrated than that of the Christian and Free Democrats. It still incorporates vestiges of the encapsulated and disciplined "proletarian" membership party that was established more than a hundred years ago and became the model for the "democratic centralism" of Lenin's Bolshevik "cadre party" and its Communist offshoots throughout the world. The national CDU organization, on the other hand, dates back only to the founding of the Federal Republic and still shows its origins as a heterogeneous union of regional electoral parties established just a few years earlier. The more decentralized structure of the national CDU also reflects the greater diversity of its constituent and affiliated groups and their resistance to efforts to create a more thoroughly integrated federal party.

Under the party statutes of the SPD and CDU, the representatives of the regional organizations to the national convention speak for the entire membership and form the supreme decision-making body for the party as a whole. However, since most of their authority is delegated to the national executive committee, and most of their decisions serve only to ratify those taken elsewhere, the actual power of the convention delegates is more nominal than real.

National party conventions in West Germany are usually pretty dull. Hundreds of resolutions may be introduced, especially at SPD conventions — but normally few will pass if they are opposed by the top leadership. For the most part between 300 and 400 delegates meeting biannually for four or five days can do little more than listen to lengthy speeches and place their stamp of approval on proposals presented by the executive committee. The proceedings will be dominated by national leaders and the leaders of the strongest regional organizations and votes will reflect subnational party alignments.

Nonetheless these conventions serve two important functions. One is focused on the external relations of the electoral party. National conventions are usually held just before a federal or state election and are designed to draw wide public attention to a party's electoral candidates and platforms; before a federal election they dramatize the selection of a candidate for chancellor and demonstrate the party's solidarity behind its choice. National conventions also provide an internally oriented, integrative function for the membership party. They legitimate the authority of the national party leadership through the election or reelection of the party's chairman, vice-chairmen, and other members of the national executive committee. They may also adopt a basic party program and resolutions stating party principles that are designed to establish fundamental guidelines for the membership party and its legislative and governmental representatives. The 1959 Godesberg Congress of the SPD, for example, provided the doctrinal basis for a new course of the national electoral party by discarding most of the Marxist ideology of the old membership party. Party leaders could thereafter meet left-wing criticism of their allegedly "opportunist" tactics by reference to appropriate chapters and verses in the Godesberg program.

Between conventions, the national executive committees

and their presidiums act as the top decision-making bodies for the membership party at the federal level. The national executive committee of the SPD and the CDU consists of about thirty members who meet on the average once a month in private sessions at the party headquarters in Bonn; roughly a third belong to the inner presidium, which meets more often.

In a way, these bodies resemble the Federal Council of the state governments in the constitutional organization of the Federal Republic. They fuse separate components of the party leadership and link national and subnational party organs. In the SPD as well as in the CDU the national executive committees consist of top government leaders, legislative leaders, and regional functionaries, and reflect the balance of power among various intraparty elite alignments.

The national chairman is the official leader of the membership party and is its principal public spokesman. His formal powers are quite limited in both the CDU and SPD. At meetings of the national executive committee and presidium his vote counts for no more than those of the other members, and he may find himself in a minority. The extent of the national chairman's real influence in intraparty relations depends on the unity among the top party elites, on his personal authority and political skill, and on the power he may derive from other offices.

The first chairman of the CDU, Chancellor Adenauer, used his governmental position, his personal authority, and his great political skills to dominate the federal party; he was less influential at lower levels and left politics in the states pretty much to regional CDU leaders in exchange for their support. The second chairman, Chancellor Erhard, was unable to play a similar role, as we noted, and had to give way to Kiesinger, previously a CDU state chieftain and minister president. While he was chancellor, Kiesinger held his own in his capacity of party chairman by mediating among other members of the CDU elite. He was, however, compelled to quit as party chairman when he failed to retain the chancellorship in 1969. His successor was the leader of the CDU opposition in the Federal Diet, Rainer Barzel, who had to resign in 1972 when he proved unable to recapture the chancellorship for the union parties. The man who followed Barzel as party chairman, Helmut Kohl, was neither chancellor nor leader of the CDU in the Diet but a powerful state government and party leader. As the chancellor-designate of the CDU and CSU in the 1976 federal election Kohl was also unable to lead the affiliated parties back to national power. But unlike Kiesinger and Barzel, he retained the chairmanship of his party and remained a viable candidate for the chancellorship. He sought to enhance his chances in this respect by moving from the position of a state government leader to that of leader of the CDU opposition in the national parliament.

The SPD, as a more cohesive membership party, has been less volatile in the choice of party chairman. At this writing, only three men have held the position; two of these died in office, and all of them became chairman without a contest. The post-Nazi chairman of the party, Kurt Schumacher, kept a tight reign on the party organization in his dual roles as head of the membership party and leader of the principal opposition party in the Federal Diet. When Schumacher died in 1952, his former deputy Erich Ollenhauer succeeded him in both posts. Ollenhauer lacked his predecessor's personal leadership authority in the membership party; he was above all a loyal organization man whom other senior SPD functionaries considered one of their own. Even before his death Ollenhauer let another man assume the leadership of the electoral party as the SPD's candidate for chancellor. That man was Willy Brandt, then Lord Mayor of West Berlin. Brandt remained a state government leader when he was elected party chairman in 1963; and he kept the party chairmanship when he resigned as federal chancellor in 1974. Thereafter, the national SPD leadership was divided among Brandt, the chairman of the membership party, Chancellor Helmut Schmidt, the leader of the electoral party, and Herbert Wehner, the chairman of the SPD parliamentary party.

In sum, then, effective control over the national organizations of the major parties has rested with an intraparty elite consisting of the top federal and state government leaders, legislative leaders, and key party functionaries. Most regional

leaders have played more important roles in the affairs of the
federal party than federal leaders in those of the state parties
— especially when a party has been out of power at the national level and in power at the subnational level. At both
levels, authoritative public policymaking by governing party
leaders has moreover been shaped more by factors outside the
party organization than by official partisan policy objectives.
Insofar as the membership party provides for the constitutional expression of the "political will of the people," it does
so primarily through the selection of their parliamentary representatives.

Choosing Representatives for the People. According to the
majoritarian principles of the West German parliamentary
system, competing parties propose and the voters decide who
is to make authoritative policy decisions in the name of the
citizenry. But as in other representative democracies — including the United States — the choice of the voters is largely pre-
empted by the choice of a few political activists. The Basic
Law of the Federal Republic stipulates only that "political
parties shall participate in forming the will of the people";
however, complex nominating and voting procedures largely
structure the electoral expression of that will and allow key
members of the subnational organizations of the major parties
to select parliamentary representatives for the people.

In Federal Diet elections, as we have seen, half of the seats
go to the victors in single-member constituency races, and the
rest are apportioned among state list candidates according to
their ranking and the electoral strength of their parties. Candidates for both types of seats are recruited from a very small
pool of active party members who are willing and able to run
for the Diet. To have any chance of making the race they must
run under the label of a viable competitive party and that,
under present conditions, means principally either the CDU/
CSU or SPD. Most West Germans cast their two ballots in
federal elections as a single vote for or against a party and its
designated governmental leaders. A constituency candidate's
personal attractiveness is consequently less important to the
voters than what he stands for. This applies even more to list

candidates who get on the ticket as the representatives of social groups and interests, such as women, young people, and clergymen.

Who then is elected into the Federal Diet? A candidate who secures a place at the top of one of the state lists of the major parties — or is nominated in one of their constituency strongholds — is virtually assured a seat. In recent years this has been the case for about two-thirds of the deputies, and the pattern is likely to persist as long as no party scores a sweeping electoral victory. In both the CDU/CSU and the SPD the processes of candidate selection favor the renomination of incumbent parliamentarians; turnover among their legislative representatives has been affected more by death and voluntary withdrawal than by involuntary retirement at the hands of their party or the voters.

As we noted, there are no primary elections. Most Diet candidates are first chosen by local party leaders to contest a constituency seat and then placed and ranked on the state lists by the secret votes of the delegates to regional nominating conventions. Who gets to run in a safe or in a marginal "swing" district, and who gets on the state lists and how close to the top, is thus essentially decided by middle-range activists in the regional organizations and only indirectly by the ordinary members of the membership party.

As the ballot for a party list carries only the names of a few prominent party leaders who head the state ticket, most West German voters have no idea exactly whom they may be sending to the Diet by that route. When a constituency candidate who is also on the list captures a district, a list candidate who would otherwise not have made it will move up and get a seat as well — provided his party is entitled to it under the rules of proportional representation. On the other hand, a district candidate who is well placed on the state list is likely to make it into the Diet even if defeated in a constituency race.[7] For

---

[7] Although the proportional allocation of all parliamentary seats is based on (second-ballot) votes for electoral lists in the states, the more constituencies a party captures directly the less secure is a low place on these lists. If the SPD is entitled to 200 seats and has won 100 constituencies, the latter number will then be deducted from the former and

that reason, a constituency candidate who faced unfavorable odds in his district will almost always strive for a more promising list slot at the regional nominating conventions. If he is a prominent member of the state party he will ordinarily be successful; if not, his list position will depend on the votes he can obtain from the convention delegates. A nomination contest will usually involve a good deal of jockeying and bargaining among various intraparty factions and competing interest groups that are trying to get their people into the Federal Diet.

The national party headquarters in Bonn coordinates federal election campaigns in the states; it has, however, little or no influence on the selection of candidates for the Federal Diet. Governing party leaders are likely to be more successful than opposition leaders in promoting the nomination of individuals whom they consider particularly qualified for the legislature, such as financial experts and other specialists on public policy matters. But if they press too hard, their efforts are apt to be counterproductive; regional and local party leaders jealously guard their power of nomination and have often gone out of their way to reject candidates favored by national party leaders. Even Chancellor Adenauer lacked sufficient influence to overcome this problem, and his efforts to introduce additional national party lists got nowhere. In federal parliamentary activities, government as well as opposition leaders depend therefore all the more on intraparty discipline and elite collaboration. And in pushing for a particular course of action in the Federal Diet they have to consider that its members are tied to sponsors and clients in the constituency and state organizations of the membership party.

---

only 100 SPD list candidates will get into the Diet. By the same token, if the party should win only 50 constituencies, 150 list candidates will get seats.

CHAPTER VII

Pressure Group Politics

IN THE FEDERAL REPUBLIC, as in the United States, responsible public officials are constantly confronted with the necessity for choice among competing demands on a wide range of issues. A pluralist society gives rise to many diverse policy interests, and a regime based on the consent of the governed must provide extensive opportunities for their articulation.[1] However, giving voice to such demands does not ensure their satisfaction. Democratic principles may call for responsive policymakers and policy implementation may be more effective when it takes account of the wishes of the affected population. But no government can accede to all demands, no matter how democratic it may be and how hard it may try to accommodate conflicting interests. The nature of the political system and the dynamics of the policy environment — as well as personal preferences and associations — cause policymakers to be more responsive to some expressed demands than to others and to vary in their susceptibility to pressure from different interest groups.

[1] Interest articulation is the political process through which individuals and groups make overt demands for the satisfaction of their values by the decision makers in a community or state. According to the nature and intensity of their claims, their perception of political alignments, and the access channels which appear available to them, people choose the means of interest articulation that seem most convenient and most likely to obtain the desired results.

THE ORGANIZATIONAL IMPERATIVE

The processes of interest articulation and accommodation conform closely to the highly formalized patterns of mass representation and elite interaction that generally prevail in West German politics. The Basic Law, as we have seen, designates the political parties as the principal nongovernmental agents for the coordinated flow of domestic policy demands into the governmental system. Interest associations provide a complementary organizational link between state and society.

The Basic Law does not explicitly recognize interest associations, but it grants all citizens the right to form and join such groups, provided they are not in conflict with the criminal code or "directed against the concept of international understanding." Pressure group politics designed to promote or prevent decisions by authorities of the state are shaped by several factors. First, access to the "right" people is restricted by the sheer size and complexity of the political system and the multiplicity of competing demands for authoritative action or inaction. In this respect, West German conditions for interest articulation are not very different from those in similarly constituted advanced industrial countries. Second, the organizational framework and operative rules of the present regime favor access through carefully regulated legal procedures. These funnel multiple policy demands through screening agents before they get to authoritative decision makers. Third, there are the prevailing political norms, which identify legitimate interest articulation with law-abiding behavior. As we noted earlier, the efforts of left-wing radicals to win mass support by taking pressure group politics into the streets have usually been counterproductive; they led to stronger public demand for law and order.

For the average West German the opportunities for direct individual endeavors to obtain interest satisfaction from public officials are limited by law. The ordinary citizen may express his demands through his vote, through administrative and judicial agencies of the state, and by personal appeals to political leaders, such as his parliamentary deputy. Some well-placed persons among the nonelites may also have informal access to influential people, through family connections and friends in high places. But especially in national politics such bonds no longer carry the weight they did under former German regimes and still do in other countries.

Most citizens of the Federal Republic feel that they can do little or nothing to influence political developments, as we noted in Chapter IV. But there are others who believe that ordinary people can have a voice in public policymaking if they join together for legitimate collective action. A rather novel form of such collective action (for Germans) has been the so-called citizen initiatives that have emerged in recent years. Most of these have been temporary and single-issue civic action groups which, here and there, have proven to be quite effective instruments of pressure group politics at the grass-roots level. For example, groups of parents have demanded and obtained more public funds for nursery and primary schools; neighborhood groups have succeeded in blocking the urban renewal plans of local government officials and real estate speculators; pressure from environmental protection groups has led to tighter controls over urban industrial pollution and traffic patterns.

These associations are, however, limited in scope and size. With the notable exception of civic action groups that have sought to block the construction of nuclear power plants, they usually do not extend into regional and national politics. And, like the political parties, they have recruited only a small minority of West Germans. Moreover, most of the participants come from middle- and upper-income groups and are identified with vested interests that are not shared by the general public.

Far more West Germans, though still a minority, belong today to one or more of the regular interest associations. Such organized pressure groups have generally been considered the most adequate means for mitigating the apparent political impotence of the "little man" through collective action. National and international opinion polls indicate that not only ordinary people in the Federal Republic, but West German elites as well, are far more likely to single out formal interest associations as the most effective agents for influencing public policies than are their counterparts in the United States, Britain, and Italy. West Germans tend to consider these organizations less partisan than the political parties and, therefore, as calling for less of a political commitment; at the same time they are believed to secure more tangible and specific policy benefits for their rank-and-file members than catch-all electoral parties do.

In contrast to the major parties, West German interest associations are not organizations for the recruitment of policymakers and do not try to gain general control over policymaking. By law and by custom they defend and promote the particular interests of social, economic, and cultural segments of the public. They will intermittently seek to influence policymaking and the day-to-day flow of policy demands, but only on certain issues and on behalf of ostensibly nonpartisan interests. Unlike the political parties, interest associations thus have special clienteles rather than broad ones. And to the extent that the major parties have become less closely identified with special interests and more concerned with winning votes through the aggregation of many interests, they have also become blunter instruments for the realization of particular policy demands. For that purpose, the pressure group politics of interest associations have consequently become even more important in governmental affairs than previously.

THE REGULAR REPRESENTATION OF ORGANIZED INTERESTS

Regular interest groups come in all shapes and sizes in the Federal Republic. Some are quasigovernmental organizations and others are strictly private associations. Some identify their nonpartisan objectives with causes that are said to be in the general public interest and others clearly demand satisfaction for special interests. The League of German Taxpayers, for example, claims to serve the general welfare in its battle against "wasteful" public expenditures, and the League for the Freedom of Science, an organization of conservative university professors and politicians, maintains that it fights for individual liberty and democracy in West Germany when it asks that the state protect the "legitimate" rights of academicians against attacks from radical students. The activities of such organizations as the Forest Owners Association, on the other hand, openly serve the special interests of a specific clientele. And the domestic and foreign policy demands of the Expellee and Refugee Associations are put forward on behalf of Germans who fled their homes in Eastern Europe after World War II.

West German interest associations are more inclusive, more tightly organized, and occupy a more privileged position in public policy processes than their American counterparts. In certain respects their activities are more closely regulated than in the United States; in others, less so. In fact, if not in name, some of the most important associations antedate the present regime; they are elements of socioeconomic and cultural continuity in a country that has been marked by sharp political discontinuities. Lingering identifications with religious, status, and occupational groups — dating back to the Industrial Revolution and beyond — still affect the policy objectives and pressure group activities of the churches and such associations as the League of German Artisans. At the same time, the effect of more recent changes in West German society and politics is reflected in the preeminently material and pragmatic perspectives of most interest group leaders and members and in the style of collective bargaining in contemporary pressure group politics.

The formal rules of representation that prevail in the governmental and party system also apply to the articulation of organized interests. Ostensibly the policy preferences voiced by pressure group leaders reflect those of their clients but often these clients exercise little or no control over their official spokesmen. This is most obvious in the case of the Roman Catholic hierarchy and other appointed functionaries, but it also applies to elected interest group leaders who are only indirectly chosen by the membership.

The extent of the influence of interest group representatives in the councils of government may be based on their personal prestige and connections, on the status of their office, on evidence of mass support for their demands, and on legal and normative criteria endorsing the "proper" representation of elements considered important in West German society — or on any combination of these. Some pressure group leaders may thus gain attention, if not results, as the presumed spokesmen for persons they only nominally represent and who may not even belong to their organizations. Compulsory membership in interest groups or a high degree of solidarity in voluntary associations may allow others to claim solid backing from their constituents.

In federal, as in state and local politics, interest associations endeavor to influence public policies principally by the following methods: (1) assuring themselves of ready access to key points in authoritative decision-making bodies through the recruitment, placement, and sponsorship of public officials sympathetic to their claims; (2) allocating effective authority to those political positions which are most accessible to them; and (3) having their goals and methods accepted by influential veto groups and, less frequently, by the general public.

How these methods are specifically employed may vary a good deal from group to group and issue to issue. In some cases such activities will be carefully shielded from public view, in others interest group leaders will openly seek to mobilize mass opinion in order to bring pressure to bear on public officials or to replace them. Depending on what they want, when, and from whom, various pressure groups will direct their efforts to different issues and decision makers. For instance, a business organization may concentrate on economic matters subject to federal legislation and seek to influence relevant federal ministries and parliamenary committees; a pressure group associated with the Roman Catholic church, on the other hand, may be primarily interested in educational policies under the jurisdiction of the states and pursue its objectives at the local and regional level.

A detailed description and analysis of the entire network of interest associations in the Federal Republic would take up the remainder of this book. There are thousands of such organizations — many with overlapping memberships — including at least 1800 national ones. However, we will confine our discussion principally to the most influential pressure groups in federal politics. In general the patterns that prevail there are duplicated at lower levels of the political system.

Compulsory and Voluntary Organizations. Some West German interest associations are specifically established by law, in accordance with corporatist principles going back to the Middle Ages, to represent certain common interests. Prime examples are the occupational "chambers" (*Kammern*), which have their roots in the corporate guilds of former times. Unlike the American chambers of commerce, these are quasi-governmental organizations of public law, which exercise compulsory jurisdiction over their members and are supposed to link key sectors of the economy to the state. Most private producers engaged in agriculture, commerce, and manufacturing, as well as members of the so-called free professions — such as self-employed physicians and lawyers — must belong to appropriate local chambers, which determine and enforce rules of occupational standards and conduct. The leading functionaries of these chambers not only represent their members in pressure group politics, but exercise derivative governmental authority over them.

These multiple economic and political functions give considerable weight to policy demands put forward on behalf of the chambers since their quasiconstitutional status makes them one of the most important associational structures providing for an orderly relationship between the economic and the political systems. To coordinate and articulate common interests, the local chambers in most of the West German states form regional groupings; their national federations in turn are supposed to defend and promote the interests of the constituent chambers at the federal level of government.

Other associations involved in politics are not based on compulsory membership. These include traditional institutional groups explicitly endorsed and supported by public authorities, particularly the major churches, as well as a host of voluntary organizations for the promotion of symbolic causes and material interests. Some are comprehensive associations performing various tasks and pursuing numerous goals, others have a single main purpose. Religious associations, for example, minister not only to the spiritual needs of their members, but engage in educational and social welfare activities regulated by public authorities. Major business and labor organizations are concerned not only with strictly economic problems, but with social and cultural policy matters. On the other hand, many smaller interest associations — such as the Pensioners' League and the League of War Victims — promote the explicit and exclusive political demands of highly particularistic clienteles.

Although such voluntary associations lack the quasigovernmental authority of the occupational chambers, they are also not as tightly controlled by agencies of the state. At the same time, they are less closely associated with the political parties than interest organizations under former German regimes and in other European countries. Under the present regime these interest associations consequently enjoy quite a bit of political autonomy and flexibility as ostensibly nonpartisan pressure groups.

Sometimes a relatively insignificant pressure group may score a success thanks to an intensive publicity campaign, an exceptionally fortuitous combination of circumstances, or a temporary alliance with politically more powerful forces. A touch-and-go electoral battle, for example, may afford the leaders of a small, but tightly organized and united group unusual opportunities to trade their support for desired commitments from party candidates. On the whole, however, the greatest political influence rests with the official and unofficial spokesmen of the large national organizations. Formal and informal interelite channels permit them to exert direct pressure on leading party and governmental functionaries: at the same time, the major interest group elites command substantial resources for applying indirect pressure through influential opinion leaders and expressions of mass support for their demands.

Influence through Functional Representation. Whereas American public officials may pay attention to the demands of interest group spokesmen if they wish, West German officials are legally bound to do so. As in most European countries, institutionalized rules for the functional representation of pluralist interests allow pressure groups to bypass the political parties and inject themselves directly into policymaking.

Numerous law and administrative regulations give formal sanction and encouragement to the long-established practice of direct contacts between interest associations and agencies of the state. Thus, in all of the states of the Federal Republic various consultative bodies attached to governmental organs transmit interest group wishes to public officials. In Baden-Württemberg, for example, representatives of the principal economic organizations are regular members of the regional planning council. The same is true in the public media: spokesmen for all of the major interest groups sit on the supervisory boards of the states' radio and television networks along with representatives of the principal political parties.

Similar arrangements exist at the federal level of government. The administrative procedures of the various ministries require that when they draft a bill for submission to the legislature — and most laws originate that way — they must consult the official representatives of the appropriate peak interest organizations (*Spitzenverbände*) and consider their wishes. Effective associational interest articulation through such formal channels is further facilitated by numerous ministerial advisory councils of nongovernmental experts connected with interest groups. For example, the West German Advisory Council of Economic Experts (*Sachverständigenrat*) is not a governmental body, in contrast to the American President's Council of Economic Advisors. However, its influence on public policy is more far-reaching since its task is to provide for the coordination of public and private economic activities at all levels of government. Such harmonization, as its name indicates, is also the official function of the "Concerted Action" (*Konzertierte Aktion*). It meets periodically in secret for an exchange of views between top officials of the Federal Bank and the Federal Ministries of Economics, Finance, Labor, and Agriculture on the one hand, and leaders of the corresponding major peak interest associations on the other.

Functional representation also provides for the coordinated

articulation of nonpartisan sectional and local interests in national pressure group politics. Various subnational governmental units are represented by their respective peak associations, the League of German Cities (*Deutscher Städtetag*) thus represents the particular interests of large urban municipalities, and the League of German Towns and Communities (*Deutscher Städte- und Gemeindebund*) those of smaller municipalities.

These legal arrangements have two chief consequences. First, they encourage behind-the-scenes interelite bargaining and accommodation among pressure group spokesmen and key public officials. Such institutionalized practices are favored by both sides on the grounds that direct negotiations among functional policy specialists facilitate the orderly processing of interest group demands outside the public arena of partisan controversy and party strife.

Second, these procedures induce the rank-and-file members of interest associations to depend on their formal representatives to obtain satisfaction for their policy demands and compel the constituent organizations of federal peak associations to rely on top interest group elites who have direct access to national policymakers. Here, too, the formal justification for such organizational arrangements is that they provide for the efficient and stable transmission of policy inputs from a pluralist society to the state. The intended object is to prevent the inundation of federal agencies by amorphous individual and group demands and to allow interests to be aggregated and adapted before and while they are considered by executive, legislative, or judicial organs of the Federal Government. From a comparative perspective, as a perceptive observer has noted, West German arrangements for the national representation of functional interests constitute "an especially clear instance in which entirely formal considerations can increase the power of federated groups and their key functionaries and thus have a major effect on the structure of organized interests." [2]

2 Reinhard Bendix, *Nation Building and Citizenship* (New York: Wiley, 1964), p. 133.

Influence through Political Representation. Structures for the functional representation of organized interests, as well as the judicial system, permit West German pressure groups to bypass party and governmental channels of political representation. However, these means also limit their opportunities for influencing the formulation of public policies, and most pressure group leaders therefore try to keep other means available. Experience has taught them that competing interest groups may neutralize each other, especially if they pursue conflicting demands by way of the governmental bureaucracy or the judiciary alone; they have learned that civil servants and the courts may decide that acceding to pressure group demands would not be in the public interest or would violate legitimate principles of law and justice. Moreover, the formal routes of access leading through the major peak associations frequently compel the constituent organizations to subordinate their particular demands to those of the larger federations and generally place smaller interest associations at a disadvantage.

For these reasons pressure group leaders endeavor to develop and maintain close relationships with the manifest political leaders who are recruited by and from the major parties. And here the degree of mutual interdependence, of agreement on basic political principles, and of reciprocity in the exchange of benefits is all-important. Party government leads interest group elites to seek influence over the composition and actions of the political elites while these, for their part, compete for the allegiances of diverse elements in a pluralist society. The power of interest group elites in the political arena will accordingly be enhanced if they can demonstrate their ability to promote or frustrate the objectives of particular political leaders, parties, and factions; these, in turn, will be most accommodating to the demands of those pressure group leaders they consider most effective.

The specific methods employed by interest association leaders to influence authoritative policies through political channels vary a good deal with particular pressure groups, parties, and circumstances, and are frequently obscure.[3] The general

[3] Whereas the activities of organized pressure groups in other advanced industrial countries, notably the United States, have been explored quite

public has been rather critical and suspicious of such activities — even when they are legal; on several occasions, pressure group politics in election campaigns have backfired, harming the parties as well as interest organizations. Elected officials and people who want their jobs therefore try to avoid the political stigma of identification with special interests and to conceal their obligations to pressure groups. At the same time, as we have seen, the major parties — and especially the CDU/CSU — provide for the representation of special interests in their organizations and on their electoral tickets and endeavor to accommodate pressure group demands in their programs.

In general, there are four methods through which pressure groups seek to influence party leaders in government and parliament: (1) attempts to obtain direct representation in the major party organizations, particularly among their leaders; (2) attempts to gain access to governing party elites through formal and informal, direct and indirect party contacts; (3) attempts to use party contacts to provide both governing and opposition party leaders with selective information and interpretations on particular policy issues (for example, articles in elite publications and "expert" testimony and memoranda supporting interest group objectives); and (4) offers of electoral assistance to friendly politicians and threats of mobilizing a pressure group's members and financial resources against those who oppose its policy demands.

Electoral pressure group politics today carry less weight than in the early years of the Federal Republic. First of all, interest associations can apparently no longer persuade politicians to quite the same extent that they can deliver the votes of their own members. Second, even the largest and politically most active pressure groups have evidently been unable to induce significant sections of the electorate in general to support their friends and punish their enemies; their publicity campaigns

---

extensively, this is not the case for the Federal Republic. Though the West German press and opinion polls attribute a great deal of influence to such groups, very little concrete information about their actual effect on policymaking is available. The few studies on the subject have dealt mostly with the period before 1960 and have tended to be either descriptive historical accounts or rather abstract legalistic analyses.

on behalf of particular parties and candidates have thus proven to be rather ineffective. Third, new laws providing public funds for campaign expenses and sharply restricting private contributions have reduced the importance of financial support from pressure groups. Political leaders have consequently been less ready than formerly to accede to the demands of interest organizations at election time and to compete for their support with preelection legislative gifts.

As these means have lost effectiveness, other means for exerting influence on political leaders have become more important to West German pressure groups. On national issues these involve principally the effective representation of their policy interests by members of the federal government, by the delegations of the state governments in the Federal Council, and by deputies in the Federal Diet. In this respect traditional patterns of functional representation that bypass political parties have been complemented by the marked increase in collaborative interelite relations between manifest and latent political leaders as we noted in Chapter V.

The major interest associations have been particularly successful in placing their spokesmen in authoritative decision-making bodies. Key officials in federal ministries have frequently been recruited from corresponding interest groups and sometimes returned to them after leaving office. For instance, the heads and leading members of the Ministry of Labor usually come from the trade unions and those of the Ministry of Agriculture from the farmers' organizations. Even when the bonds are not so close, federal ministers and their principal subordinates tend to act as the spokesmen of their respective interest group clients in formulating public policies.

Such relationships are considered to be mutually advantageous, and West German government leaders welcome and encourage them for more than narrow partisan reasons. They are thought to furnish the political leaders of the state with expert advice and special information not available through other sources, such as on the secret flow of foreign funds into and out of the private economic sector and on the well-guarded investment plans of West German industrialists. These contacts are also believed to provide governmental policymakers with exceptional opportunities for hearing and considering interest group demands and complaints out of the public view. For instance, they are said to be most helpful for weighing the pros and cons of contemplated fiscal measures designed to influence the patterns of wages, prices, and profits. Finally, the representation of private interests in the executive branch of the government is thought to be particularly useful for facilitating interelite negotiations prior to a policy decision and for obtaining the cooperation of the affected interest groups in its implementation.

Lobbying is at least as prevalent in West Germany as it is in the United States. Several hundred national organizations maintain offices in the capital city of Bonn to provide them with close contacts between their headquarters and government and party agencies. In West Germany, professional lobbyists are not required to list their names and sponsors in public registers, but they are likely to have better access to federal ministries and legislative bodies if they do. For example, only those interest group spokesmen who are registered with the Federal Diet will normally be allowed to voice their views at public hearings of its committees or be asked to submit written statements. When this regulation was instituted a few years ago, all sorts of associations entered their names in the register, from the very largest to some with as few as eight formal members.

On the whole, middle-range lobbyists may be less closely controlled than in the United States, but they also have a less significant role in policymaking. In the first place, negotiations on issues involving the major interest associations almost always reach into the top echelons of the peak organizations and the government and focus on direct contacts among corresponding elites. Second, national and subnational legislative organs are less important targets for pressure group politics than in the American federal system, though more so than in such unitary and parliamentary systems as the British. In West Germany, interest group leaders concentrate especially on the executive branch because it is the source of crucial administration regulations and most legislation. Bills introduced by the executive normally become law, whereas bills that originate in the legislature and legislative amendments opposed by the government usually do not. For example, between 1953 and 1973, about two-thirds of the bills sponsored by the Federal Government were approved by the Diet, whereas only roughly a third of those submitted by its members were passed.

Interest group representation in West German legislatures is more conspicuous than in the United States. Under the rules of the Diet its members are required to reveal their affiliations with organized pressure groups and on this evidence alone the groups appear to be well represented. Functionaries of business, agricultural, and religious associations are to be found especially among deputies of the CDU/CSU and FDP, whereas trade union officials are more apt to be deputies of the SPD. However, all of the parties in the chamber include numerous members of these and other interest groups. Moreover, the official listings do not mention more covert links to pressure groups, such as those of deputies who may have temporarily severed formal connections but continue to maintain informal interest group ties.

Whether overtly or covertly, such legislative representation of vested interests is particularly pronounced in the committees of the Diet, where most of its policy actions take shape. Through committee assignments, party leaders have enabled various pressure groups to be especially well represented in committees that deal with matters touching on their interests. Most of the legislative maneuvering and bargaining among pressure group spokesmen occurs in the private sessions of these committees and of the corresponding "study groups" (*Arbeitskreise*) of the different parties.

All of this should not lead us to overestimate the effect of pressure group politics in the Diet. West German interest associations must contend not only with the fact that the Federal Government normally exercises tighter party control over the Federal Diet than the American executive does over the Congress, but with constitutional provisions that impose tighter limits on the policymaking powers of the Federal Parliament. For instance, neither of its two chambers can compel the government to increase its budgetary proposals. Under these conditions interest groups normally turn to parliament only if they cannot receive satisfaction from the executive branch, and then usually to get desired changes in governmental bills rather than entirely different legislation. The significance of legislative pressure group politics is thus measured not so much by the number of interest group representatives in the Diet as by the amendments that become law through its actions. In this respect, interest associations have generally been more effective as veto groups than as promotional groups, and they have achieved more minor than major changes in governmental bills.

THE BIG FOUR

As we have said, economic values and, to a lesser extent, religious values are basic sources of subcultural group identification and political alignments in the Federal Republic. In pressure group politics these key values take the form of organized interests that focus on socioeconomic and sociocultural issues (*Wirtschaftspolitik* and *Kulturpolitik*) and are reflected in the preeminence of four major associational constellations: the national producers associations of agriculture, business, and labor, and the religious organizations of the Roman Catholic and Protestant churches.

The leaders of these associations constitute a large part of what we have called the latent political elites. They exert pressure on the manifest political elites when public policies seem likely to affect their group. Governmental, administrative, and party leaders are usually very attentive to their demands, but especially so if they believe that policy implementation could be stymied by the major interest group elites. In the case of the principal economic associations, effective interest articulation depends largely — though not entirely — on the strength of the shared material objectives of their respective members and on their leaders' commitment to an instrumental, pragmatic view of the state's socioeconomic functions in a dynamic policy environment. In the case of the religious association, effective articulation rests primarily on the persistence and legitimacy of traditional norms that have allowed the religious elites of the two major churches to claim a special role in state and society as the guardians of ethical standards and public morality.

Business Organizations. Big business, tightly organized into national interest associations and dominated by a few men, was the most powerful private interest group in pre-Nazi Germany and played a prominent part in mobilizing the Nazi economy for war. After 1945, the Allied occupation powers sought to diminish the concentration of West German business establishments, but such measures proved to be temporary; with postwar recovery big business regained its pre-eminent position in both economic and political life.

However, due to the increased specialization and internationalization of the West German economy, the homogeneity of the big business associations is today a matter more of form than of fact. At the same time, however, institutional arrangements and the structure of the German economic system provide greater mutual cooperation among German businessmen than is found among their American counterparts, particularly in the key economic sectors dominated by a few giant commercial and industrial concerns.

The collective political interests of the business community are formally represented by all-inclusive employers associations organized along regional and functional lines. Every employer of more than two or three workers is a member of local and regional chambers of industry and trade, as well as of specific occupational associations, which in turn are organized into federated groups. Nationally these organizations are united in various peak associations — such as the Federal Association of German Bankers — which employ a full-time staff to look after their constituents' interests. At the apex of all these groups stands a triumvirate of federated peak associations whose leaders serve as the formal spokesmen for the political demands of the business community as a whole.

The Diet of German Industry and Commerce (*Deutscher Industrie-und Handelstag,* DIHT), the national peak association of the chambers of industry and trade, is the least involved in federal politics. It does some lobbying and public relations work on behalf of its rather amorphous business clientele and occasionally lends its unofficial support to conservative candidates for public offices. The Federation of German Employers' Associations (*Bundesvereinigung der deutschen Arbeitgeberverbände,* BDA) is a more active group, particularly as a national spokesman for business on policy matters relating to labor and social issues. As a counterpart to the peak trade union associations, it seeks to promote the political interests of employers through lobbying and public relations work.

The third member of the triumvirate, the Federation of German Industry (*Bundesverband der deutschen Industrie,* BDI), is politically the most active and influential. Its membership encompasses thirty-nine affiliated national federations representing all branches of German industry and, through them, 98 percent of German industrial concerns. The Industrial Federation devotes much of its budget to publicity work designed to provide a favorable climate of political opinion for the promotion of its policy interests.

The leaders of the three peak business associations frequently collaborate in national pressure group politics. Cooperation is facilitated by overlapping membership in top organs and a broad but diffuse interelite consensus on the political interests of business relative to those of other societal groups. The presidents and executive directors of the industrial and employers federations sit as observers at one another's board meetings; in fact, in the mid-1970s one man was president of both peak associations. The two organizations jointly sponsor the Institute of German Industry which conducts leadership conferences on policy issues involving business interests and turns out a large volume of research reports and analytical studies on political developments. Several coordinating committees, such as the Joint Committee of German Trade and Industry, provide additional formal links among the top business pressure groups.

Many leading members of the peak business associations, moreover, maintain close informal relationships that extend throughout the Federal Republic. Elite business clubs and "luncheon groups" periodically bring them together. A "supper club" meets regularly in Düsseldorf and reportedly "the decisions made around its tables play a major role in West German industry and, indeed, the entire economic life of West Germany."[4]

Recent West German elections have indicated that the peak

---

[4] Philip Shabecoff, "When the Waiter Brings Coffee, Germans Talk Turkey," *The New York Times,* January 21, 1966.

business associations do not command sufficient popular support to mobilize substantial voting power on behalf of their policy demands. Furthermore, they lack the internal solidarity of some smaller promotional groups due to the heterogeneity of business interests in a pluralist society. Although their constituent organizations have been able to use contacts with political and administrative elites to promote or block specific policy measures, the three associations have largely confined their joint efforts to more general business objectives. They have thus opposed the expansion of public economic enterprises and the extension of state controls over the exchange of goods and services in the private sector. They have also fought against anticartel legislation and regulations designed to curb the power of big business in setting prices and allocating markets, and have lobbied against "codetermination" laws that allow employees to participate in the direction of both public and private enterprises. But apart from such general issues, the business elite has found it difficult to achieve and maintain a united front through the peak associations.

Business associations, like other pressure groups, endeavor to use various routes of access to policymakers. One of these is the Federal Parliament. Estimates of the number of Diet deputies with direct or indirect connections to business organizations have varied widely; roughly 20 percent have been business managers, independent entrepreneurs, and functionaries of employers' associations, and, over the years, about two-thirds of these deputies have been identified with the interests of industry. By far the largest number have been Christian Democrats, and most have not been members of the businesse elite. Few top business leaders have sought to get into the legislature, though conservative politicians have often called for more prestigious business representation in the chamber. Most prefer to play a less conspicuous role in public affairs, and those who have sought election have frequently been unable to get nominated even by the CDU/CSU. Business pressure groups have, however, not lacked helpful friends in the Diet, especially among the members of its key economic committees and party study groups. These friends have served as contacts and lobbyists for the employers associations in their relations with the federal executive.

At the national policymaking level, business spokesmen have found it most effective to present their demands directly to the chancellor or his closest advisers and key ministers. At lower levels of the executive branch, more highly formalized institutional arrangements — as well as patronage appointments from the business community — have provided access to key members of the civil service. In addition, party channels can promote close relations among top business and governing political leaders, especially if the latter are conservative Christian Democrats or Bavarian Christian Socialists. These tend not only to be particularly sympathetic to the views of the business community and to have been recruited from its ranks, but to be closely associated with the nongovernmental Economic Council (*Wirtschaftsrat*). This group represents about 80 percent of the roughly 1000 enterprises that account for more than half of the business turnover in the Federal Republic and, though formally independent of the CDU/CSU, it is in effect a powerful wing of the two union parties.

None of this, however, means that the leaders of big business organizations and enterprises form a dominant power elite or belong to a homogeneous ruling class. Not only are countervailing domestic and foreign factors in the policy environment too strong to make this possible, but the contemporary business elite lacks the necessary attributes. In comparison with its predecessors, it contains more economic subgroups with different — and often competing — policy interests on specific issues. The business elite is also now more international in its composition and outlook than formerly and less disposed to identify its own interests with the national interests of a German state. And the business elite, and particularly its younger members, is no longer committed to exclusive and distinctive big business orientations dividing it sharply from other leadership groups and political elements in the country.

With the passing of the traditional, patriarchic German owner-entrepreneurs — such as the Krupps — and their replacement by the managerial executives of national and multinational corporations, a new outlook has emerged. It rejects a special ideological "ethos" and political "calling" for business leaders in favor of cost and benefit considerations in domestic and foreign economic relations. There is a far greater readiness than formerly to bargain with employee representatives of the so-called social partners without involving public authorities. There is also far greater willingness to rely on political leaders and civil servants for governmental policies that will safeguard private business interests under a "social market economy" of free-enterprise capitalism in a social service state. Various studies have shown that most members of the present business elite believe that they have neither the time nor the skill to devote themselves very much to party politics. As they see it, their task is to make money for themselves and their clients; that of the public policymakers is to provide them with favorable conditions for the pursuit of profits at home and abroad.

Labor Organizations. Employee associations constitute the largest alignment of occupational pressure groups in the Federal Republic. Their membership is, however, far less inclusive than that of the employer associations. The growth of labor organizations has not kept pace with the expansion of the work force, especially not in the private service sector. In the mid-1970s organized labor thus took in only about four out of ten West German employees.[5] (See Table VII.1.) Proportionate membership strength is, however, not an adequate measure of the trade union leadership's qualitative influence over public policy processes. No West German government, whatever its partisan complexion, can today ignore the spokesmen of organized labor; public officials at every level of government depend on their cooperation for the effective implementation of socioeconomic policies.

The strategic role of the labor elite in the contemporary political system is unprecedented in German history for several reasons: (1) Independent employee organizations include

[5] In the early years of the Federal Republic close to half the employees were trade union members, but rising prosperity and the mass recruitment of women and foreign workers into the economy reduced the relative strength of organized labor, particularly among the expanding group of low-skilled, salaried service employees.

Table VII.1. *Organized Labor (1974)*

Percentage of work force in employee associations			
Wage and salary earners	39	Salaried employees	22
Manual workers	45	Civil servants	76

Membership of major employee associations	
German Confederation of Trade Union (DGB)	7,167,923
Metal Workers Union	2,460,697
Public Service Workers Union	997,771
Chemical Workers Union	454,793
German Confederation of Civil Servants (DBB)	728,047
German Salaried Employees Union (DAG)	454,793

a larger percentage of the labor force than under previous regimes (they did not exist in the Nazi era). (2) Socioeconomic developments have greatly increased the importance of the particularly highly organized areas of skilled industrial and public service employment. (3) The membership and leadership of the labor organizations are more unified and integrated into the political system than in former times. Whereas the German labor movement was once deeply split into bitterly feuding Socialist, Communist, Catholic, and liberal trade unions, such ideological divisions no longer exist. As full-fledged members of the policymaking stratum all of the top union leaders not only endorse, but strongly support the present constitutional order.

The rules for representing collective policy demands in effect allow labor leaders to speak for all employees, whether organized or not. Formal arrangements assume that unorganized labor shares the socioeconomic interests of trade union members; nonmembers thus derive "free-riders" benefits from pressure group achievements. Thus, if organized labor scores gains in social security, fiscal, and wage and hour legislation, in regulations concerning the labor courts for employer-employee disputes, or in extending codetermination laws to more business enterprises, unorganized labor is considered to profit from these accomplishments as well. We have here one more example of West German legal provisions designed to ensure orderly and stable policy processes in a pluralist society through interelite negotiations and bargaining among leaders representing different interests.

In comparison with their counterparts in other non-Communist and industrially advanced countries, West German labor leaders have been able to depend on a very high degree of cohesive rank-and-file support. The trade unions, like other formal nongovernmental associations in the Federal Republic, are required by law to be democratically organized in accordance with the usual graduated methods of representation. Top labor leaders are thus only indirectly elected by the rank-and-file members and only indirectly accountable to them. They have generally been responsive and responsible to the membership, but they also have had a good deal of autonomy in defining and representing the membership's specific policy interests. In this regard their authority has been sustained within their respective unions by the solidarity and discipline of the membership, by strong organizational bonds, and by tight leadership control over middle-level union functionaries and internal media of communications.

The leaders of organized labor have access to many key public officials, both through formal channels of functional and political representation and through informal contacts. Most also command substantial financial resources for the promotion of their policy interests. In addition to income from membership dues, trade unions derive profits from numerous economic enterprises, such as banks, publishing houses, insurance companies, apartment complexes, and breweries. These funds support public relations and lobbying activities. They also enable the peak associations and the richest unions to maintain a professional staff of labor lawyers and specialists who furnish labor leaders with expert information and advice on various policy problems.

The preeminent peak association of organized labor is the German Federation of Trade Unions (*Deutscher Gewerkschaftsbund,* DGB). In 1972, its predominantly male membership took in practically all organized industrial workers, more than two-thirds of organized white-collar employees, almost half of organized civil servants, and a third of the entire labor force. About eight out of ten DGB union members are today wage earners; the rest are mostly low- to middle-level salaried employees and civil servants.

The DGB is neither divided into a large number of amalgamated occupational unions, like the British Trade Union

Congress, nor split into industrial and craft unions, like the American AFL-CIO. It consists of sixteen national unions, which are organized by economic sectors and may include both production and service workers. The federation takes no part in collective bargaining with employers, and its constituent organizations engage in political activities of their own. The peak association functions primarily as their joint pressure group in federal politics. Its activities are financed by the member unions, and their leaders collectively determine DGB positions on national public policy issues. The top functionaries of the three giant unions that contribute most of the funds and members to the DGB (see Table VII.1) also carry the most weight in its councils and command the largest voting blocs at its conventions. The federation's national chairman has virtually no independent authority and serves primarily as its leading spokesman and chief administrative officer at the DGB headquarters in Düsseldorf.

The two smaller peak associations of organized labor are less inclusive than the DGB and more closely identified with traditional status differences between blue- and white-collar workers. However, with the waning of such distinctions, their leaders have increasingly discarded the notion of a distinct corporate identity for their members and have come to share the pragmatic trade union outlook of the DGB elite.[6]

The German Salaried Employees Union (*Deutsche Ange-stelltengewerkschaft,* DAG) split off from the DGB when the Federal Republic was established. Its founders held that white-collar employees did not share the outlook and interests of manual workers — who then as now, predominated in the DGB — and would be better served by a separate organization. As it turned out, most salaried employees did not care to join any labor organization, and most of those who did preferred

[6] In recent years the waning of socioeconomic differences between wage earners and salaried employees has been particularly pronounced among middle-income and young age groups. West German labor laws still retain some of the traditional distinctions; however, labor contracts in both public and private employments have increasingly discarded them in favor of differences in pay and fringe benefits based on experience and skill. At the same time, differences in the life-styles of manual and white-collar workers have gradually given way to common mass consumption patterns.

the DGB. The notable exceptions have been high-level employees in private enterprises who hold technocratic managerial positions; the ones who are not members of business but labor associations are likely to belong to the DAG.

Whereas the Salaried Employees Union has thus not been a strong rival of the DGB in obtaining the allegiances of white-collar workers, the German Federation of Civil Servants (*Deutscher Beamtenbund,* DBB) has been a more successful competitor in the particularly highly organized sector of public employment. The DBB and DGB represent about an equal proportion of the three-fourths of civil servants who are union members, but most of those in the higher ranks — including university professors and judges — belong to the DBB. Unlike other employees, servants of the state may not strike against their employer under West German law, but they also enjoy greater job security and more generous retirement benefits. Their positions in governmental agencies and the heavy overrepresentation of former or temporarily retired civil servants in West German legislatures have, however, permitted their associational leaders to advance the collective interests of these appointed public officials quite effectively by other means.

West German trade unions have thus far been much less militant in pursuing their interests than organized labor in Italy, France, and Britain. The right to strike for political as well as economic reasons is anchored in the constitution, but it has not been used often. In comparison with other leading industrial, non-Communist countries, including the United States, the Federal Republic has had exceptionally few major strikes. The leaders of organized labor have generally considered it neither necessary nor desirable to resort to this ultimate weapon, and West German employees have infrequently engaged in wildcat strikes in defiance of the trade union leaders' wishes and contractual agreements. Labor laws provide heavy financial penalties for unions that strike in violation of existing contracts and labor leaders have usually found both governments and private employers ready to negotiate new agreements when faced with the prospect of a crippling strike.

The trade union leadership has on rare occasions used the

threat of a strike to back up its pressure group demands in the political arena. In 1951, for example, DGB leaders said they would call a general strike if the Federal Government did not push a codetermination law for the coal, iron, and steel industries through parliament; their demand was met. In 1966, the threat of a strike by the Ruhr coal miners induced the Federal Government to arrange for a settlement underwritten by public subsidies to the mine owners. At other times such threats not only proved less effective, but provoked strong counterproductive public criticism of the unions and their leadership. For instance, in the late 1960s organized labor failed to block legislation providing for the suspension of certain sections of the Basic Law in the event of a "constitutional emergency." The trade unions had to be content with provisions that appeared to safeguard the right to strike. On this, as on other occasions, labor leaders staged mass demonstrations in support of their demands, but for the most part they have preferred to achieve their pressure group objectives through less dramatic interelite negotiations.

The extensive functional and political representation of organized labor under the prevailing regime affords its leaders manifold opportunities to promote their clients' interests out of the public view. In addition to their participation in numerous governmental and quasigovernmental bodies, labor leaders have direct and indirect access to political leaders through the major parties. DGB and other union officials wield influence in the CDU/CSU through the labor wing of the Christian Democrats, though not nearly as much as in the Social Democratic party. Relations between the DGB and SPD functionaries are especially close due to extensive overlap in the membership and objectives of their respective organizations and a corresponding degree of interdependence. When the Social Democrats have held the reins of government they have been particularly receptive to the demands of the DGB elite; at the same time, they have been able to use common short-range and long-range policy considerations to temper such demands.

On the face of it organized labor is strongly represented in the Federal Diet. The proportion of trade union members among the legislators has greatly increased since the establishment of the Federal Republic; in 1949 it was 25 percent, in 1977 it was 50 percent. Most of these deputies have belonged to DGB unions and the Social Democratic party but they have also included members of other employees' associations and as much as a fifth of the CDU/CSU deputies.

It would, however, be a mistake to take these numbers as a measure of trade union influence over legislation. Not only have practically all laws passed by the Diet government originated in the executive branch, but most deputies affiliated with trade unions are merely nominal members. Only 10 to 15 percent have been active trade union functionaries who manifestly represent the interests of organized employees in the Federal Diet and, above all, in appropriate parliamentary committees. Even those do not constitute a solid labor bloc since rivalries among the peak associations and differences in the policy concerns of various trade unions are reflected in differences among their parliamentary spokesmen. In this respect deputies associated with business and agricultural pressure groups have demonstrated more cohesive strength. Employee representatives on both sides of the aisle have occasionally banded together to promote the passage of legislation favored by most trade unions or to block measures opposed by them. But usually such interest alignments have yielded to party alignments between government and opposition deputies in the final vote. Rather than cross party lines and violate party discipline, the friends of organized labor have preferred to promote its cause in the privacy of preliminary intraparty councils and secret parliamentary committee sessions.

For labor leaders, as for other vested interest elites, the primary target for pressure group politics is not the legislative but the executive branch of government. Here parliamentary deputies, party functionaries, and administrative officials affiliated with organized labor have served as its emissaries to the Federal Chancellor's Office and the Ministry of Labor. Such links were significantly extended and assumed increasing importance when the Social Democrats assumed leadership of the government in 1969, in a coalition with the FDP.[7]

7 In 1974, one-third of the members of the Federal Government, all Social Democrats, were former leaders of DGB unions and a number of its key parliamentary secretaries had previously held important positions in such unions.

The Social-Liberal Coalition of the 1970s — like similarly constituted state governments — pointed up the particular significance of such interpersonal ties when the SPD is in the government but compelled to share control of the executive branch with a junior partner. On the one hand, a Social Democratic majority within the government provided DGB leaders with greater opportunities to advance their policy interests than under a government led by Christian Democrats. Effective trade union pressure was thus largely responsible for the passage of tax reform and social welfare legislation opposed by business and its friends in the FDP. On the other hand, the commitment of DGB leaders to the SPD and its coalition with the Free Democrats imposed restraints on what they could seek from the Social Democratic chancellor and ministers. The latter held that although close collaboration between the SPD and the Labor Federation was essential, it called for a mutually beneficial exchange. Consequently they asked for at least as much support from organized labor as they would give. More particularly, they insisted that responsible "labor statesmen" had to adapt their demands to what prevailing political and economic conditions would permit and support the coalition government even when its policies appeared to conflict with the immediate interests of their clients. Insofar as pressure from below would allow them, the DGB leaders were accommodating.[8]

The moderate course pursued by the trade unions over the past thirty years has led foreign observers as well as West German political leaders to give organized labor much of the credit for the exceptionally high degree of political stability in the Federal Republic.[9] Radical left-wingers inside and out-

---

[8] For the sake of maintaining harmony in the governing SPD/FDP coalition the DGB leadership agreed, for example, to a compromise formula on its codetermination demands for the extension of labor participation in management. And when inflationary pressures and rising unemployment produced serious economic problems for the government, its Social Democratic members were able to persuade the union leaders to moderate their demands for higher wages and better social benefits.

[9] As SPD chairman and former chancellor Willy Brandt put it, for example, to an American audience in 1975: "If we are in fact in a better [economic] position than many others, and if social peace has been kept to such a remarkable degree, one explanation is that we have reduced the

side the labor movement contend, however, that such stability has been maintained by the ruling establishment — including union leaders — at the expense of the "working class" and for the benefit of big business. In their view, class conflict is inherent in a capitalist state and economy and the "real" interests of labor are not served by the pressure group politics of labor statesmen. Accordingly, they have sought to raise the class consciousness of rank-and-file members of the Labor Federation and the Salaried Employees Union and urged them to obtain more militant leadership through mass action, wildcat strikes, and shop council elections.

Many of these efforts to radicalize the labor movement have come from "young Turks" among middle-level union functionaries who are better educated than most workers and may even have gone to a university. Whether they will become tomorrow's labor leaders and whether they will then pursue an equally radical course remains to be seen. Thus far at least, most union members have loyally supported the more moderate policies of their present leaders. Older trade unionists are more conservative and have little use for aspiring leaders who share neither their background nor their outlook. Foreign workers and younger trade unionists who are less content with their lot under the prevailing system have been somewhat more susceptible to left-wing agitation.

The present labor leadership has either sought to tame the radicals in the unions or to expel them, for they represent a challenge not only to its performance but to its conception of organized labor's proper role in state and society. First, the labor chieftains consider the unions integral components of a democratic and pluralist system of competing interest groups. Second, they believe that popular and elite differences on specific policy issues must not be allowed to disrupt a more

antagonism between capital and labor. . . . Our trade unions play an important part in our economic and social life, a part far beyond their traditional roles. If there are fewer social tensions in the Federal Republic of Germany than in many comparable countries, this is not only a matter of per capita income but primarily the result of a development directed toward more social democracy." (Speech in New York before the American Council on Germany, March 25, 1975 [distributed by the German Information Service]).

fundamental consensus on the principles and rules of that system. In this regard West German labor leaders consider a basically harmonious relationship between the unions and other organizational structures in the country best for the particular interests of labor and for the public interest.

From this point of view divisive conflict ideologies and sharp adversary relationships between employees and employers seem retrogressive rather than progressive, and more likely to weaken than to strengthen the solidarity of wage and salary earners and their support for the prevailing regime. Reformist strategies and tactics that appear opportunistic and short-sighted to their left-wing critics are in the opinion of labor's present top leaders properly undogmatic and realistic. Like their American counterparts, they believe that the political activities of the unions should focus primarily on bread-and-butter problems and avoid doctrinal commitments to state ownership, income equalization, and similar "dogmatic" solutions. They are more concerned with governmental tax policies, budget allotments, and vocational training programs than in furthering class-conscious labor unity, and they prefer to bargain amicably with their business adversaries rather than fight them. They are willing to collaborate with employers' associations in opposing the demands of agricultural and foreign pressure groups and with religious organizations in promoting social welfare legislation. And though West German labor leaders may occasionally still employ traditional working-class rhetoric to rally their supporters, they make little use of it in their dealings with other elites and the general public.

On the whole, then, the contemporary labor elite is an important element of what we have called the policymaking stratum of the Federal Republic. It has a major stake in the preservation of a regime that has integrated organized labor into the political system and provided its leaders with prominent participant roles in public affairs. Top labor functionaries today generally share the pragmatic outlook of key political, administrative, and business leaders and consider themselves fully competent to represent the best interests of organized as well as unorganized labor in pressure group politics. Their identification of these interests with material benefits has been conditioned by an era of rising affluence in which organized labor grew from an underprivileged social stratum to one of the most prosperous employee groups in the world. Labor chieftains who now direct vast economic organizations and participate in the management of both private and public enterprises are no less interested than government and business leaders in keeping an essentially capitalist economy on track at maximum safe speed. The policies advocated by union leaders may not always correspond to those favored by employer groups, but basically they are the same arguments for sustained economic growth, for they are based on the notion that the bigger the pie the greater will be labor's share.

Farmers Organizations. West German farmers, unlike their American counterparts, have been represented in governmental and quasigovernmental bodies by the spokesmen for complementary rather than rival agrarian pressure groups. All proprietors are required by law to belong to the corporate units of the national League of Agricultural Chambers (*Verband der Landwirtschaftskammern*). Most of them are also voluntary members of the League of German Farmers (*Deutscher Bauernverband*) and affiliated with an association of agricultural banks and cooperatives (*Deutscher Genossenschaft und Raiffeisenverband*). These three peak organizations have formally distinct functions, but their overlapping membership, leadership, and policy demands have united them informally in the so-called Green Front for the political promotion of agricultural interests.

The functional and political representation of agricultural interests under the present regime has provided the leaders of this alignment with extensive access to public policymakers. In national pressure group politics they have maintained particularly close ties with Christian Democratic leaders and key officials in the Ministry of Agriculture. Since the establishment of the Federal Republic about 10 percent of the deputies in the Diet have been farmers. Most of these are members of the CDU/CSU; virtually none belong to the SPD. Unlike the largely nominal trade union members, and even more than the representatives of business interests, these legislators have constituted a solid bloc in the lower house of the Federal Parliament. Led by active or former functionaries of the agricultural associations, they have vigorously fought on behalf of the Green Front in its committees and party caucuses. The contents of the annual package of farm legislation known as the "Green Plan" provides one of the principal and most conspicuous measures of the farm lobby's effective influence in the Federal Government and Federal Parliament.

Throughout the 1950s and well into the 1960s — when a conservative coalition of Christian and Free Democrats controlled the government and both houses of parliament — the Green Front exercised a great deal of influence over agricultural policies. Its leadership displayed a remarkable capacity for obtaining tax concessions, guaranteed price supports, and generous subsidies for its clients, but especially for the full-time farmers.[10] These achievements were aided by the ability of the farm lobby to promote and exploit a favorable climate of opinion — especially among the conservative older leaders and supporters of the ruling parties. Many of these considered the regular farmers the mainstay of esteemed traditional virtues in an advanced industrial society and believed that it was therefore the responsibility of public authorities to safeguard a life-style associated with the pastoral tranquillity of rural areas.

More pragmatic political considerations were, however, no less important in winning the support of the dominant government and party elites for the demands of the agricultural lobby. The FDP as well as the CDU/CSU depended then heavily on votes in rural districts where the Green Front commanded a loyal and cohesive following that strongly supported its

---

[10] Under the Adenauer government organized agriculture scored for example a major triumph with the Agricultural Act of 1955, which called for generous government assistance to the farmers on the grounds that they had failed to profit as much from postwar economic recovery as business and labor. And in the early 1960s the leader of the Farmers League refused to agree to the abolition of agricultural tariffs with members of the European Economic Community until he received assurances from the Erhard government that his clients would receive long-term public assistance to enable them to adjust to new competitive conditions.

efforts to promote the interests of West German farmers against the competing claims of organized labor, big business, and foreign importers of agricultural products. Especially in the northern and southern regions of the Federal Republic, independent farm proprietors and their families were committed to support the Green Front not only because they shared socioeconomic interests, but because they had a common political outlook derived from the corporate traditions of an exclusive agricultural estate. Older full-time farmers — who were particularly attached to such subcultural "in-group" sentiments — played leading roles in local and regional recruitment organizations of the Christian and Free Democrats and used their influence on behalf of the Green Front.

Organized agriculture was "a real power" in pressure group politics, asserted the head of the Farmers League in 1966, because the exceptional unity and qualitative strength of its supporters made up for its numerical and financial inferiority to big business and labor. At the time the claim seemed still valid to most observers but already a bit hollow to a few. Since then it has become increasingly evident that the Green Front has lost a great deal of the popular and elite support it once enjoyed. In comparison with equivalent organizations in other major advanced industrial countries — notably the United States, France, and Japan — West German agricultural associations have in recent years experienced a particularly precipitous decline in political influence. Thus, whereas the power of the trade unions has grown and that of big business has remained great since the establishment of the Federal Republic, that of the agricultural lobby has clearly diminished.

Government measures designed to enhance the competitive viability of West German agriculture through the elimination of small and unprofitable enterprises have been a product as well as a source of this decline. As a product, they reflect the delayed political effects of structural socioeconomic changes. The solid support which the farm lobby could once marshal behind its efforts to block or drastically modify public policies was gradually eroded as more and more farmers and children of farmers went into better paying industrial and service occupations. The farming population dropped from more than

5 million in 1950, to about 2 million in 1972, and full-time farmers, the most loyal supporters of the farm lobby, had by then dwindled to less than half that number.

At the same time, governmental policies have promoted the flight from the land. Under the terms of a European Common Market agreement, small marginal farmers are gradually being eliminated as protectionist agricultural subsidies are reduced. Under present plans, the entire West German farming population is to be cut to a mere million by 1980. In that event the relative numerical strength of the agricultural pressure groups will become even smaller, but their loss may prove to be organized labor's gain.

These developments need not lead to the collapse of the Green Front. Even under the Social-Liberal Coalition of the 1970s it remained strong enough to give its spokesmen considerable influence over the formulation and implementation of governmental agricultural policies. Farm production in the Federal Republic has tripled since 1950, and a lobby representing a few economically important producers may be able to hold its own in future pressure group politics.

By present indications, however, the Green Front may find it much more difficult than in the past to wring concessions from the dominant policymakers — even if they should be Christian Democrats. Inflationary pressures have intensified the unwillingness of business and labor groups to absorb the cost of hidden farm subsidies in the form of taxes and higher food prices. The largely export-oriented patterns of the West German economy do not favor the counterclaims of agricultural interests, since these tend to raise the competitive prices of industrial producers. Thus, if current trends continue, the Green Front may increasingly be forced to fight a rearguard battle to save what it can for its remaining clients.

Religious Organizations. The religious organizations of the Roman Catholic Church and the German Evangelical Church (EKD) make up the fourth constellation of key pressure groups. Separation of church and state as we know it in the United States exists neither in form nor in fact. Religious leaders are more closely involved in public policy processes and their political influence has been far more pronounced than in most other advanced industrial countries.

The free exercise of religion is a private matter under the Basic Law, but its organized expression is not. All religious associations are bound by legal regulations, and the two major churches are very special institutions of public law. As such they are subject to the constitutional authority of the state, but they are also entitled to privileged support and protection from the state.

These formal reciprocal arrangements have given West German religious leaders strong reasons, as well as opportunities, for engaging in pressure group activities. In this respect, the effective political representation of their policy demands in legislative bodies has become less important as religious affiliation has played a diminishing role in West German elections. However, the persistence of traditional corporatist principles providing for the functional representation of the major religious groups in public affairs has sustained the influence of religious leaders at the policymaking level.

As we noted earlier, nine out of ten West Germans are under law either certified Protestants or Roman Catholics in roughly equal proportions. Most attend religious services infrequently, if ever. But all of them are required to pay a surcharge of 10 percent or more of their income taxes, which the government turns over to their respective churches. "Opting out," of this arrangement is difficult and rarely happens. For most West Germans this church tax is a legal obligation imposed on them by the state. According to a recent opinion poll, less than half would pay an equal amount voluntarily if it were to be abolished, a fifth would contribute less, and another fifth nothing. The churches receive, moreover, a good deal of tax-exempt income from extensive property holdings.

Some of this income is used by the churches for strictly religious activities, but most of it goes into their numerous social services — such as orphanages, nursery schools, hospitals, retirement homes, and sundry charities. Religious organizations have therefore a considerable stake in government fiscal policies that affect the size of their chief sources of income and are bound to oppose tax measures that would give them less.

At the same time, religious leaders have a major stake in maintaining legal arrangements under which they are neither directly responsible to public authorities for the expenditure of church funds, nor accountable to nominal church members who have no control over the functional representatives of their ostensibly collective religious interests.

In all of the states of the Federal Republic constitutional and other legal provisions call for clerical participation in the formulation and implementation of social and cultural policies. Clergymen have, for example, a voice in the operation of the public educational system and sit on the supervisory boards of the radio and television networks. Similar arrangements for the functional representation of religious interests prevail at the national level of government. Both of the major churches have quasiambassadorial clerical spokesmen in Bonn and furnish information and advice to appropriate federal agencies, particularly the Ministry for Family Affairs. Thus, the formal organization of the political system affords officially recognized religious interests extensive opportunities for presenting their demands to key public officials.

These arrangements have lent legitimacy to clerical pressure group politics, but they do not fully account for the prominent role of religious elites in an otherwise increasingly secularized polity. Three factors have come into play here. One has been authority attributed to religious leaders on political matters touching on public faith and morals. Most West Germans may not be particularly devout, but they do associate ethical standards of propriety with "Christian" beliefs and values. Such convictions are vestiges of traditional religious loyalties among both Protestants and Catholics, especially in the older generations. They are intertwined with strong popular sentiments against "godless" communism and other radical Marxist creeds, and they also reflect an emotional reaction to a prosaic and materialist mode of life in an advanced industrial society. The anticlerical movements and religious conflicts of former times are gone from West German politics.

A second factor that has lent weight to the prominence of clerical elites in public affairs has been the belief of political leaders that organized religion is a major stabilizing element in

West Germany. Clerical leaders are considered influential opinionmakers by the political elites, and a public pronouncement by a Protestant or Catholic bishop is taken to express more than a strictly personal viewpoint. No major political figure has recently been willing to invite trouble by criticizing the clerical hierarchy, at least not in public. Religious leaders, in turn, try to apply indirect pressure on policymakers through the force of public opinion. Clerical positions on public issues are put forward in sermons, in the mass-circulation religious press, in resolutions and memoranda from the governing bodies of the major churches, and in pastoral letters from the Catholic bishops. Such opinion-molding efforts have been particularly intense at the grassroots level, notably in the small towns and rural areas of Bavaria where Catholic priests often play leading roles in the dominant Christian Social Union.

A third and less conspicuous factor has been interelite ties between the clerical hierarchy on the one hand and high party functionaries and public officials on the other. Such bonds have been cultivated on both sides because both have found them to be advantageous. Lay leaders of the two principal churches have played important intermediary roles in both of the major parties. These roles have been more evident in the CDU/CSU, but the less emphatically "Christian" SPD has also given prominence to its contacts to the clergy. Former President Gustav Heinemann, for example, was a leading member of the Protestant laity, and Defense Minister Georg Leber of the Catholic. These interpersonal relations have been facilitated by a network of religious interest associations and nonpartisan institutes affiliated with one or another of the major churches.

The formal representation of religious interests in public affairs provides for absolute parity between Catholics and Protestants. The leadership of organized Catholicism has, however, been by far the more active and militant force in pressure group politics. It has been more united in its political objectives and more determined in their pursuit, and it has commanded a much larger base of dedicated supporters. There are special associations for Catholic employers and Catholic employees, Catholic men and Catholic women, Catholic parents and Catholic youths. Devout members of the church belong to at least one of these supposedly nonpartisan mass organizations, which usually work together in national pressure group politics. The Catholic Bureau and the Catholic Club in Bonn coordinate their activities and the mass circulation Catholic press serves as the medium for internal political communications from the clerical and lay leadership to the members. For the smaller political and elite public the church sponsors special political publications, such as the weekly *Rheinischer Merkur,* and maintains Catholic academies that serve as conference centers for meetings and discussions on current political problems.

Organized Catholicism has generally been a conservative element in West German politics. Most of its leaders have held that Catholic policy interests fare best under governments controlled by the CDU and CSU and have therefore backed the union parties at election time. Devout Catholics have followed suit by voting overwhelmingly for CDU/CSU candidates (see Table VI.1, p. 185). Until farily recently the clerical hierarchy urged them to do so in pastoral letters calling for the election of candidates embracing "Christian" principles. Individual bishops have continued the practice in such Catholic strongholds as Bavaria, but it has become less common as governing SPD leaders have sought to collaborate more closely with the hierarchy. The leaders of Catholic lay organizations have, however, remained consistent supporters of the CDU/CSU both as a governing and an opposition party.

In years ahead such a one-sided coalition strategy may suit neither the interests of the Christian Democratic leaders nor those of the Catholic lobby. The former have recently found the solid support of organized Catholicism to be a mixed blessing for a supposedly interdenominational party; it has provided them with the votes of a declining number of devout Catholics, but it has cost them those of an increasing number of more nominal Catholics as well as Protestants. The Catholic lobby, on the other hand, has recently suffered a series of major defeats because it did not have sufficient popular and elite support; most notably it failed in its battles to maintain a separate system of denominational schools and to prevent the passage of more liberal divorce and abortion laws.

By all indications Catholic power in West German pressure group politics is diminishing. In certain areas of the Federal Republic, notably in Bavaria, organized Catholicism is likely to remain influential in regional and local politics for some time. However, in national politics the erosion of its influence appears irreversible. The Catholic clerical elite may adopt less doctrinaire, partisan, and exclusive strategies to save what it can. But the hierarchy would find this course difficult to take, since it involves an unavoidable dilemma. The Catholic lobby might benefit from more flexible collaboration with a wider range of elite groups, especially under Social-Liberal governments. However, it can ill afford to ignore the sentiments of conservative clergymen and lay officials down the line whose uncompromising militancy has provided organized Catholicism with much of its strength in pressure group politics.

The fact that once very rigid lines between Catholics and Protestants have all but disappeared would seem to make the Protestant sector of organized religion the most obvious partner for the Catholic. But because Protestants are more loosely organized and ideologically diversified than Catholics such collaboration has thus far been rather limited in national pressure group politics.

The activities of the Catholic lobby are still colored by vestiges of the bitter battles fought by a religious minority against a ruling Protestant establishment in the former German Reich. Those of the Protestant lobby, on the other hand, reflect a decided break with the traditional union between church and state. The spokesmen for organized Protestantism represent an interest alignment in a pluralist polity that is neither as powerful as big business and labor nor as cohesive as organized Catholicism.

The Protestant Evangelical Church is a predominantly Lutheran confederation of provincial churches that exercise no direct control over affiliated religious interest associations. Its ministers and lay leaders may wield a good deal of individual or collective influence in regional and local politics, but in national affairs they have often lacked a common denominator for their specific policy demands. The orthodox Lutheran clergy has generally favored a course of minimal explicit involvement in partisan politics and has primarily sought to achieve its policy objectives less overtly through the functional representation of Protestant interests. There is a politically outspoken minority, but frequently it is divided by differences between conservatives and reformers on particular policy issues, such as the need for compulsory religious education in the public schools and a liberalization of abortion and divorce laws.

The resulting problem of achieving a consensus within the Protestant elite therefore requires a good deal of preliminary deliberation and consultation. Consequently, when the leadership of the Evangelical Church has spoken out in public it has usually commanded considerable attention among the political public and elites.

In the late 1960s and early 1970s, for instance, a series of memoranda from the Synod of the EKD called for a more flexible government policy of accommodation with the East European countries, a subject that had previously been taboo in official circles. In the face of bitter opposition from the refugee pressure groups, the collective authority of the Protestant elite contributed significantly to making the issue a matter of legitimate public discussion and thereby smoothed the way for a new phase in West German foreign policy.

Subsequently the Synod addressed itself in 1973, to two highly contentious domestic issues, the legitimate use of violence and the extension of the welfare state. On the former it cautiously allowed that "Christian" principles might justify revolutionary action against an inhumanitarian, oppressive regime, but said that it was to be condemned in a state where human rights were respected and changes were possible by peaceful and democratic means. On the latter the Synod declared that the socioeconomic inequities in an advanced industrial society required that the state provide more adequate social security and public assistance to the socially disadvantaged and physically handicapped, especially old and sick people and poor families with many dependent children.

Protestant political activities have on the whole been wider in scope at the elite level and narrower at the mass level than Catholic ones. Leaders of the Evangelical Church and its affiliated organizations have played prominent roles in the

CDU/CSU, SPD, and FDP, as well as in the trade unions and the major business associations; Protestant interest associations have at the same time been less partisan in pursuing pressure group objectives than their Catholic counterparts and have collaborated more readily with governments of different political complexions. Conferences at "Evangelical Academies" have brought Protestant theologians together with leaders from other spheres of public life, and with foreign leaders, for free-wheeling discussions on a wide range of current political issues — for instance on ways to overcome international and domestic sources of political tension.

The influence wielded by the Protestant elite has, however, obscured the fact that its popular base is rapidly dwindling. Most Protestants have become rather casual members of their church and young people especially are turning their backs on it entirely. A 1973 survey of West German Protestants, for example, found that a mere 14 percent attended religious services regularly, 27 percent went only occasionally, 40 percent rarely, and 19 percent never. The most frequent reasons cited by the respondents for a sharp drop in church attendance were (1) that the traditionalist theology of Protestant clergymen was out of tune with modern times and (2) that now, as in the past, official Protestantism was too closely identified with the ruling establishment.

The leaders of the Evangelical Church are very concerned about such signs of mass alienation, but they are divided about the causes and cures. Elements that have been moving toward the political left blame the church for failing to reform its body and doctrine; in their view it can regain mass support by taking the lead in a fight for "social progress" in West Germany. Conservatives, however, hold that evangelical Protestantism has failed to tend its fundamental religious roots and should confine its political activities to strengthening socioeconomic and cultural harmony and "morality" in private and public affairs. Which of these factions will prevail over the long run remains an open question, but in any event Protestant pressure groups are likely to become less important in national politics.

PRESSURE GROUP POLITICS AND PUBLIC POLICIES

In the Federal Republic, as in other countries, pressure group politics are both sources and products of authoritative public policies. Governmental actions may reflect interest group demands, they may give rise to such demands, and they may curb pressure on public policies. In West Germany this reciprocal relationship between pressure group inputs and governmental outputs is conditioned by the dynamics of a particular policy environment and by particular patterns of interaction among the general public, specific interest groups, the major parties, and agencies of the state.

As we have seen in this chapter, the legitimate expression of pressure group demands is tightly structured in accordance with the representative principles of the present regime. Explicit legal provisions for the functional representation of organized interests connect the principal pressure groups directly to executive agencies of the state; more indirect and informal arrangements provide for the political representation of organized interests in elective bodies through their ties to the major parties.

As we have also noted, West German pressure group politics have been marked by the corporatist vestiges of a preindustrial society. Present patterns reflect progressive and mutual adaptation between the pressure group subsystem and other components of the ongoing political system, a development that has been particularly pronounced in economic policymaking. Though traditional forms of functional interest articulation continue to have some importance, pressure group politics have by and large come to conform to socioeconomic, cultural and political circumstances that are very different from those of previous German regimes.

On the whole, interest organizations are today less closely controlled by the state, less intimately associated with political parties, and more flexible in their pressure group strategies and tactics than formerly. Most are no longer identified with sharply segmented subcultures, and interest group differences tend to involve particular policy issues rather than more profound doctrinal disputes. For example, the failure of an emphatically "Christian" trade union movement testifies to the detachment of organized labor from clerical as well as anticlerical ideologies. And as the encapsulated ideological camps of the past have gradually dissolved, tenuous and transitory pressure group coalitions on specific policy issues have become far more common.

The more heterogeneous the membership of an interest association, the more difficult it is to achieve internal consensus on its policy objectives. For the sake of at least nominal unity, cross-pressures arising from plural interests and competing affiliations must be accommodated by restricting and diluting the areas for collective political action. Particularly in the large peak associations of organized business, labor, and Protestantism, the autonomy of the constituent groups has been promoted by different policy concerns. Employer and employee associations in one economic sector may, for instance, join forces to further their common policy interests against those of a similar alignment identified with another sector. The peak business organizations include associations of importers and exporters who may collaborate on some policy issues but compete on others. Occupational interests may sometimes unite public employees organizations on policy matters relating to the salaries and pension rights of their members and at other times lead to conflicts within and between such associations.

Another major feature of contemporary pressure group politics is that they exclude most West Germans and involve primarily interelite relations. The organizational rules and actual operation of the prevailing regime have served to institutionalize mutually advantageous exchange relationships among key interest group functionaries, party leaders, and public officials. As noted earlier, bargaining, reciprocal adaptation, and compromise have come to characterize interaction among polyarchic elites in a pluralist state and society; these patterns extend across occupationally segmented interest groups and make for basically harmonious relationships among their leaders, and between these and the manifest political decision makers.

But though interest group elites may command extensive

means for influencing public policies, they are constrained in the demands they can make and the means they can employ to realize them. One reason is the formal and informal "rules of the game" for legitimate pressure group politics. A second reason is cultural norms place the interest of state and community above those of special vested interests and establish public officials as the legitimate arbitrators among competing pressure group demands. There are also cross-cutting popular and elite allegiances, which may override identifications with "nonpartisan" interest groups and induce political participants to disregard such identifications for the sake of partisan objectives or party discipline. And, finally, there is the pluralism of competing elites involved in policy processes, which disperses rather than concentrates the power of organized interests.

These constraints curb the political influence of even the most powerful pressure groups. They allow party leaders and high government officials to aggregate, balance, and, if need be, reject pressure group demands in the name of "larger" public interests. And they enable these leaders to avoid commitments that would make them the instruments of any particular interest association or interest group alignment. Control over public policies rests in the last analysis with elected and appointed public officials, and the extensive intrusion of the authority of the state into West German society provides these officials with considerable power to curb pressure group demands.

It would seem then that the prevailing regime provides for effective checks and balances in the relationships between organized interest groups, political parties, and agencies of the state. But this matter has been disputed over the years. According to their leading spokesmen, the various pressure groups are constructive and stabilizing elements in a democratic state and pluralist society because they constitute orderly channels for transmitting diverse demands to the authoritative policymakers. These claims are, however, disputed by West Germans who assert that the entire pressure group system has gotten out of hand or, at least, that some of its principal components exercise far too much influence at the expense of public interests, particularly those of people who do not belong to interest groups.

A good deal of this criticism has focused on the activities of the major producers and religious organizations. On that score Table VII.2 shows some rather significant shifts in public

Table VII.2. *Pressure Groups Considered to Have Too Much Influence (in rounded percentages)*

	Mass opinion[a]		Elite opinion[b]
	1962	1971	1972
Big business	59	26	34
Trade unions	37	46	45
Agriculture	32	14	45
Catholic Church	46	23	41
Protestant Church	8	8	30

Source: [a]*1962:* EMNID Institute, *Informationen,* July 1962. *1971:* E. Noelle-Neumann and E. P. Neumann, *Jahrbuch der Oeffentlichen Meinung 1968–73* (Allensbach: Verlag fuer Demoskopie, 1974). [b]U. Lange-Hoffman et al., *Westdeutsche Führungschicht* (Universities Kiel and Mannheim, unpublished, 1973).

opinion, as well as rather pronounced differences between contemporary popular and elite opinion. Notice that the proportion of West German adults who felt that big business, agricultural organizations, and the Catholic Church wielded too much power declined appreciably from 1962 to 1971, whereas the proportion attributing excessive influence to the trade unions increased substantially.[11] The 1972 survey of elite opinion (which included major interest group leaders) reflects more pluralist and balanced perceptions of the relative power of the big four at the policymaking level. You can see that the elites are far more inclined than the general public to consider the Protestant Church too influential and to attribute excessive power to big business, argricultural organizations, and the Catholic Church. One explanation for these differ-

[11] To some degree, but by no means entirely, these differences probably relate to the fact that in the first period the country was governed by a coalition of conservative Christian and Free Democrats and in the second by the Social-Liberal Coalition of the SPD and FDP.

ences may be that the elites have a keener appreciation of the actual patterns of influence in pressure group politics; another might be that in West Germany, as in the United States, leading public officials and competing elite groups often consider the other side in pressure group politics all too powerful.

Be that as it may, the really important question is what political consequences follow from these attitudes. And here we find that when influential opinion leaders resort to attacks on the "excessive" power of a particular interest group in the heat of an electoral campaign, or a battle over some policy decision, the effect may be more far-reaching than intended. Such charges tie in with popular hostility toward the entire pressure group system and thus sow seeds on fertile ground.

As we noted, most West Germans are at best only nominal members of interest associations, and those who do not belong to any are especially likely to distrust them all. These sentiments have been encouraged by prominent journalists and academicians who have sharply condemned the ostensibly enormous power of the major pressure groups. Public officials have been charged with serving them all too readily or, at least, with failing to keep them under control.

According to the most vehement of these critics the present situation is intolerable and requires major changes for the sake of the public interest — which some of them identify with the interest of the West German state or society and others with the personal welfare of the common people. Some highly critical observers maintain that governmental executive agencies should be given more authority to hold the pressure groups in check whereas others want the political parties to exercise greater dominance over the interest associations. Reduced to their essentials, the proposed alternatives to catch-as-catch-can interest group pluralism are thus either a less democratic administrative state or a more democratic party state. As we shall see in the next chapter, such either-or "solutions" are based on oversimplified and distorted interpretations of policymaking processes in the Federal Republic.

CHAPTER VIII

Policymaking

WHO MAKES OR SHOULD MAKE authoritative policy decisions, for what purposes, in what manner, and to what effect is at the heart of West German politics. As in other countries, disputes on this score are based on conflicting policy premises, conflicting policy preferences, and conflicting evaluations of the outcome of action or inaction on the part of leading public officials. In contemporary West Germany, such controversies range from substantive ideological cleavages between conservative proponents and radical critics of the regime to procedural disputes among and within agencies of the state; they divide voters, parties, and pressure groups, as well as policymakers and would-be policymakers.

The federal chancellor may make a policy declaration that his government intends to, say, reduce taxes and expenditures in the public sector to provide more investment capital for economic growth and employment in the private sector. The parliamentary opposition is likely to profess to share his concern about a lagging economy, but condemn his program as the wrong way toward a desirable objective. Its spokesmen may contend that it would be better to put more money into public works or into direct subsidies for ailing business enterprises. Other critics may maintain that short-term measures will not solve long-range problems posed by the nature of the West German economy, such as its trade dependency or its capitalist organization. Then, again, they may argue that other issues are even more pressing, for instance, threats to civil liberties or public security.

Because "open government" and free-wheeling debate on public issues are political norms, policy conflicts are likely to be more visible in the Federal Republic than in many other countries. Particularly — but by no means exclusively — around election time, adversaries to policy disputes will bid for public support by vigorously defending their position in parliament, in the mass media, or even in the courts. As a result — and especially when they capture headlines — such controversies often seem more profound and less susceptible to resolution than they are in fact. Then, too, a good many disputes are not only waged but settled out of the public view in party councils, government agencies, and legislative committees. This is all the more likely when policy issues are complex or politically sensitive and when efforts to achieve compromises involve few key decision makers. In these cases differences are likely to surface only when some or all of the participants feel that they have more to gain than to lose by calling them to the public's attention.

In any event, the authoritative resolution of policy conflicts rests ultimately with the organs and agents of the West German state. Constitutional arrangements provide these with legal control over the formulation of public policies and the operation of the contemporary political system enables them to exercise that control. Our principal concern in this chapter will be with national policy issues and their processing by national public officials. Though measures adopted by subnational components of the state may at times have more than a local or even regional effect, policy decisions affecting the entire country are usually made at the federal level of government.

THE CONTEXT FOR POLICYMAKING

The outstanding feature of the present policymaking system is representative and responsible party government, as we have seen. And we also noted that the decisions of governing party leaders are conditioned by demands for and constraints on policy actions. Some of these demands and constraints are the results of legal arrangements that restrict as well as legitimate the activities of public authorities. Others arise from a dynamic policy environment that generates domestic and foreign problems and structures policy responses. These factors, in turn, enter in different forms at various times into patterns of collaboration and conflict among members of the general public, the political public, and the elites of the Federal Republic.

Under the terms of the Basic Law, you will recall from Chapter II, the federal executive and bicameral parliament are assigned primary legal responsibility for translating the policy intentions of leading public officials into authoritative rules, such as changes in the constitution, a treaty, a budget law, or a government decree. Administrative and judicial agencies are charged with interpreting and applying general rules in specific cases (see Figure VIII.1).

This formal distinction, however, obscures the fact that in West Germany, as in the United States, judicial and administrative bodies may also shape, if not make, policy. Various top federal courts may do so in the process of reviewing executive legal ordinances and administrative regulations, and the Federal Constitutional Court in passing on the compatability of policy measures with the Basic Law. Consider, for example, that certain sections of the federal constitution are not subject to amendment and that for these sections neither the lawmakers nor the voters, but the constitutional court is the final legal authority. The judicial review decisions of the court have repeatedly compelled executive and legislative officials to discard or modify policy measures; such rulings led Chancellor Adenauer to abandon his effort to create a federal television network in the early 1960s and forced the Federal Parliament to come up with a less restrictive campaign finance law in the late 1960s. In both cases the government had the votes, but not the legal power to overrule the court; at other times the lawmakers have had the authority to overrule, but not the necessary votes. In formulating a law or implementing regulations, policymakers are therefore likely to take into account the reaction of the courts and tailor their measures so they will pass judicial muster.

Similarly, actions taken or not taken by the Federal Bank

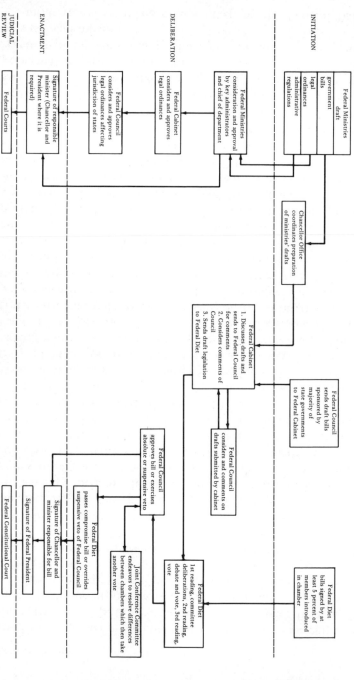

Figure VIII.1. *Formal Federal Rule-Making Procedures*

under its statutory mandate to sustain monetary stability have often had a decisive effect on the formulation of domestic and foreign policies in the executive branch. And the cumulative spinout of ostensibly policy-implementing activities by federal regulatory agencies, public authorities in the states, and such paraconstitutional bodies as the occupational chambers, have occasionally given a special twist to federal policies that was neither intended nor anticipated by their originators.

How socioeconomic conditions and other environmental factors enter into West German policymaking processes we saw in Chapter III. As we noted there, these shape and are shaped by governmental actions. Available economic resources, for example, influence the size of the federal budget; on the other hand, the allocation of tax assessments and the distribution of public funds affect the amount of money West Germans can put into savings, business investments, and private consumption. In international affairs the Federal Republic's membership in the European Community and the North Atlantic Treaty Organization involve commitments that limit its leaders' freedom of action; and the extent to which they honor these commitments affects in turn West Germany's relationship with its economic and military partners.

Here we need to remember that West German foreign policies are directed toward other states and their governments, whereas domestic policies concern the authoritative distribution of public benefits and obligations within the Federal Republic. This is not just a formal but a practical distinction when it comes to policymaking. Inside the country public officials not only decide who is to get and who is to do what, when, and how; they command extensive means to enforce their decisions. Not so in foreign affairs. There the use of force in support of policy measures is out of the question and West German policymakers are compelled to rely on diplomatic persuasion, economic inducements, and propaganda — and on favorable circumstances — to realize their intentions. Their ability to obtain what they seek may be promoted or hindered by international conditions, but in any event tends to depend on factors largely beyond their control. At the same time we must remember that domestic and foreign affairs are so closely intertwined in West German public affairs that domestic policy issues are frequently colored by foreign policy considerations and foreign policy decisions influenced by domestic policy concerns.

Policymaking in the Federal Republic is finally conditioned by the patterns of political orientations and relations we examined in preceding chapters. These structure the processes of interaction between organs of the state on the one hand, and voters, parties, and pressure groups on the other. It is especially in this respect that public policies in the Federal Republic can be the consequences as well as the sources of political controversies; they may reflect as well as produce domestic demands on and supports for the policymaking system and specific policymakers; they may conform to as well as mold the climate of political opinion and the effective distribution of political resources for influencing policy actions.

The high degree of institutionalization of the present regime and the characteristics of the contemporary political culture enhance the legal authority of public officials; but they also require them to conform closely to established governmental roles and procedures. As agents of the state these key decision makers are expected by most West Germans to provide for the public welfare and the resolution of policy conflicts within the limits of law and popular consent.

The stratified patterns of political influence permit the general public to express its policy demands and grievances at election time, but largely limit more direct participation in policy formation to the elites and the political public. When it comes to authoritative decisions, West German socioeconomic and political pluralism is primarily reflected in the efforts of government, party, and pressure group leaders to make specific measures conform with their personal preferences or those of their clients. And the management and resolution of attendant policy conflicts on specific issues is usually a matter for negotiations among key public officials and other policymakers. Thus far, at least, there have been few profound interelite conflicts over the nature and direction of public policies. Some issues, such as relations with the German Democratic Republic and other Communist countries, have produced dramatic clashes among West German leaders; however, they have not been the products or causes of irreconcilable conflicts. A high degree of agreement on basic regime principles and procedures, and comparatively well-functioning arrangements for the management of policy disputes, have sustained the collective authority of official decision makers.

A substantial part of national policymaking involves automatic procedures and mundane issues that arouse little or no public controversy and concern. A good many governmental measures are designed by civil servants in appropriate executive departments and are routinely approved by their superiors — and, if required, by the Federal Cabinet, Chancellor, and Parliament. Much of the legislation turned out by the Federal Diet and Council has dealt with noncontroversial governmental bills that have been passed as a matter of course with the votes of the opposition as well as ruling parties. Pressure groups, you will remember, are likely to fare best under these circumstances and to find it more difficult to gain their policy objectives when they become embroiled in partisan controversies and in jurisdictional disputes among public authorities.

Still, there have been and will be divisive policy issues that are not very readily disposed of by common agreement. In fact, there are many indications that these issues are likely to become more numerous and basic. On such issues, the ability of key decision makers to resolve interelite conflicts becomes a crucial prerequisite for the effective implementation of public policies.

ISSUES AND ANSWERS

Policymaking revolves essentially around the decisions of governmental authorities to do or not to do something about public issues, to give priority to some matters, and to handle policy problems one way rather than another. These processes require first of all the identification of policy problems and objectives; second, a ranking by importance; and third, opportunities to choose among alternative courses of action. Thus, if West German officials do not recognize the existence of an issue requiring a policy response, they will not even consider appropriate government measures; if they see some issues as more important than others they will attend to them first; and if they believe that they have no options, their policy response will proceed from this assumption.

Any of these points can pose policy questions that lead to policy conflicts when politically influential West Germans disagree on the answers. To begin with, such disputes may focus on what constitutes a policy problem. For example, there is likely to be little argument if the issues are the preservation of peace and prosperity but a good deal more when it comes to the inequitable distribution of incomes in the Federal Republic. Some policymakers hold that the latter is not a problem, or at least not a public one demanding authoritative reform measures. They therefore oppose laws and regulations that, in their view, constitute unwarranted and harmful interference with the distribution of rewards for private initiative and individual enterprise in a free market economy. Others maintain that income inequality is not a private matter but a policy issue involving the general welfare. For them the question is consequently not whether it is a public problem, but what government authorities should do about it.

Whether the desirable is also possible under prevailing conditions is another question. Here conflicting views of the policy environment can first of all lead to disputes over policy priorities. Thus West German leaders who share policy concerns and objectives may differ on the relative significance of particular public issues and problems.

For example, top West German officials — like their American counterparts — have disagreed in recent years over whether it was more important to curb rising prices or to check mounting unemployment, and to what extent measures to encourage economic growth should take precedence over measures to control industrial pollution and urban congestion. Social Democratic and Free Democratic coalitions have been divided over whether trade union demands for more industrial democracy and income equality were more pressing than threats from the business community that such measures would stifle managerial initiative and profit incentives. Conservative Christian Democrats have insisted that a decline in public morality and civic discipline is a vital policy issue because it threatens to undermine the authority of the state and its agents. Proponents of immediate socioeconomic reforms, on the other hand, maintain that rising social tensions make it more urgent to provide for greater equity in the distribution of opportunities and the allocation of goods and services.

Conflicting perceptions of the international policy environment have led to similar controversies within the policymaking stratum over priorities in the conduct of foreign relations. For instance, policymakers who believe that the Soviet bloc poses a grave and sustained threat to the security of the Federal Republic hold that primary emphasis must be placed on appropriate countermeasures, above all joint defense arrangements with the United States and other NATO allies. Those who consider the danger not as serious, and the opportunities for mutually beneficial trade relations with the Communist countries more promising, argue that at least as much stress should be placed on economic considerations.

But let us say that a sense of common purpose or compelling environmental circumstances cause West German decision makers to agree not only on the pressing importance of a public problem, but on the most desirable policy response. It will then not necessarily follow that there will be no further differences among them about what should and can be done. Disputes on this score may arise from conflicting assessments of their freedom of choice, from conflicting views of appropriate procedures, and from conflicting perceptions of the consequences of contemplated policy decisions.

Domestic and foreign efforts to influence the output of West German policymaking organs are predicated on the assumption that authoritative public officials have at least some choice among alternative courses of action. At the same time, such endeavors are usually directed toward narrowing the range of options acceptable to the relevant decision makers and toward persuading them that the favored decision would also be the best decision. For example, the efforts of foreign leaders to influence the course of West German policies have often been aimed at reducing the choices for West German decision makers to a point where the actions sought by foreign leaders would seem far more attractive to them than any conceivable alternative. In domestic politics similar strategies are employed by governmental and nongovernmental elites to achieve or prevent particular policy actions by executive, legislative, and judicial bodies.

These efforts are most effective when the ultimate decision makers conclude that other options are out of the question. For instance, most West German leaders today believe that security considerations permit no alternative to close collaboration with the United States; the military and diplomatic benefits for the Federal Republic are said to outweigh the attendant economic costs and foreign policy constraints.

On the other hand, efforts to influence policy are less effective when the decision makers believe that they have other feasible options and are sharply divided on the extent of their freedom of choice on a particular policy issue. For example, less developed countries have found it difficult to wring economic concessions from the Federal Republic because West German leaders have not thought it absolutely essential to satisfy such demands and have held conflicting views about the necessary extent of foreign aid.

As a rule, West German decision makers seek to increase their room for bargaining maneuvers and conflict regulation by endeavoring to keep options open and extending the range of feasible choices in the formulation of domestic and foreign policies. Chancellor Adenauer was particularly skilled in this respect — both in his negotiations with foreign governments and in his dealings with elite alignments at home — and as a result he was singularly successful in achieving his policy goals.

The issue of options also enters into disputes over how West German policymakers should pursue their objectives. Such disputes may revolve around questions of form and questions of method; more often than not they will involve both.

Controversies on matters of form usually involve conflicting interpretations of constitutional and other legal rules for policymaking. For example, the question of whether a policy measure requires only the approval of the Federal Diet or that of the Federal Council as well can lead to clashes between the two chambers, especially when the opposition in the Diet has enough votes in the Council to block such legislation. Or the point at issue may be a jurisdictional dispute between state and federal authorities, or between departments of the federal executive. Then, too, controversies of this sort may arise over the question of whether formal rules calling for interest group consultation and parliamentary committee deliberations have been properly observed in the course of policy formation.

Disputes over method concern essentially different estimates of what is necessary and what is available to achieve particular policy aims. West German decision makers may want to get at the roots of current economic problems, but if they disagree on where these roots lie they will also disagree on feasible solutions. For example, according to Chancellor Helmut Schmidt, the domestic price inflation of the mid-1970s was primarily attributable to external causes that demanded international solutions through intergovernmental negotiations. However, according to the critics of his economic policies it was a homemade inflation caused by excessive governmental expenditures and could only be cured through a domestic austerity program. But what expenditures should be cut was another question — in effect, a political one. It was answered differently by various party and pressure group leaders in terms of their conflicting political interests and values. That left it to the Schmidt government to come up with an authoritative solution in the form of a budget that made no one happy.

This dispute underscored the fact that controversies over policy methods are inextricably interwoven with conflicting evaluations of their consequences. Some of Chancellor Schmidt's economic consultants argued that if the economy was to get moving again at an optimum rate, social service expenditures would have to be cut to the bone; some of his political advisors insisted, however, that if this were done it would have dire electoral consequences for the chancellor's party, the SPD.

On this point, consider two ongoing disputes relating policy methods to their anticipated consequences. In foreign affairs, one group of policymakers holds that closer trade relations with the German Democratic Republic will lead to a gradual liberalization of its political system; another group maintains that this will only strengthen the Communist regime. In domestic affairs, left-wing Social Democrats assert that tighter state control over private business investments will enhance the efficient mobilization and allocation of economic resources; their conservative opponents predict, however, that such measures will stifle individual initiative and talent and lead to an authoritarian command economy run by a vast and inept government bureaucracy.

In short, arguments over the choice of methods are conditioned by differences over their expected effects. Among West German policymakers disputes of this sort usually focus on three questions. One is whether formal decisions can be effectively implemented. For example, government leaders have been divided over the feasibility of wage and price controls for checking inflation. A second question is whether a proposed policy action may be counterproductive — or, at least, too risky to chance. Thus arguments in favor of wage and price controls have been met with counterarguments that such measures would only intensify inflationary pressures through a black market. A third question is whether efforts to deal with one set of issues may not create problems in other spheres of policymaking. For instance, suggestions that domestic economic difficulties might be eased by reducing military expenditures have invariably run up against predictions that such reductions would expose the Federal Republic to Soviet blackmail and antagonize its allies. Similar policy controversies have been provoked by friction between government endeavors to sustain the Federal Republic's strong competitive position in world markets and simultaneous diplomatic efforts to maintain close political relations with the United States and fellow members of the European Community.

All told, then, West German policymaking is subject to controversies over means and ends. On such occasions arguments for and against one or another course of action are presented and disputed in terms of "if-then" propositions that point policy deliberations toward a future state of affairs. In this section we have emphasized some major conflict issues, but we must not forget that many less conspicuous and less broad-gauged problems also pose policy questions. How they are authoritatively answered, if not settled, depends largely on who is involved, under what circumstances, and with what considerations in mind.

THE EXECUTIVE ARENA

The management of the national policy agenda — and of attendant policy conflicts — rests first and foremost in the hands of top officials of the Federal Government. Remember that under the constitutional allocation of powers federal authorities are in charge of foreign relations and most domestic policymaking. Furthermore, the executive branch has access to more extensive sources of policy-relevant information than other branches of government, nongovernmental organizations, and the press.[1] Insofar as such information furnishes executive officials with exclusive intelligence, it can give them a decided advantage in their dealings with outsiders.

Of course, preeminence in policymaking is one thing; control over policymaking is quite another. The Federal Government as a whole has rarely, if ever, been able to make policy unilaterally in every area under its formal jurisdiction. And particular government leaders have time and again been compelled either to abandon cherished policy objectives, or to make haste slowly and, frequently, to settle in the end for less than what they wanted.

To begin with, a large part of what goes on a government's policy agenda — and in what order — is not simply up to its leaders. There are matters they are obliged to deal with under the laws of the Federal Republic and its treaty commitments. For instance, the executive branch is required by the constitution to submit a balanced annual budget to parliament, and it is bound by West Germany's membership in the European

1 The Federal Government thus receives all sorts of privileged information through exclusive diplomatic and military channels, through inter-elite ties and intelligence agencies, and from expert consultants and advisory bodies. Periodic polls sponsored by the government furnish its leaders with a reading of the climate of public opinion for current policymaking, while the planning staffs in various ministries and the chancellor's office collect and process information for future policy actions.

Community to take all necessary measures for implementing EC decisions through domestic regulations. Then there will be developments emphasizing or deemphasizing particular issues and policy demands for government decision makers. An upcoming election, for example, may cause government leaders to put off the introduction of unpopular economic measures and make them especially sensitive to pressure from party and interest group elites. Or urgent problems may suddenly be thrust into the executive arena by unanticipated developments, such as the severity of the West German energy crisis and economic recession of the 1970s.

The range of items that the leaders of the Federal Government may choose to place on or leave off their policy agenda, or to assign a different order of priority to, is thus limited. Here the programmatic commitments of ruling parties, the personal preferences of key executive officials and their relationship with other policymakers, and the extent of policy consensus in the councils of the Federal Government are likely to be particularly important. Consider, for example, that the conservative government of Konrad Adenauer put much greater stress on internal and external security issues than the Social-Liberal Coalition headed by Willy Brandt, but far less on domestic reforms and friendly relations with Communist countries. And whereas under CDU Chancellor Ludwig Erhard explicit government planning programs were anathema, members of the Brandt government were initially seized by a virtual planning euphoria.

Procedures for processing the policy agenda in the executive arena have been practically as important as its contents in shaping the policy output of the Federal Government. Here we must note that although parliamentary party government has made for closer executive-legislative policy coordination than in the United States, pluralism *within* the Federal Government has been far more pronounced in West Germany. One reason is that all governments have been coalitions with factional cleavages within and between the ruling parties. Another is that the persistence of time-honored departmental prerogatives has accentuated the structural segmentation of the executive branch and complicated the coordination of functionally interrelated policymaking tasks.

Under so-called *Resort* principles, precise legal regulations define the special responsibilities of decentralized government departments and assign to a dozen or more ministries exclusive original jurisdiction over specific spheres of policy formulation. The Ministry of Economics has thus the authority to deal with some aspects of foreign trade, but others come under the aegis of the Ministry of Economic Cooperation, and the preparation of the government budget is the business of the Ministry of Finance. All matters touching on relations with East Germany are the concern of the Ministry of Intra-German Relations, whereas diplomatic relations with other Communist states are dealt with by the Foreign Ministry.

Overlapping partisan and bureaucratic politics may consequently delay, if not prevent decisive government action on pressing policy problems. The partisan dimension for policy conflicts in the executive arena is defined by the shifting complexion of political alignments and the degree of policy consensus in party governments, the bureaucratic dimension by the range of policy differences among civil servants in autonomous government departments. Both dimensions for potential disputes over ends and means reflect the pluralist patterns of checks and balances in the West German policymaking stratum, especially in the executive arena. Personal and factional rivalries among elites inside and outside the Federal Government are apt to become interlaced with internal controversies over appropriate policy objectives, priorities, and procedures. At the same time, effective agenda management by the executive as a whole depends on the cohesiveness of its top political officials — chancellor, ministers, state secretaries, and key division chiefs — and on the loyal support of the regular career civil servants in the bureaucratic substructure. Unresolved policy disputes within the Federal Government are likely to weaken its influence in the arenas of parliamentary and federal politics and, consequently, its authority in domestic and foreign affairs. Government leaders therefore consider effective arrangements for the consensual resolution or, at least, the containment of such conflicts a crucial prerequisite for the smooth operation of the executive policymaking system.

The coordination of government policies calls first of all for broad-gauged agreements among the executive and legislative leaders of the ruling parties on what needs to be done and how. These understandings usually provide top government officials and their advisers with fairly general policy guidelines that allow for a good deal of flexibility in executive decision making. Specific policy options and action proposals are formulated by staff officials in appropriate ministries and submitted to the Federal Cabinet by way of intra- and interdepartmental screening processes.

Coalition politics and the organizational segmentation of the Federal Government have served to underscore the coordinating roles of the Federal Chancellor and his chief assistants. The chancellor's office has grown over the years from a small secretariat into a staff of some 400 employees. Its chief may be a minister or state secretary, but will in any case be a political appointee chosen by the chancellor to help him harmonize particularistic ministerial policies for which he alone is ultimately responsible to the Federal Diet. This task usually calls for skill on the part of the chancellor and for circumspection on the part of the chief of the chancellor's office. The record of various incumbents has been rather mixed. Adenauer, for example, used his assistant Hans Globke well; Brandt's less diplomatic and more independent lieutenant Horst Ehmke antagonized the department heads and complicated rather than facilitated the chancellor's coordinating efforts. But even Adenauer, at the very height of his imperious chancellor democracy, was far more effective in coordinating the foreign than the domestic policy action of his government.

The Basic Law, as we noted in Chapter II, gives the chief of the Federal Government substantial control over executive policymaking (see pp. 20–23). However, his powers are not nearly as vast as those of the American or French president. West German ministers, on the other hand, have enjoyed a good deal more latitude in running their departments and in shaping their particular policies than their counterparts in the United States and France. The chancellor's constitutional right to create and abolish ministries, to choose the members of his government and to determine its policies, has been sharply curbed by the practices of coalition politics. Moreover, under the procedural rules of the Federal Government, he cannot compel a department head to follow a specific course. Nor can he bypass the authority of a minister who will not cooperate; he can only request his resignation or ask the federal president to dismiss him, and neither course may be politically feasible.

Coalition politics have provided the most obvious constraints on the chancellor's control over federal ministers. The number and allocation of cabinet portfolios are usually crucial in the formation of governing coalitions; disputes on that score have sometimes required weeks of preliminary bargaining among party and interest group elites. Organized labor has to be accommodated with a man of its own at the head of the Ministry of Labor and the farmers' associations with an acceptable minister of agriculture. Important party factions have to be represented, and a powerful party leader is unlikely to settle for anything less than a major cabinet post, such as minister of foreign affairs, defense, economics, or finance. This is not just a matter of prestige; government position may hold out the promise that the incumbent will be able to enhance his political reputation and advance his policy objectives by placing his personal imprimatur on particular government actions. In recent times, three out of four successful aspirants to the chancellorship — Erhard, Brandt, and Schmidt — promoted their claims to the top position in that manner.

Once a government is in place, the jurisdictional prerogatives of the ministers will further limit the chancellor's control over policy formation. Their partisan and personal interests now combine with the special policy concerns of their ministries to reduce the chancellor's freedom of choice and to complicate the development of cohesive executive policies. Much depends on whether ministers can strike a balance between their individual roles as department heads and their collective roles as members of the chancellor's cabinet. In the former capacity they represent the particularistic concern of their departments in relations with the chancellor, fellow ministers, legislators, and the public; in the latter they represent the common political objectives of a party government in their relations with subordinates in the federal bureaucracy and the interest group clients of their departments.

On the whole, federal ministers have identified themselves

more with their departmental than with their cabinet functions — and all the more so the longer they have stayed with one department. One reason is that elite and popular opinion has judged their performance in office on the strength of their ability to promote policy demands associated with their ministries. A closely related reason is that ministers have depended on the loyal services of their in-house bureaucracy and in return have felt obliged to look after its interests, especially in budgetary allocations. A third reason is that ministers have relied on staff briefings and position papers that present policy issues in terms of a restricted departmental focus rather than overall government objectives.

In effect, the combination of coalition politics and ministerial prerogatives has allowed the chancellor and his office only limited control over policymaking in the executive arena.[2] As we noted earlier, how much use the chief of government can make of his formal coordinating powers depends largely on his personal authority in a government of ruling party leaders. On the other hand, the autonomy of a department head and his influence over government policies will be all the greater the less he is politically beholden to the chancellor and the more the chancellor depends on his cooperation and that of the minister's supporters inside and outside the executive branch.

The policy actions of the Federal Government have always been the products of collegial decision making — less so in Adenauer's days and more so since then. The chancellor, unlike the American president, does not have the legal right to disregard or overrule his cabinet on major policy issues, but ministers need the support of the chancellor and a majority of their peers to obtain necessary cabinet approval for their policy proposals and for senior appointments in their departments. By the procedural rules of the Federal Government, the Federal Cabinet must give its formal blessings to the govern-

---

[2] See Renate Mayntz and Fritz W. Scharpf, *Policy-Making in the German Federal Bureaucracy* (New York: Elsevier, 1975) and Neville Johnson, *Government in the Federal Republic: The Executive at Work* (Oxford: Pergamon, 1973) on this and other matters discussed in this section.

ment's budget and all other legislative measure and legal ordinances before they can be submitted to the Federal Parliament. It is also the ultimate authority for settling policy disputes in the executive arena. A federal minister will therefore not normally seek cabinet approval for a policy measure unless he knows he can get it, and he will try to resolve policy differences with the chancellor and other ministers before they reach the cabinet.

By enabling a chancellor to promote or block policy action by the Federal Government, these formal provisions tend to strengthen his authority as its chief executive; by compelling him to base his own policies on a ministerial consensus, they also tend to weaken it. Should most cabinet officers refuse to go along with the chancellor, he would have four legitimate recourses: he can (1) defer to their wishes, (2) request their resignation, (3) ask the federal president to dismiss them, or (4) press them to change their minds — if need be by threatening to ask the Federal Diet for a personal vote of confidence or to bring down the entire government with his own resignation.

An astute chancellor will see to it that such conflict situations do not arise, especially if he lacks the resources for mobilizing decisive outside support on his side. All of the above four contingencies would reflect on his performance as chief executive and might even cost him his job. Chancellor Erhard's inability to surmount conflicts with his ministers, for example, led to his involuntary retirement. Chancellor Adenauer, on the other hand, would avoid such confrontations by staging tactical policy retreats and agreeing to face-saving compromise solutions in the name of government harmony.

For the sake of his public image, a chancellor must at least appear to be in control of a united Federal Government — even if he is not in fact. The more fragile an alliance of powerful party leaders and the greater the divisive pressures from the outside, the more important it is that he be able to manage and contain internal policy controversies. He cannot allow partisan and bureaucratic conflicts to paralyze the policymaking functions of the Federal Government and he cannot permit any minister to saddle him with responsibilities for policies he does not endorse. Take the case of Karl Schiller, an unprecedented "superminister" who headed both the finance and economic ministries in Chancellor Brandt's first Social-Liberal Coalition cabinet. Schiller worked for some time in close collaboration with the chancellor and initially enjoyed strong elite support inside and outside a government that commanded only a bare majority of the Federal Diet and none in the Federal Council. However, when Schiller's policies led to bitter disputes with fellow ministers, Brandt evidently welcomed, if not encouraged, the resignation of a man who lacked an independent power base in the ruling Social Democratic party.

The pluralist constraints on joint policymaking in the Federal Government have emphasized the importance of harmonious associations among its top officials. A good working relationship between chancellor and ministers holds mutual advantages, and it is particularly essential for close collaboration between the principal majority and minority party leaders in coalition governments. CDU Chancellor Kurt Kiesinger thus worked in tandem with his SPD Deputy Chancellor and Foreign Minister Willy Brandt in the 1966–69 Grand Coalition of Christian and Social Democrats. When Brandt became chancellor of the subsequent Social-Liberal Coalition, he teamed up with Walter Scheel, the leader of the FDP; the pattern was maintained by their immediate successors — SPD Chancellor Helmut Schmidt and FDP Deputy Chancellor and Foreign Minister Hans-Dietrich Genscher. Along with other key governmental and legislative leaders of their respective parties, these men settled outstanding policy differences in the ruling coalitions and forged agreements outside rather than inside the formal sessions of the Federal Cabinet. For instance, in 1974, cabinet approval of the federal budget was ensured after a series of informal meetings at Chancellor Schmidt's vacation home; and in the following year the Social-Liberal Coalition leaders resolved their differences on a new codetermination law in a similar fashion.

Policy disputes in the executive arena are most likely to become enmeshed in bureaucratic politics when they involve departments with competing pressure group clienteles. For example, officials of the ministries of agriculture and finance may lock horns over the size of tax benefits for the farmers and those of the ministries of economics and labor over the formulation of measures affecting wages and prices. Such interbureaucratic conflicts are apt to be all the more intense when they engage civil servants who have pursued most or all of their careers in a single department; these tend to be the most jealous guardians of their ministry's prerogatives and to identify themselves closely with the promotion of its particular policy interests.

The executive policymaking system is designed to prevent such bureaucratic controversies or, if that is not possible, to resolve them at the earliest possible stage. To begin with, low-ranking department officials are not likely to get very far with their policy proposals if their superiors believe that these proposals will run into trouble at higher department levels. Second, the heads of government departments are unlikely to consent to proposals that will provoke strong opposition from their ministerial colleagues or the chancellor. Third, institutionalized arrangements for resolving policy conflicts between departments call for interbureaucratic negotiations between senior officials that will produce a compromise solution at the subcabinet level. If differences persist, the state secretaries may enter the fray on behalf of their minister, and the chief of the chancellor's office may endeavor to act as an honest broker.

The Federal Cabinet as such has consequently been a more deliberative than decision-making organ. It normally meets about once a week, mostly to listen to expositions of current policy problems by the chancellor and various ministers and to consider appropriate government responses. Perfunctory approval of a particular course of action or inaction usually follows from preliminary understandings among top political officials and senior civil servants. The cabinet's formal authority to settle policy disputes has been rarely exercised. Its members may agree to disagree if differences have not been resolved at an earlier stage; more likely, the chancellor will put off a cabinet decision, rather than let it come to a vote that might split or, at least, reveal cracks in his government.

THE LEGISLATIVE ARENA OF THE FEDERAL DIET

For most West Germans the popularly elected lower house of the Federal Parliament is the most conspicuous arena of national policymaking. Its public plenary and committee sessions are covered by the mass media and schoolchildren from all over the country are taken to watch "democracy at work" from the visitors' gallery of the chamber. But for all that, what the ordinary citizen reads, sees, and hears gives him a rather limited and not particularly impressive picture of the policymaking functions of the Diet.

Nominally, the Diet has rather extensive constitutional powers in this respect since all laws and treaties of the Federal Republic require its approval. In actual fact, the chamber as a whole has, however, appeared to wield only very limited influence over authoritative policy choices and consequently has not been held in particularly high public esteem.

The initiation, formulation, and enactment of legislation has generally been controlled by the Federal Government and its legislative managers. Roughly 85 percent of the bills passed by the Diet between 1949 and 1973, originated in the executive branch; in contrast, only about one-third of the bills introduced from the floor of the chamber became law, and then only by consent of the Federal Government. Most deputies on both sides of the aisle have had to confine their efforts to shaping specific details in domestic legislation, usually on behalf of particular partisan and pressure group interests.

One major reason for the predominance of executive authority in the legislative arena is that the directly elected representatives of the people labor under the same handicap as lawmakers in other advanced industrial countries. That is, the vast scope and complexity of policymaking inhibits the effectiveness of deputies, who lack the expertise, information, and supportive services available to executive leaders. Recent measures have somewhat improved that situation by providing the Diet and its component parties with more office space and a larger staff. In this respect West German deputies are now better off than members of the British House of Commons, but still far less so than American congressmen. Nor do they wield as much of the critical power of the purse over governmental revenues and expenditures. The Diet not only has to share this legislative authority with the Federal Council of the state governments; it also may not increase or shift allocations in the Federal Government's proposed budget without the consent of the finance minister. Moreover, its fiscal powers have been further limited in recent years by governmental planning programs that have tended to structure legislative appropriations for scientific research and development and other key areas of national policy.

A second and related reason for executive predominance is that the constitutional authority of the Diet has been profoundly affected by the evolution of party government and party alignments in the Federal Republic. The authors of the Basic Law built on nineteenth-century principles of parliamentary government and sought to prevent excessive bureaucratic and legislative control over policymaking through a system of checks and balances between executive and legislature. What they did not anticipate was, first, that both would become controlled by the leaders of just one or two parties, and second, that party government would penetrate deeply into the executive bureaucracy and also reduce the autonomy of the direct representatives of the electorate. Both developments have provoked a good deal of critical comment from West German political observers. Those who hold that the authority of the state rests on the shoulders of a nonpartisan civil service establishment charge that party government has led to the politicization of the federal bureaucracy; those who identify a democratic regime with parliamentary control over policymaking maintain that party government has led to the bureaucratization of legislative politics and made the Diet an abject instrument of the executive.

In contrast to the United States, top officials of the West German Federal Government participate directly in legislative processes. Government bills are shepherded through the Diet by the chiefs of appropriate departments and their principal lieutenants and government leaders can at any time intervene in policy disputes; they may not only ask to be heard but must be allowed to voice their views in plenary or committee sessions of the chamber. The chancellor, ministers, and parliamentary state secretaries may intercede as members of the executive branch or as members of the legislature; regular state secretaries and other key civil servants play less conspicuous roles as representatives of their political superiors in committee meetings of the lower house and in private conferences with Diet deputies.

In marked contrast to parliaments under former German regimes and in other countries, the Federal Diet has not provided the public with the spectacle of constant and bitter confrontations between executive and legislative leaders and between governing and opposition parties. Although major controversies may occasionally surface in the public media — especially at election time — policy conflicts and attendant bargaining negotiations in the Diet have been confined almost entirely to nonpublic meetings of its committees and party caucuses. Plenary meetings of the chamber are essentially ritualistic public performances for the legitimation of antecedent policy decisions in these bodies.

The Diet as a whole meets four or five times a week. The chamber is rarely crowded except for important votes; it is particularly empty on Friday afternoons, when most deputies rush back to their home bases for weekend politicking. On the average, only about a tenth of the legislators will be there, though committee sessions and party caucuses may not be scheduled at the same time. Deputies are fined by the interparty Council of Elders for unexcused absences, but they usually just sign in and then go to work in their offices. More often than not, they are simply too busy with other matters to go to plenary meetings.

Members in attendance tend to pay little or no attention to the business at hand. Spectators will normally see them at their desks catching up with other work or reading newspapers, strolling through the aisles and chatting with colleagues and assistants, and leaving the chamber at frequent intervals to attend to outside business — such as meeting a constituent or lobbyist. But then neither the deputies nor, for that matter, the spectators have usually much cause to follow the proceedings in the front of the chamber with rapt attention. Most of the time is taken up with dry reports by committee chairmen and with highly technical platform lectures from subject matter specialists designated by the leaders of the governing and opposition parties.

Scheduled plenary debates are likely either to reiterate already well-known partisan positions for further public consumption or to be so complex that they fail to capture wide public interest. Questions and interpolations addressed to members of the government may touch off an unscheduled debate, especially if they are put by prominent opposition deputies and focus on controversial policy issues. But even on such occasions the procedural rules of the diet allow for little spontaneous give and take. So-called major and minor inquiries must be submitted in writing and this requirement allows government spokesmen to come back with carefully prepared replies, if they consent to answer at all. Moreover, since major inquiries require the signature of thirty deputies and minor inquiries that of fifteen, backbenchers have little chance to get into the act without the consent of their parliamentary party leaders. In fact, they have practically no opportunity to be heard except in oral questions from the floor — and these almost always deal with some minor problem, such as the proper application of legislative or administrative measures in specific instances of interest to a deputy and his constituents.

Measures designed to attract more public attention to plenary debates have addressed themselves more to form than to substance. For example, recent reforms provide that speeches may no longer be read from manuscript and must be limited to forty-five minutes; other proposals — for example, that the Diet adopt a more intimate seating arrangement under which government and opposition benches would face each other, as in the British Commons — came to naught.

The root of the matter is that executive leaders have usually discouraged and legislative leaders have not sought frequent debates on policy issues, regardless of the parties in power. Ruling party elites have not considered them either necessary or useful for efficient and responsible government, and opposition party elites have generally refrained from using their limited means to force such debates. The traditions, organization, and style of West German parliamentary processes, and the patterns of West German party government, combine to emphasize the legislative rather than the educative functions of the Diet. The survival of the Federal Government is not decided by plenary debates in the chamber and they do little or nothing to enlighten a public that neither knows nor cares very much about their contents to begin with. Legislative policymaking is thought to be far more important — not only by most of the Diet's deputies, but by their party and pressure group clients.

In short, most plenary meetings of the Diet are pretty dull affairs, though they have occasionally been enlivened by demonstrative interruptions from the floor and touch-and-go votes in a narrowly divided house. The public media have therefore made all the more of exceptional dramatic clashes between proponents of ostensibly sharply conflicting policy positions.

A more meaningful measure of the legislators' role in policymaking is provided by the activities of the major organizational components of the Diet — its parliamentary parties and committees. The former are the setting for intraparty disputes in the legislative arena, the latter for interparty conflicts. They are connected through the specialized working or study groups (*Arbeitsgemeinschaften*) formed by the legislative committee members in each parliamentary party. Consequently, these deputies represent not only their party and its clients in the Diet committees, but also the cross-party policy interests of their particular committee and its constituencies in the caucus meetings of the parliamentary parties.

As we noted in Chapter VI, the members of the parties in the Diet are tied to local constituencies and regional party organizations, to various ideological camps and vested interest organizations. The resulting pluralist patterns in the parliamentary parties resemble the patterns of executive pluralism in the Federal Government and require equivalent arrangements for internal conflict management and policy coordination. The major difference is that in the legislative arena such arrangements are not shaped nearly as much by formal rules;

informal bargaining processes therefore play a correspondingly greater role in the resolution of policy disputes within the parliamentary parties.

The constitutional lawmakers do not simply dance to the tune of their legislative leaders; ruling party elites cannot ignore opposition in the parliamentary parties in pushing for a particular course of action. They lack the means to enforce their wishes and may have to go to a good deal of trouble to persuade reluctant deputies to buy a controversial measure. Chancellor Adenauer usually delegated this task to his legislative lieutenants; in more recent times both chancellors and ministers have made it a practice to argue their points personally in party caucuses.

Caucus meetings are subject to democratic procedures for arriving at a common policy position. When an issue gives rise to significant internal disagreements there may be extended deliberations, and if these fail to produce a consensus the party leaders will usually call for a vote. However the Basic Law allows deputies to disregard the outcome. In the SPD a high sense of party loyalty and discipline has almost invariably led dissenters to adhere to majority decisions on votes in the Diet and its committees; Christian and Free Democrats have been more prone to disregard them, especially if their dissent is backed by powerful party or interest group factions or secured by a safe seat in the Diet.

Legislative committee meetings take up a large part of the deputies' time. The reason is that they are unwilling to approve skeletal laws that would give the Federal Government great leeway in interpretation and application and consider it their duty to submit bills to meticulous consideration in committee. In part this outlook is a legacy of German parliamentary traditions, which define highly explicit legislative codification as the principal means of popular control over the executive. In part, too, it is based on the deputies' belief that the input of pluralist interest demands in the Diet can be most adequately and efficiently processed through the committee system of miniparliaments. Moreover, committee assignments provide both majority and minority party members with opportunities to look after the needs of their pressure group clients and their local constituencies in specific policy outputs.

How much influence Diet committees wield over policymaking is a matter of considerable dispute among West German political observers. Some argue that the Diet "has disintegrated into a conglomerate of incoherent, highly specialized committees and working groups which are coordinated only by the leaders of the parliamentary parties, and whose horizons remain limited to narrowly defined areas of specialization." [3] In this view, the committees are totally dependent on guidance from the ministerial departments and are bureaucratic in their working patterns and in the perception of their tasks. Other observers maintain that "an elaborate committee structure with the most influential parliamentarians of all parties as chairmen of the important committees will assure the West German parliament of a degree of substantive influence in policy processes that is not found in the classical parliamentary systems." [4] In this view, the Diet, through its committees, is seen as closer in power to the American Congress than to legislatures in other representative democracies.

Judging by past experiences, it would appear that the influence exercised by Diet committees depends on their spheres of jurisdiction and on particular circumstances. Committees that deal with key areas of policymaking — such as the foreign affairs, defense, and budget — have tended to be most closely guided by cues from the executive branch; more highly specialized committees — such as the Agriculture Committee, the Committee for Urban Affairs and Home Construction, and the Committee for Labor and Social Affairs — are more autonomous and more amenable to interest group pressure. Consequently deputies who are primarily concerned with attending to the needs of particular constituencies are likely to prefer a seat on the latter type of committee, whereas those who are

[3] Joachim Hirsch, "Scientific-Technical Progress and the Political System" in Klaus von Beyme (ed.), *German Political Studies*, vol. I (London-Beverly Hills: Sage Publications, 1974), p. 119.

[4] Mayntz and Scharpf, *Policy-Making in the German Federal Bureaucracy*, p. 36.

more interested in broader domestic and international issues opt for the former.

That circumstances may make a difference in the policy influence of Diet committees can be shown by two illustrations. During the Grand Coalition between the CDU/CSU and SPD in the late 1960s, the committees wielded an unprecedented degree of power and were often able to block or significantly change legislative proposals of the executive branch. Just because the government was based on an overwhelming parliamentary alignment between the two major competitive parties, it could not automatically rely on the support of a disciplined majority on specific issues. Policy differences that could not be settled in the executive arena were often resolved by compromise agreements in legislative committees. The second illustration is the situation when the opposition in the Diet commands sufficient votes in one or both houses of the Federal Parliament to block key policy objectives of the Federal Government. The Social Democrats were in that position in the 1950s and early 1960s, when the CDU/CSU led the government; the Christian Democrats in the 1970s, when the SPD headed the Social-Liberal Coalition. In both instances the parliamentary opposition employed the leverage of its veto power in the legislative arena to extract substantial concessions from the government in committee meetings of the Diet.

THE FEDERAL ARENA

The governments of the ten constituent states of the Federal Republic play major roles in national policymaking. Their importance is all the more noteworthy in the light of recent efforts in other advanced industrial countries, including the United States, to curb the concentration of public authority through regional devolution. Territorial dispersion of decision-making sites is said to extend the opportunities for democratic participation and control. It is also said to promote political harmony by allowing for a more effective expression and accommodation of sectional interests than in a centralized state. And it is held to increase the efficiency of the public administration and its responsiveness to popular needs and demands.

Informed observers are divided over how far any of these claims have been sustained in the Federal Republic, and whether for better or for worse. Some laud the principles and practices of West German federalism for enhancing democratic pluralism, as well as political stability and administrative efficiency in government. Others maintain that they make it singularly difficult for the Federal Government to cope with pressing national policy problems, or that they serve to promote and legitimate the joint executive authority of federal and state leaders.

The patterns of conflict management in the federal arena are first of all conditioned by formal rules for integrating national and subnational institutions. As we noted in Chapter II (pages 15–32), the Basic Law both fuses and divides the constitutional powers of federal and regional authorities and interposes state structures between central and local organs of government. And we observed in subsequent chapters how both are reflected in the electoral system and in the organization of political parties and pressure groups. The key agencies for countrywide policy coordination are intergovernmental committees, the Federal Council, and the top echelons of the major parties and interest associations. The principal mechanisms of the resolution of policy conflicts are negotiations among officials of the central and state governments, bargaining between federal and state party leaders, and adjudication by the Federal Constitutional Court.

Three developments have especially affected policymaking in the federal arena. The effective autonomy of the states has diminished over the years as the scope of federal regulations has increased. The progressive nationalization of public policy problems has furthermore eroded the legislative authority of the state parliaments and accentuated the role of the state governments in the formulation of policies for the entire country. And policy disputes in the federal arena have come to focus largely on issues related to differences in the political economy of the various states as sectional religious distinctions have become less important in West German politics.

The state governments are legally empowered to develop common policies on their own — that is, without the participation of federal organs — in two areas. One covers issues that fall under the exclusive jurisdiction of the states, principally control of the primary and seconda schools, the public media, law enforcement, and local government administration. The other concerns the few matters that remain subject to the policies of the state governments because federal authorities have not exercised their overlapping legislative powers.

In these spheres interstate negotiations resemble international negotiations among sovereign countries in that no state government can be compelled by the others to follow a particular course of action. State officials deal with each other in regular ministerial conferences and special joint commissions as the spokesmen for parliamentary state governments with similar, but not always identical interests. For example, diverse regional concerns and traditions have complicated efforts to coordinate local government operations, and sharp ideological differences among state government leaders have surfaced in disputes over the contents of a standardized school curriculum. Policy conflicts on such issues can be settled only by mutual agreement. Even then, there is no assurance that a settlement will be implemented in all the states. State officials may turn out to lack sufficient authority in their governments and parliaments to deliver what they agreed to. In any event, more often than not the mutual understandings will be kept in general terms and the more precise implementation will vary a good deal from state to state.

The state governments have been impelled to strive for more "self-coordination" under the pressure of expanding federal authority. Most often this takes the form of executive agreements on joint formulas for the solution of shared policy problems. For example, when in the early 1970s, the demand for higher education became greater than the available space in the most popular fields, the state governments established joint admission standards and selection procedures for the state universities. However, voluntary self-coordination has proven most difficult under the unanimity rule in interstate negotiations, and the nature of their common policy problems has largely compelled the state governments to rely increasingly on federal regulations and funding. Their disputes over policy contents and procedures have to a corresponding extent shifted more and more from the subnational to the federal level of decision making.

The federal policymaking system may be compared to a wagon wheel. The outer rim consists of the state parliaments and administrative agencies at the periphery. They are joined to the center by the spokes, the state governments. The Federal Council, at the hub, connects the state governments to the Federal Government and the Diet. As a permanent assembly of their delegates, the council fulfills two primary functions. It stands apart from the national executive and popularly elected lower house as an instrument for the defense and promotion of the interests of the state governments and their particular clients. But it is also a part of the Federal Parliament and, as such, serves to coordinate the formulation of national policies with their implementation by subnational organs of government.

In a strictly legal sense the council is not, like the United States Senate, a coequal chamber of the national legislature. Although the upper house considers all bills passed by the Diet, it cannot block legislation that falls under the exclusive jurisdiction of federal authorities, most notably defense and foreign policy measures. Its approval is needed for constitutional amendments — which require a two-thirds majority vote — and for laws that come under the joint legislative powers of federal and state authorities.[5] But here the Federal Constitutional Court has ruled that legislation derived from a law already approved by the chamber does not require its consent. And though the Federal Cabinet must submit all of its legislative proposals to the council before they are formally introduced in the Diet, it does not have to accept changes recommended on a majority vote of the state governments.

However, these formal provisions convey only a very limited picture of the state governments' actual involvement in the formulation of federal policies. In 1973, one out of two laws required the approval of the Federal Council, compared to

[5] If such a measure is defeated by a two-thirds vote in the Council it can become law only if it is subsequently approved by a two-thirds majority in the Diet.

one out of ten in 1949. And the state governments have lately performed an increasing number of so-called joint tasks with the Federal Government. A compromise formula for more "cooperative federalism" has led to a proliferation of inter-ministerial planning committees of executive officials from the central and state governments. These bureaucratic organs develop national programs for urban and regional economic development, for scientific research and educational projects, for coordinated federal and state budgets, and for federal financial assistance to the states. Such projects are in turn translated into broad-gauged legislative proposals of the federal and state governments which, in effect, leave the state diets with no other choice but to accept or reject them in their entirety. Consequently, the state diets will almost invariably give their approval without much ado — especially when they would otherwise forfeit federal matching grants. In late 1975, for example, a general higher education law that emerged from six years of hard bargaining between federal and state officials was quickly passed by both the federal and state parliaments.

In the Federal Council the state governments are in some ways in a stronger position relative to the Federal Government than are the members of the Diet. Unlike the lower house, the upper one cannot be dissolved in the event of a conflict with the national executive and the Federal Government is thus more amenable to compromise. The state governments can also deal with the Federal Government on a more equal basis than the deputies because their own civil servants provide them with a much larger and more knowledgeable staff of expert advisers. And although the Federal Government may not make the Diet privy to its deliberations and may deny it a good deal of policy-relevant information, formal rules as well as practical considerations require that the state governments be kept informed.

All legal ordinances of the Federal Government, and all of its administrative regulations that affect the states, must have the approval of the Federal Council (see Figure VIII.1). But beyond that, both the national executive and Diet need to take into account the fact that the effective implementation of most domestic policy decisions is the business of the state governments. Although the latter are bound by the Basic Law to execute federal regulations faithfully and uniformly, they must be allowed a good deal of leeway in the interpretation and application of such measures.

As a rule, every Federal Government will do its best to work in tandem with the state governments. The greater their cooperation, the less cost and effort has to go into coordinating activities of the small supervisory staff of the federal civil service. Moreover, the Federal Government has really not much choice but to rely on the voluntary compliance of each state government. What are its alternatives? Apart from withholding funds for specific revenue sharing projects, it can either bring a recalcitrant state government before the Constitutional Court — which may involve protracted and chancy proceedings — or it may seek majority support from the Federal Council for the application of the as yet untried measure of federal enforcement. These legal alternatives may serve the Federal Government as bargaining weapons, but they are rather blunt instruments.

The state governments, for their part, have a vast stake in the formulation of federal policies, for they are touched by virtually all of them. Federal legislation determines how much each state will get of the tax revenues that flow into the national treasury.[6] Federal measures designed to steer the national economy shape the resource base for state and local taxes and, therefore, what subnational governmental authorities can collect or must borrow to meet expenses. In this regard the size and shape of the federal budget and federal grants are particularly important, not only for the economic well-being of the state governments but for their political fortunes. Consider, too, that federal policies on regional economic development and domestic welfare legislation, on foreign trade and investments and the employment of foreign workers, and so forth, have a very decided effect on socioeco-

---

[6] Some 60 percent of all tax revenue goes into the national treasury; of this, about two-thirds goes to federal agencies, most of the rest to the state governments, while local governments receive by far the smallest share.

nomic conditions in the various states. And note that state authorities rely on federal organs for information and procedural arrangements that will enable them to discharge their assigned tasks properly. The police functions of the states are one example. The uniform application of federal traffic regulations and internal security measures throughout the country calls for means of enforcement that all the state governments will consider technically feasible and adequately funded.

As in the United States Senate — though not to the same extent and in the same manner — the representatives of states with small populations wield a disproportionate degree of influence in the Federal Council (Table VIII.1). Although the distribution of the citizenry among the states has shifted quite a bit, the allocation of seats in the chamber has not changed since the establishment of the Federal Republic. Remember that each state government controls at least three and at most five unit votes. Consequently, the government of the city-state of Bremen can cast as many votes as that of the Saarland and that of Lower Saxony as many as the government of North Rhine-Westphalia. In effect, the bargaining powers of the small states is particularly great on issues that find the chamber narrowly divided.

Because the state governments play a greater and more direct part in national policymaking than in the United States, interstate party alignments are also more important in West Germany. At the same time party affiliation does not carry as much weight in the federal arena as in the legislative arena of the national Diet.

Since the establishment of the Federal Republic, the major parties have waged a continuous battle for a decisive majority of the state votes in the Federal Council. But neither the governing nor the opposition parties in the Diet have ever been able to count on a durable, favorable plurality or, better yet, a two-thirds majority in the other house. Not only have parliamentary elections and changing coalitions in the states led to partisan realignments in the chamber, but party loyalties have often proven less important than the promotion of particularistic sectional interests by the state governments.

Party unity across state lines is usually strongest when policy

Table VIII.1. *The Political Economy of West German Federalism (1972–73)*

	Percentage of Federal Council seats	Percentage of total population	Percentage contribution to national taxes	Per capita tax index	Percentage of economic product		
					Agriculture	Industry	Trade and services
Federal Republic	100 = 41	100 = 58.5 million	100 = DM 216 billion	100 = DM 3594	3	52	45
Northern States							
Schleswig-Holstein	10	4	3	72	7	43	51
Hamburg	7	3	10	336	0.6	41	58
Bremen	7	1	2	215	0.9	46	53
Lower Saxony	12	12	8	65	6	50	44
Central States							
North Rhine-Westphalia	12	29	29	103	2	54	44
Hesse	10	9	10	105	2	48	50
Rhineland-Palatinate	10	6	5	75	5	55	40
Saar	7	2	1	69	2	52	46
Southern States							
Baden-Württemberg	12	15	16	105	3	58	39
Bavaria	12	18	15	85	4	53	43

Sources: Calculated from data in *Statistisches Jahrbuch für die Bundesrepublik*, 1973, 1974, passim.

disputes in the federal arena are dominated by sharp partisan conflicts in the national parliament. It also tends to prevail in controversies between the state governments over cultural policies that fall under their ·exclusive jurisdiction, such as educational reforms. At other times particular policy issues will produce shifting cross-party alignments that find the members of parties opposed to each other in the Federal Diet, on the same side in the Federal Council and in interstate conflicts. A common attachment to regional autonomy has thus time and again united governing Christian Socialist leaders in Bavaria and governing Social Democratic leaders in the city-state of Hamburg as the principal defenders of states rights against the encroachment of the central government.

Policy disputes in the federal arena are especially likely to transcend party ties when they involve issues related to differences in the political economy of the states (see Table VIII.1). For example, the heavily industrialized states do not share the problems of those where agriculture remains important. Or take recent controversies over a national program on energy resources. Here the different party governments of states with a particular interest in the use of native and foreign coal supplies have stood in opposition to a united front of those with an economic stake in the utilization of imported oil and natural gas. And note, above all, the persistence of intergovernmental conflicts over the distribution of national tax revenues among the states. Under the prevailing formula the four richest states subsidize public services and economic development projects in the other six. Their governments seek to recapture as much as possible for their own use. On the other hand, the states with large populations demand a more equitable per capita distribution, whereas the smaller and poorer states want both more than they contribute and more than they can claim on the basis of population.

The state governments, like the deputies of the Diet, take most of their policy cues from the Federal Government. Although they have the collective authority to introduce federal legislation through the Federal Council, they have seldom done so and then only on minor, noncontroversial matters. Policy conflicts in the federal arena are therefore usually prompted by actions of the national executive, either directly or by way of the Federal Diet. Correspondingly, the management of such disputes also rests principally with officials and legislative agents of the Federal Government. How they are dealt with depends on the nature of the issues and the alignment of political forces.

Differences over administrative procedures are normally resolved through interbureaucratic negotiations. These are conducted almost entirely out of the public view and far from partisan strife by federal and state civil servants. For the most part, they concern complex but mundane issues, or entirely nonpartisan issues, which the respective government leaders are content to leave their subordinates to settle inside and outside the committees of the Federal Council. Expected and actual electoral outcomes seldom impinge on such negotiations, and the rare deadlocks have been invariably due to the intrusion of more profound disputes on the content of federal policies or constitutional issues. Disputes between federal and state government leaders on such substantive issues have only rarely ended up in the Federal Constitutional Court. Usually they are decided in the Federal Council. And if the Federal Government lacks the votes to have its way, it is likely to modify its position. Moreover, the Federal Government will endeavor to formulate its policy proposals in such a manner that it will not have to stage a public retreat in the face of opposition in the council. The demands of the controlling majority are accordingly frequently anticipated when a law or ordinance is drafted and often need not even be made explicit; an unspoken threat of rejection in the upper house can suffice. If need be, negotiations will continue while a bill is considered by the Diet, and in this stage, bargaining within and among parties will be particularly important. Should a bill be nonetheless defeated in the council after passage in the lower house, a compromise solution may still emerge from secret deliberations in the standing conference committee of the two chambers. Thus, of about forty-two bills which the council vetoed between 1969 and 1976, all but two were ultimately approved in an amended form.

THE SYSTEM IN OPERATION

We observed early in this chapter that major controversies in the policymaking stratum have been rare in the Federal Republic. And as we also noted, when disputes do arise they tend to be settled through behind-the-scenes negotiations among the elites rather than on the open stage of West German politics. Conspicuous conflicts in authoritative decision-making arenas are accordingly atypical, but they illuminate interrelationships and processes that are obscure at other times. Let us therefore conclude this chapter by taking a look at six such cases. Each of them, in various ways, illustrates the close connection between formal structures and political dynamics in a pluralist context for policy conflicts and their management.

ANTITRUST LEGISLATION

The Policy Problem. Soon after the establishment of the Federal Republic, the CDU-led coalition government of Chancellor Adenauer became embroiled in a major policy dispute over innovative antitrust legislation.[7] Business cartels that had flourished under earlier regimes and survived regulatory efforts by the occupation powers were blossoming again; the question at issue was what the authoritative decision makers could and would do about this development.

Initial Actions (1950–53). The first round in the extended battle over cartel legislation was fought principally in the executive arena. It involved three sets of leading contestants: the allied high commissioners for Germany, the big-business elite, and the Adenauer government. The joint American-British-French High Commission (HICOC) exercised far-reaching collective authority over policymaking, since the Federal Republic had been granted only limited sovereignty

[7] Case study based on Gerard Braunthal, "The Struggle for Cartel Legislation" in James B. Christoph and Bernard E. Brown (eds.), *Cases in Comparative Politics,* rev. ed. (Boston: Little, Brown, 1969), pp. 187–206.

by the three former occupation powers. HICOC demanded speedy action on stringent antitrust legislation that would prevent any kind of cartel. West German industrial leaders, on the other hand, were just as adamantly opposed to such measures. The Adenauer government, in the middle, was thus confronted with strong countervailing pressures. The situation was further complicated by two additional factors. One was that economic growth through industrial exports had high priority on the government's policy agenda and that here the powers represented on the High Commission were also major competitors. The other problem was that the ruling parties and their supporters in the business community were internally divided on cartel control.

The CDU Minister of Economics, Ludwig Erhard, was a fervent proponent of maximal competition in a free enterprise system and wanted to outlaw trusts while maintaining a minimum of state control over the economy. The cartel division of his department prepared a government bill to this effect which Erhard presented to the Federal Cabinet in March 1951, for its necessary approval. Prolonged deliberations at the top of the executive branch followed because the tripartite High Commission maintained that the proposed legislation did not go far enough whereas the business lobby held that it went too far. A year went by and, in March 1952, the cabinet was ready to approve the submission of a compromise bill to the Federal Parliament. It provided for the prohibition of industrial cartels and for an enforcement agency, but dismissed HICOC demands for the outlawing of cartels in agriculture, banking, and transportation.

Even before this measure was formally introduced in the Federal Diet, it encountered strong opposition from the Federation of German Industries. The BDI maintained that it was willing to accept controls over industrial cartels, but not their total prohibition. This produced a deadlock between Erhard, who threatened to resign, and leading industrialists, who informed Chancellor Adenauer that they might withhold contributions to the Christian Democratic campaign in the coming 1953 election. Broader domestic and foreign policy considerations induced Adenauer to support Erhard's position, but with the end of the legislative period, the initial government bill died in the Economic Affairs Committee of the Federal Diet.

Bargaining and Negotiations in the Executive Arena (1954–55). The second round in the battle over anticartel legislation featured a sparring match between Economic Minister Erhard and West German industrialists. Intervention by the High Commission ceased to be a significant factor, since the three Western powers gradually turned over their authority to the Federal Government and, in May 1955, granted full sovereignty to the Federal Republic. In domestic politics, the CDU/CSU now held a majority in both houses of the Federal Parliament and the SPD opposition was also in favor of outlawing industrial cartels. In February 1954, the Adenauer coalition cabinet approved a new Erhard bill to this effect and, on the face of it, speedy legislative passage seemed ensured. However, the government bill was not even to be submitted formally to parliament for another year; the industrialists were by no means ready to surrender, and Erhard delayed introduction in the hope of overcoming their opposition.

According to constitutional procedures, the proposed measure was initially sent from the cabinet to the Federal Council for preliminary consideration. While the upper house sat on it for three months, it became evident that the CDU/CSU's nominal parliamentary majority — and SPD support — did not ensure easy passage for the government bill. The heterogeneous Christian Democratic party and business elites were deeply split on the issue. Under pressure from industry leaders, representatives of CDU/CSU-dominated state governments in the Federal Council recommended changes to the cabinet that weakened some key provisions of the Erhard bill. The cabinet considered it advisable to accept a number of these suggestions and Erhard, in lengthy negotiations with BDI spokesmen, agreed to accept further emasculating amendments when the government bill reached the Federal Diet.

Conflict and Conflict Resolution in the Legislative Arena (1955–57). The third and final round in the battle over anticartel legislation took place in the Federal Diet. Its fate there shows what can happen when a strong pressure group fails to obtain satisfaction in the executive arena and is able to exploit the division of the governing parties on policy issues in the lower house of parliament.

In March 1955, the government's regulatory bill was formally introduced in the Federal Diet with its first reading and entered the usual committee stage. Five committees were to deal with its contents for more than two years, but for the most part the legislative struggle between the proponents and opponents of effective regulations focused on the deliberations of the Economic Affairs Committee. Two bills, one more and one less restrictive, were introduced by deputies of the governing CDU/CSU, but neither received much support. The government's proposals, on the other hand, were endorsed by a single-issue majority coalition composed of left-wing Christian Democrats, most Free Democrats, and the opposition SPD.

In view of this alignment, the industry lobby sought to keep the government bill bottled up in the Economic Affairs Committee with the help of its accommodating CDU chairman. When that did not prove possible, the BDI sought in vain to get Chancellor Adenauer to withdraw his support. However, it was more successful in applying both direct pressure on individual CDU/CSU deputies and indirect pressure through their party organization. Though the BDI was unable to block the Federal Government's regulatory proposal altogether, it managed to win further exemptions through compromise solutions to bitter committee battles.

Policy Enactment and Its Effects. In the summer of 1957, the final committee version of a much watered-down government bill was passed without much further debate in its second and third reading by the Federal Diet. The Federal Council went along, the federal president attached his signature, and in January 1958, a cartel control law at last went into effect — eight years after the first try. Many of the deputies who had voted for it declared themselves far from satisfied with a policy measure that was so much weaker than the original Erhard proposals. However, business leaders who had opposed restrictive legislation from the outset considered the emasculated law still too severe. But they found they could live with it. Its administrative implementation by the new regulatory cartel office demonstrated that the concessions won by business pressure groups safeguarded many of the old practices in restraint of trade. The industrial lobby made no attempt to repeal the law and was able to block efforts to strengthen it substantially.

SUBSIDIES FOR THE RAILROADS

The Policy Problem. In 1953, the publicly owned federal railway system was in deep financial trouble and the CDU/CSU-dominated Federal Government of Chancellor Adenauer was legally bound to come to its rescue.[8] The plight of the railway system was essentially due to two factors. One was that it was obligated to maintain regular services on unprofitable lines, the other that it had to transport unwieldy cargoes at fixed low rates in the face of growing competition from private truckers. The problem for the government was to obtain ameliorative legislation that would provide the railway system with more income without reducing existing services and increasing charges.

Policy Formulation and Conflict in Executive Arena (1953–54). The Adenauer government started from the position that closing down the unprofitable operations or raising the passenger and cargo rates of the railroads was out of the question. The only feasible alternatives appeared to be (1) massive government subsidies, (2) measures to improve the competitive position of the railroads in relation to private trucking, or (3) some combination of the two. In the summer of 1953, the government settled on the third option, but it realized that its legislative proposals would have to take into account potential opposition from trucking firms, from their suppliers and customers, and from commercial concerns that did their own trucking. It therefore sought a measure that

[8] Case study based on Gerard Braunthal, *The West German Legislative Process: A Case Study of Two Transportation Finance Bills* (Ithaca, London: Cornell University Press, 1972).

would provide for new highway construction on behalf of these interests and, at the same time, provide subsidies from new taxes for the railroads and transfer a portion of long-haul trucking to the railroads' ownership.

Since the contemplated solution to the problem was first of all a revenue matter, the task of drafting a transportation finance law fell initially to appropriate officials in the Ministry of Finance. But as it also involved the concerns of other government departments, these civil servants were under instructions to consult officials from the Ministry of Transport and the autonomous Federal Railway Administration. Almost at once, interbureaucratic conflicts arose that eventually took in the ministries of justice, economics, and foreign affairs and cabinet-level political officials. At issue were such questions as whether and how much to increase taxes on motor vehicles, transportation, and motor fuel and whether to introduce tolls on the superhighways. The departments and their chiefs approached the problem from their particular perspectives and those of their respective interest group clients. For example, the Ministry of Finance sought to change the existing tax structure to increase revenues for the railways, whereas the Ministry of Economics held that such a change would harm industrial expansion by cutting into the profits of private automobile construction and trucking concerns.

By early 1954, interministerial negotiations had failed to resolve these differences. Opposition SPD deputies in the Federal Diet began to question the Federal Government's ability to cope with the problem, and embarrassed Christian Democrats pressed their government leaders to come up with an agreement. At the same time, major interest groups — notably the Federation of German Industries (BDI) and the German Federation of Trade Unions (DGB) — endeavored to influence the shape of the government bill, though with little effect. The intense governmental controversy was veiled in exceptional secrecy and the mandatory consultations with concerned interest organizations were kept to a minimum. Moreover, both of the major peak associations of business and labor were internally divided on the issue. In the BDI, for example, steel producers identified their interests with substantial aid to the railroads, whereas the manufacturers of motor vehicles saw this aid as contrary to their interests. In the DGB a similar conflict along functional lines set the Federation of Railroad Workers against the Federation of Public Service and Transport Workers.

Policy Conflict and Conflict Resolution in the Legislative Arena (1954–55). In March 1954, the Federal Cabinet gave its reluctant approval to a proposal that still did not suit some of its members, especially the Minister of Economics Ludwig Erhard. From there the bill took its usual course to the Federal Council for preliminary consideration. The pressure groups on both sides of the issue persuaded the state governments to recommend a substantial number of changes. On return of the bill, the cabinet accepted about half of these and in June 1954, sent the amended government bill to the Federal Diet for its first reading. At that point the disagreement in the Federal Government and among CDU/CSU deputies was underscored when a Christian Democrat took the unusual step of introducing a rival proposal from the floor — one that came closer to the wishes of the Economic Ministry. Even more exceptional was that when the two proposals went to the Economic Affairs Committee of the Diet, the Economic Ministry went out of its way to indicate its opposition to the official government bill. This, in turn, prompted the Federal Cabinet to reconsider and reaffirm its collective endorsement of the government's measure. Nonetheless, legislative passage of the government proposal was still not ensured. Contending alignments of bureaucratic, partisan, and pressure group interests fought over the contents during lengthy deliberations in the Committee for Finance and Taxation. Deputies of the government's own party battled for major changes and the votes of the opposition Social Democrats were needed to defeat their amendments before the government bill was reported out of committee for a second reading and vote in the Diet.

The bill passed its second reading despite an intensive lobbying campaign by its diehard opponents. Their efforts to mobilize public opinion against the measure failed, probably because the bill was too complex and technical to command wider attention. But even after preliminary passage, there were last-minute efforts to change the bill through amendments from the floor when it came up for a vote on the third and final reading. All of them failed. The government's proposal took its last hurdle in the Diet easily, and then was approved by the Federal Council without significant amendment. With the signature of the federal president, the transportation finance law took effect in April 1955.

Although the final version of the law conformed essentially to the original draft of the Ministry of Finance, it also bore the marks of the conflicts, bargains, and compromises that accompanied its course from initiation to enactment. Of the thirty-one original clauses, only nine remained unchanged; four were altered in interdepartmental bargaining, two were amended by the Federal Council, and sixteen were changed in the Federal Diet. Throughout, the federal chancellor and his chief of staff in the chancellor's office acted as brokers in the resolution of bureaucratic, partisan, and pressure group disputes that led to the law's final passage.

COST SHARING

The Policy Problem. The vast majority of West German employees are covered by mandatory medical insurance programs run by private companies but regulated by public authorities.[9] In May 1957 — after five years of controversy and shortly before federal elections — the CDU/CSU-dominated Federal Parliament enacted a health insurance reform law sponsored by the Adenauer government. It maintained a formula under which all of the funds for sick-leave payments and medical bills were provided by the insurance companies and employers; the latter, particularly, were required to pay larger amounts than before. In view of rising medical costs this requirement did not sit well with the business community, and its leaders demanded a new formula that would require direct contributions from the insured. After receiving assurances on this score from the Christian Democrats, the business elite gave

---

[9] Case study based on William Safran, *Veto-Group Politics: The Case of Health Insurance Reform in West Germany* (San Francisco: Chandler, 1967).

large sums to the CDU/CSU electoral campaign and, after the landslide victory of Adenauer's party, pressed for a speedy return on its political investment.

Policy Response and Conflict in the Executive Arena (1957–60). In October 1957, Chancellor Adenauer honored his party's policy commitments to the business community. In a policy statement to the newly elected Federal Diet, he announced that his government intended to introduce legislation that would make patients shoulder a portion of their medical costs. This requirement provoked at once strong public counterpressure from interest groups opposed to such cost-sharing, a strategy that interfered with the usual procedures for discreet negotiations between appropriate government departments and nongovernmental peak associations. The Federal Chamber of Physicians (BAK) objected in the name of the entire medical profession; it took the position that the proposed measure would lead insured persons to consult their doctors less frequently and held that this would be good neither for public health nor for the economic well-being of the doctors. The Federation of German Trade Unions also opposed the measure, declaring that it was a scheme designed to benefit big business and the medical profession, and that it would deprive low-income workers of adequate medical care. The opposition Social Democrats endorsed this view, whereas members of the labor-wing of the Christian Democrats voiced more cautious reservations — at least in public.

During the following year, the Adenauer government did not let these objections deter it from its chosen course. Under the organization of jurisdictional authority in the executive branch, the task of translating the general policy aim of the political leadership into a specific government bill fell to the Ministry of Labor. Its officials had closer connections to the trade unions than those of other concerned departments — notably, the ministries of health, economics, and finance — and they were more sympathetic to the wishes of organized labor. Labor representatives sat on a special advisory committee of the Labor Ministry that had a major hand in working out a first draft. But whatever influence labor may have exerted was

evidently undercut by countervailing pressure from the business elite during subsequent interdepartmental negotiations;
in October 1958, a special cabinet committee presented the
public with a list of "basic principles," which called for cost-
sharing as a means to stem the growth of a welfare state men-
tality in the country. The Federation of German Employers'
Associations expressed its wholehearted approval, whereas the
German Trade Union Federation reiterated its adamant opposition. The medical profession was deeply divided on the issue;
the Association of German Physicians endorsed cost-sharing,
whereas the Federal Chamber of Physicians and the Federal
Association of Medical Insurance Physicians rejected it.

The Federal Government was apparently taken aback by the
strength and vehemence of the opposition to its plan. Although it published the text of a cost-sharing bill in December
1958, the cabinet did not formally approve it for another year.
In the interval the Ministry of Labor engaged in lengthy negotiations with the critics of the government proposal, but these
failed since the ministry was neither willing nor able to scrap
previous agreements with other departments and pressure
groups. The government reportedly considered dropping its
plan altogether before the conflict spilled over into the legislative arena, but decided to go ahead when the Social Democratic opposition challenged it to take that risk.

Sustained Conflict (1959–61). Ordinarily, the government's
proposal would have been approved by the Federal Parliament without much difficulty since the Christian Democrats
controlled both houses. As it was, the prospects for passage
became increasingly remote as the policy conflict moved into
the legislative arena. In November 1959, the Federal Cabinet
sent the bill to the Federal Council for preliminary consideration; cost-sharing was rejected by a committee of that chamber,
but was rescued by its supporters in plenary session. The
Federal Cabinet thereupon reaffirmed its endorsement of the
bill in February 1960, and dispatched it to the Federal Diet.

In the meantime, the opponents had launched a concerted
pressure group campaign that was designed to block the bill in
the Diet. The trade union elite staged mass rallies and ob-

tained commitments from Christian Democratic deputies that they would not support cost-sharing. The leaders of the medical organizations opposed to the concept mounted a simultaneous lobbying drive that reached a quite unprecedented scope for these professional groups; as a result, medical leaders who endorsed the proposal considered it necessary to meet with the chancellor and emphasize their support.

The first reading of a bill in the Diet is normally a routine affair. However, in this instance, the opposition SPD used the opportunity to stress the government's failure to adequately consider the objections of the trade unions and medical associations; furthermore, CDU deputies went out of their way to voice their reservations. Next, the bill went to the Diet Committee on Social Policy whose members, regardless of party, had particularly close associations with the trade unions. In the course of the committee's deliberations, spokesmen for some twenty-eight interest groups opposed to and in favor of cost-sharing argued their case; representatives of the Federal Government sought to steer the bill past the committee stage before it could be caught up in the 1961 election campaign for a new Diet. However, in the light of this forthcoming event, deputies from all parties were increasingly sensitive to mounting pressure group opposition on the outside. The leadership of the Federal Association of Insurance Physicians warned that their members would go on strike if the Diet should pass an unsatisfactory law and the DGB elite mobilized its mass membership against the government bill.

Conflict Resolution (1961). Although the Diet Committee on Social Policy decided to report out a cost-sharing bill for a second reading vote by the entire house, the government proposal was clearly in trouble by late 1960. Opinion polls suggested overwhelming public disapproval, and when spokesmen for the medical opposition sought out Chancellor Adenauer in December 1961, he was ready to stage a strategic retreat. Adenauer acknowledged that the critics had not been properly consulted and placed the blame on government bureaucrats and deputies of his own party; these, in turn, felt that the chancellor had let them down after they had worked hard to realize his announced objective. The chancellor then tried to negotiate a compromise, but in the end was persuaded by other leaders of his party that the best political course was to let the bill die in committee. In early February 1961, the Social Policy Committee of the Diet voted to give it no further consideration.

EMERGENCY POWERS

The Policy Problem. For close to a decade after its establishment, the independence of the Federal Republic was limited in a potentially crucial respect.[10] The United States, Britain, and France retained the legal right to declare a state of domestic emergency and to intervene with their military forces in the event "a serious disturbance of public security and order" should threaten the maintenance of a democratic regime or the safety of their troops in West Germany. They were pledged to renounce their prerogatives as soon as appropriate national legislation furnished West German authorities with equivalent emergency powers. In order to provide such legislation the Basic Law had to be amended as it did not provide for such comprehensive powers. And such an amendment required a two-thirds majority vote in both houses of the Federal Parliament.

Initial Actions (1958–61). The first efforts to effect the necessary constitutional changes came to grief in the legislative arena of the Diet because of irreconcilable differences between the governing and opposition parties. Both sides agreed in principle that West German authorities should assume the emergency powers of the three Western allies, but they sharply disagreed on the content of appropriate measures. The conservative ruling coalition of Christian and Free Democrats led by Chancellor Adenauer maintained that the executive had to

---

[10] Case study based on Gerard Braunthal, "Emergency Legislation in the Federal Republic of Germany" in Henry S. Commager et al, *Festschrift für Karl Loewenstein* (Tübingen: Mohr, 1971). See also R. J. C. Pierce, "Federal German Emergency Powers Legislation," *Parliamentary Affairs* 12 (1969): 216–25; Carl C. Schwertzer, "Emergency Powers in the Federal Republic of Germany," *Western Political Quarterly* 12 (1969): 112–21.

be able to act swiftly and decisively in times of crisis to protect the fragile constitutional order. However, the Federal Government needed the votes of the opposition Social Democrats and these were not prepared to go along unless several stringent conditions were met. Above all, they insisted that basic civil liberties had to be safeguarded and executive powers carefully circumscribed if emergency powers were to be employed to maintain and not subvert West German democracy. Social Democratic party and labor elites and their supporters pointed out that constitutional emergency powers had been employed by executive officials to undermine and ultimately destroy the democratic Weimar Republic. The leadership of the German Federation of Trade Unions particularly opposed any measure that would allow the Federal Government to curb the rights of organized labor — especially the right to stage a general strike.

The Adenauer government's drive for crisis powers got off to a bad start in 1958, when Interior Minister Gerhard Schröder declared that an emergency would be "the hour of the executive." His statement provoked a storm of controversy as members of the attentive political public took it to mean that parliament would be allowed only a minor role under the pending government proposal. Over the following year the staff of the Interior Ministry drafted a constitutional amendment under Schröder's supervision, which was revised in numerous consultations with officials of other federal ministries and CDU/CSU-controlled state governments. Social Democratic party and labor leaders, however, were not drawn into these secret intragovernmental deliberations and did not learn about the contents of the government proposal until it was approved by the Federal Cabinet in 1960. They immediately announced that they could not support the text as it stood, because it made no distinction between internal and external emergencies and lacked adequate guarantees against a misuse of the Federal Armed Forces to quell domestic disturbances.

The government nevertheless sent its version to the Federal Council for preliminary consideration. There it encountered a host of objections from Social Democratic state governments.

The cabinet chose to ignore them when the measure came back and dispatched it to the Federal Diet, where the proposed constitutional amendment died in committee at the end of the legislative period. With a federal election in the offing, both the governing and the opposition parties were unwilling to seek a compromise solution, and that finished the first try.

Elite Negotiations, Public Controversy, and Conflict Prolongation (1961–65). The 1961 election kept the conservative coalition in power and parliamentary party alignments essentially unchanged. However, with the election out of the way, political observers expected that a compromise would now be possible. Chancellor Adenauer named a new interior minister, Hermann Höcherl, who appeared more conciliatory than his predecessor and more willing to consult with the SPD and labor leaders and to accommodate their demands. After lengthy interelite negotiations, Höcherl obtained cabinet approval for a constitutional amendment that met many, but by no means all, of the objections to the ill-fated earlier version. In November 1962, the new government text was dispatched to the Federal Council, which recommended a number of changes. The cabinet accepted only half of these and then sent the proposal to the Federal Diet. There it remained in committee for more than two years while governing and opposition party leaders continued to bargain for a compromise solution.

By the time the legislative period drew to a close in mid-1965, the Federal Government evidently believed that no further interparty differences stood in the way of parliamentary approval before the impending Diet election. But then the SPD leadership suddenly announced that it could not give its consent to the constitutional amendment after all because it still considered some emergency provisions entirely unacceptable. In fact the SPD leaders had yielded to heavy pressure from the DGB elite which told them to withhold their assent if they wanted the electoral support of organized labor. Such pressure was all the more telling since a coalition of trade unionists, prestigious academicians, and Protestant theologians, assorted pacifists, and radical leftists had launched an unusual, fervent civic action drive against emergency powers among the political public. Ordinarily, such a campaign to block legislative action would not have been successful, but this time it coincided with the sentiments of many back-bench SPD deputies. Under these circumstances, the second government proposal could not obtain the necessary two-thirds majority in the Diet.

Elite Realignment and Conflict Resolution (1966–68). The 1965 election showed a continuing gain in votes for the SPD, but the CDU/CSU was still the strongest party. Party leaders on both sides were now ready to work out an effective compromise in collaboration with the trade union elite. At a DGB congress, top Christian Democratic and Social Democratic leaders jointly called for an end to organized labor's opposition. A breakthrough in the long dispute came with the formation of a coalition government between the two major parties in late 1966. The members of the new cabinet quickly agreed on a new text drafted by the Minister of Interior Paul Lücke and his staff. It provided that basic civil liberties, including the right to strike, would not be touched in any emergency. The compromise proposal was rapidly approved by the cabinet and the Federal Council and introduced in the Federal Diet by June 1966.

Nominally, the governing parties now had between them more than enough votes to amend the Basic Law. However, all was not yet smooth sailing. While the Diet's committees deliberated at length on the new version submitted by the executive branch, about a third of the SPD deputies joined in a dissident group that declared itself far from satisfied with the revised text. Most of the SPD leaders, however, were not willing to let demands for further major changes endanger the fragile government alliance with the CDU/CSU. As it was, the Christian Democratic leadership had trouble enough keeping conservatives in line who held that the party had already made far too many concessions to its Social Democratic partners on this and other issues. Tactical political considerations also induced the DGB elite to withdraw from the extraparliamentary opposition and accept the compromise agreement as the best it could get under the circumstances.

As a last resort, the diehard opponents of any emergency

powers mounted a massive, unprecedented campaign in 1967, to block parliamentary passage. Particularly for radical student leaders, the fight had become a battle against the entire "establishment." In order to ease this extraparliamentary pressure, Federal Diet committees invited several university professors to testify for and against the constitutional amendment in a series of exceptional public hearings. But the die had already been cast. In May 1968, emergency legislation was passed over the opposition of fifty-three deputies — one-tenth of the Diet's membership — and then approved by a unanimous vote of the state governments in the Federal Council.

THE BASIC TREATY WITH EAST GERMANY

The Policy Problem. When the SPD-FDP coalition government of Chancellor Willy Brandt came to power in 1969, better relations between East and West Germany was one of its declared policy objectives. This constituted a major departure from the previous policy of successive CDU/CSU-led governments, which had adamantly refused to accept the legality of another successor state to the former German Reich. But although German reunification "in peace and freedom" had remained official policy, quasi-official "intra-German" relations with the German Democratic Republic had grown in recent years. The Brandt government wanted to anchor these relations in firmer legal commitments by both sides as a part of its more general policy for improved relations with the European Communist countries. Accordingly, it undertook to negotiate a series of agreements with the GDR that culminated in the "Treaty on the Basis of Relations Between the Two German States" of 1972. To take effect, the so-called Basic Treaty had, however, first to be ratified by the Federal Diet, and this involved the Brandt government in a major political and constitutional policy dispute.

The Battle in the Legislative Arena (1973). Even before the Federal Government formally submitted the Basic Treaty for parliamentary approval in spring 1973, the battle lines had taken shape. On one side were the governing coalition parties, the SPD and FDP, and on the other the opposition CDU/CSU, which controlled a majority of the votes in the Federal Council. With only a few exceptions, the Christian Democrats — and especially the Bavarian Christian Social Union — were against the entire "eastern policy" of the Social-Liberal Coalition. A year earlier their opposition to treaties with Poland and the USSR had almost led to the overthrow of the Brandt government in an evenly divided Diet; it had taken an unprecedented special federal election to sustain the government's claim to popular support on the issue and provide it with a firm parliamentary majority in the lower house.

In February 1973, the Federal Cabinet submitted the treaty to the Federal Council for the usual preliminary consideration by that body. It was immediately rejected there on the vote of the CDU/CSU-controlled state governments, but this did not mean that the treaty could not be ratified. As the issue did not involve the constitutional authority of the states, the council would not be able to exercise an absolute veto, and the government had the votes in the Federal Diet to override a suspensive veto with a simple majority. Therefore, when the treaty came back to the Federal Cabinet, that body felt free to disregard the objections of the CDU/CSU majority in the Council and quickly sent the measure to the Diet for its first reading.

At this point in the proceedings, the question of the constitutionality of the treaty came to the fore and split the ranks of the opposition Christian Democrats. A minority — consisting mostly of deputies of the Bavarian Christian Social Union — maintained that the agreement with East Germany violated the Basic Law, which called on "the entire German people" to strive for the reunification of the two Germanies. Their demand that the CDU/CSU parliamentary delegations should jointly exercise their legal right to place the matter before the Federal Constitutional Court was rejected by the CDU leaders. Unlike their Bavarian CSU colleagues, most of them held that such a move promised little success and would only enhance the legitimacy of the treaty if the court should endorse it.

After that episode, the legislative battle featured a good deal of heated rhetoric on the floor of the Diet, but Christian Democratic arguments against the agreement with the GDR failed to sway the general public; opinion polls indicated that it was supported by most of the voters. In committee stage, the treaty was processed as a piece of domestic legislation and considered by the Committee on Intra-German Affairs rather than the Foreign Affairs Committee. It was ratified by the Diet in May 1973, and then went to the Federal Council. The matter of a suspensive veto by that chamber was laid to rest when the Basic Treaty was passed with the votes of the states governed by Social and Free Democrats over the sole opposition of the Bavarian CSU government; the rest of the Christian Democrats preferred to abstain rather than renew the battle. On June 6, 1973, the treaty was signed by the federal president some seven months after it had been initialed by the East and West German negotiators.

Judicial Review (1974). The Bavarian CSU undertook a last-ditch battle in the judicial arena by exercising the right of a state government to challenge federal legislation in the Federal Constitutional Court. Before the treaty had been approved by the Federal Council, the court had refused to grant the Bavarian government an interim injunction that would have halted legislative process pending a judicial decision. However, it agreed to consider the constitutionality of the treaty after it became domestic law. The case went before one of the court's two chambers, where the Bavarian government held that the treaty conflicted with the Basic Law and the Federal Government argued that it did not. In late spring 1974, the judges rendered a unanimous verdict which sustained the latter position, but with a caveat that held potentially important implications for future West German domestic and foreign policies touching on intra-German relations. The court cautioned executive and legislative public officials that they were at all times constitutionally obligated to do all they could to promote German reunification and to do nothing that would hinder it.

LEGALIZING ABORTION

The Policy Problem. When the Social-Liberal government of Chancellor Willy Brandt came to power in 1969, a new abortion law stood high on its announced policy agenda for major social reforms. Under existing regulations, abortions were permitted only in cases of dire medical emergencies, and heavy penalties were provided for all persons involved in illegal abortions. Illicit operations were, nonetheless, frequent. By current estimates, every year some 200,000 women had abortions; women who had the necessary money went to countries where abortions were legal, and women who did not obtained them where they could — which often meant with medically unqualified abortionists. Opinion polls indicated that more West Germans favored than opposed a reform law. Prominent professional women became particularly active in a drive for the abolition or at least the drastic modification of prevailing restrictions. On the other hand, the Roman Catholic Church, its lay organizations, and leaders of the preponderantly Catholic Christian Democrats, demanded that the Brandt government leave well enough alone.

The Search for a Compromise in the Executive Arena (1971–72). The Brandt government was in quite a quandary on the issue. Although its members were on the whole in favor of abortion reform, they were by no means in agreement on the precise form it should take. Moreover, the SPD chancellor and ministers — one of them a prominent Catholic lay leader — were not at all keen for a conflict with the Catholic hierarchy, as they had only recently managed to soften its long-standing hostility toward their party. Then, too, any legislative reform proposal by the government had to allow for the fact that the Christian Democrats commanded close to a majority in the Diet and controlled the Federal Council. Furthermore, it had to take into account legal considerations dictated by the Basic Law.

The difficult task of drawing up appropriate legislation came under the jurisdiction of the SPD Minister of Justice, Gerhard Jahn, who favored a measure that would permit abortions only under special conditions. His proposed limitations were more liberal than those on the books, but they were still too narrow for other members of the government. Consequent disputes among the ruling party leaders transcended bureaucratic and partisan differences and involved personal

310 *Policymaking*

convictions and religious ties. The Free Democrats were pretty well united in favor of minimal restrictions on abortions during the first three months of pregnancy. However, the Social Democrats in the government, parliament, and SPD organization were divided on the question. As a result, officials in the Justice Ministry were working on the eleventh draft for a government bill when the special election of 1972 brought proceedings to a halt.

The search for a compromise in the executive arena became all the more difficult as the public conflict became more embittered before and, especially, during the 1972 election campaign. The proponents of an end to all restrictions on abortion waged a publicity campaign that was as much directed against the restrictive measure advocated by the minister of justice as against the old regulation. The adamant opponents of any reform — spearheaded by Catholic clerical and lay leaders — were no less active. For example, they gave wide publicity to an article by an official of the Vatican which likened a liberalized abortion law to Nazi euthanasia measures for the destruction of "useless lives." And one of the West German cardinals declared that a candidate for the Federal Diet who did not explicitly reject abortion reform did not deserve the support of devout Roman Catholic voters.

Actions in the Legislative Arena (1973–74). The 1972 election gave the Social-Liberal Coalition a solid majority in the Federal Diet, while the CDU/CSU remained in control of the Federal Council. Abortion reform was put back on the policy agenda in the spring of 1973, although not by action of the Federal Government. Its failure to come up with a bill led deputies in the Diet to seize the initiative — a highly unusual step. Four alternative proposals were introduced from the floor of the lower house. One, sponsored by members of the SPD and FDP, provided for abortions during the first three months of pregnancy by agreement between patient and doctor; a second, sponsored by a smaller group of SPD and FDP deputies — including the minister of justice — was less liberal; a third proposal, introduced by a majority of the Christian Democratic opposition, was even more restrictive; and a fourth, sponsored by a group of particularly conservative CDU/CSU deputies, called for virtually no substantial changes in the existing rules.

The four bills went to the Diet's Select Committee for Reform of the Criminal Code. None of them obtained the support of a majority of its members after almost a year of public hearings and closed deliberations; all of them were reported back to the entire Diet for a second and third reading vote as a compromise in committee proved impossible. In April 1973, the most permissive proposal, providing for abortions during the first three months of pregnancy, passed by a close vote that evidently cut across party lines. Two weeks later the CDU/CSU majority of state governments in the Federal Council turned the bill down and called for a meeting of the interhouse Conference Committee to work out a compromise. That body was not convened because the Brandt government held that in this instance the consent of the Council was not required and believed that there were by now sufficient votes in the Diet to override a suspensive veto. And, indeed, the lower house passed the reform bill with the necessary majority in June 1973, and it was signed into law by the federal president. That, however, was not to be the end of the matter.

Judicial Review (1974–75). While the reform bill was still in committee, the Conference of German Catholic Bishops had called for an appeal to the Federal Constitutional Court if the bill should pass. When it did, the CDU government of Baden-Württemberg got the court to issue an injunction that prevented the new law from taking effect until a constitutional complaint by the state government could be adjudicated. In late February 1975, the Constitutional Court rendered its authoritative verdict: A majority of the justices declared the law unconstitutional on the grounds that it violated the spirit of provisions in the Basic Law which guaranteed the sanctity of life. The Court held that more permissive abortion laws in other countries could not serve as a guide for West Germany in view of its Nazi legacy.

Mass opinion polls indicated that most West Germans disapproved of the court's decision and only about a third endorsed it. But that did not alter the fact that the reform law was dead and that the old regulation remained in force until a new one meeting the court's constitutional criteria was passed. These criteria were spelled out for the lawmakers in policy guidelines which the justices appended to their decision, and which subsequently were closely observed by the Federal Government in obtaining the passage of another, more restrictive, abortion reform bill.

CHAPTER IX

Completing the Circle: Policy Fallout

THE PRECEDING CHAPTER focused on the production of so-called policy outputs by agents of the state. Now let us examine the effects, or policy outcomes, and some political feedbacks into the policymaking system.

The dynamic interrelationship between the sources and consequences of public policy has been a constant theme in our study of West German politics. Participating actors, as we have seen, do not just respond to environmental conditions; they also try to shape them, as best they can, in accordance with their personal preferences. The analysis of policy effect patterns can thus provide us with a reading of the long-range distribution of political power in terms of the lasting indentations it leaves on the topographical map of domestic and foreign affairs.

This is easier said than done when we deal with as complex a society as that of West Germany. It is usually hard to discern the full extent of policy consequences, and all the more so when they involve gradual, cumulative, and subtle developments in political relationships, social standards, and lifestyles.

In theory, public policies in the Federal Republic can have practically infinite ramifications. We may thus attribute socioeconomic and cultural changes to particular policy measures, but it is usually very difficult, if not impossible, to establish a clear cause-and-effect linkage. Frequently there is simply not enough evidence to warrant such conclusions, or the evidence can all too easily lead to distorted or spurious conclusions.[1]

A further problem is that policy fallout may have intangible effects. Take, for example, such elusive factors as "the investment mood" of the West German business community or the good will of public opinion abroad (especially in Communist countries). Both may influence demands on and support for the policymakers, but their effects are not readily analyzed.

We shall therefore confine ourselves in the following sections to a narrower range of direct and manifest policy consequences. And if socioeconomic matters seem particularly important it is because they have been — and are likely to remain — in the forefront of domestic and international political issues.

PUBLIC FINANCE

The authority of elected officials to raise and spend money is a key policy instrument at every level of government in the Federal Republic. The allocation of the costs and benefits of public expenditures affects citizens and noncitizens, elites as well as nonelites, and it enters into most disputes among parties and pressure groups. Budgetary issues, therefore, attract a particularly high degree of public attention and obtain exceptionally prominent exposure through the mass media.

Taxation. Who pays what in general taxes is as much a perennial issue in West German as in American politics. There, too, taxpayers resent apparent inequities in the distri-

---

[1] Crime statistics, for example, give us a very imperfect picture of law-and-order violations in West Germany since they list only uncovered offenses. At the same time they do not really allow us to say that there is more or less crime than in other countries because these countries may be more or less diligent in pursuing and registering criminal actions. Frequently heard assertions that the foreign workers in the Federal Republic are particularly likely to commit crimes overlook the fact that most of these are young, unattached males who, whether aliens or not, account generally for a disproportionately high number of law violations. Or consider the claim that the rising divorce rate is attributable to more liberal divorce laws. What may be no less significant is that West Germans marry at an earlier age than in the past and that more than seven out of ten remarry.

bution of the burdens and complain that they have to pay too much for what they receive in public goods and services. And political leaders are no less sensitive to such sentiments, especially around election time. If they are out of office, they will do their best to exploit those sentiments to get in. Governing policymakers, on the other hand, are cautious about introducing tax measures that are likely to prove widely unpopular. Apart from these tactical, short-run factors, tax policies have been fairly constant since the establishment of the Federal Republic and have not been substantially affected by changes in ruling decision makers.

Here we should note that national tax policies have everywhere at least two, and sometimes three, objectives. One is to provide public authorities with funds to meet their current expenses, including debt payments on money borrowed for limited periods at fixed rates. A second is to influence economic developments and, more particularly, to shape the patterns of domestic production, savings, and consumption. In addition, tax policies may be deliberately designed to structure the distribution of wealth and income in a country. But even if not, they will invariably affect it.

Now let us see how these factors work out in West Germany. To begin with, we need to remember that the policymakers are not faced with the revenue problems of a country with a subsistence economy; they can tap a per capita income that is one of the highest among leading world powers. And we must also remember that overall economic policies in the Federal Republic have from the beginning set a course for sustained productive growth through a capitalist market economy operating under a pluralist democratic system.

For these reasons, we do best to compare West German tax policies with those in similarly constituted major industrial nations. Note, first of all, that governmental revenues absorb around a fifth of the gross national product.[2] That is about the same as in the United States, less than in Britain, and more than in France and Japan (see Table IX.1).

---

[2] Gross national product figures provide a rough monetary measure of a country's total output of goods and services.

Table IX.1. *Sources of Government Tax Incomes in Major Industrial Countries*[a]

	G.F.R.	U.S.	U.K.	France	Japan
Taxes as percentage of GNP	23.8	24.0	31.7	21.8	16.2
Percentage of government income from direct taxes					
Individual income tax	36.9	45.5	39.7	21.3	26.1
Corporate income tax	7.4	14.3	9.6	10.9	28.0
Percentage of government income from indirect taxes	55.7	40.2	50.7	67.8	45.9
Total	100.0	100.0	100.0	100.0	100.0

[a]Figures are for 1969-71, but have not changed substantially.

Source: Statistical Office of the European Community, *Basic Statistics*, 12th ed. (1972), passim.

A fairly constant tax bite out of the GNP has meant that governmental revenues have increased in the Federal Republic as the national income has gone up. But here we should take account of a second important point, the nature of the West German tax system. Though corporate profits make up a major portion of the national income, they constitute an exceptionally small percentage of tax revenues (see Table IX.1). The share contributed by taxes on personal incomes is a good deal less than in the United States, but much more than in France and Japan. Indirect taxes on goods and services, on the other hand, account for at least half of the total, more than in any other major Western country, except France. Such levies are in the last analysis paid almost entirely by individual consumers, including those who are too poor to pay other taxes.

These patterns are largely the outgrowth of a basic precept of West German economic policies. We might call it the fallout principle. It is based on the notion that everybody benefits from a high rate of private investment at home and abroad; that is, the higher the profits of West German business, the more they will boost national income and general affluence. Accordingly, if corporations and individuals earn more, they will also pay more income taxes and consume more taxed products and services. And public authorities, in turn, will have more money for general welfare expenditures.

Income tax regulations are consequently designed to encourage productive investments. As in the United States, capital gains from business ventures are taxed at a much lower rate than other incomes, and income splitting among family members provides further tax advantages on gains from investments. Moreover, in the Federal Republic taxes on corporate profits are paid either by the business enterprise or by the stockholders, but not by both as in the United States.

These provisions tend to favor the wealthy more than lower-income groups. But the latter are also offered considerable tax inducements to put what money they can spare into direct or indirect investments. A series of laws passed between 1964 and 1971, for example, set forth increasingly favorable tax breaks for capital accumulation through savings deposits in banks, building and trust funds, and similar private investment institutions. The number of West Germans who took advantage of these opportunities jumped from 4 million in 1968 to 18 million in 1973 — about one out of four. Other legislation has given income tax advantages to employees participating in the profit-sharing arrangements that exist in quite a few West German business establishments, and to small investors who own so-called people's shares in such enterprises as the vast Volkswagen corporation. Of course, more extensive participation in investments involves not only a broader scattering of business profits, but a larger dispersion of losses and risks.

As we noted in Chapter III, West German income tax policies have neither sought nor produced a significant redistribution of wealth from the most to the least affluent. The richest 10 percent got more than 29 percent of all post-tax income in 1950, and more than 31 percent in 1973; at the same time the share of the poorest 10 percent increased only from 2.1 to 2.6 percent.[3] The decision makers have rather accented what they consider a fair allocation of income tax burdens. A good many West Germans are exempted from paying any income tax because they earn too little; in the mid-1970s roughly a

[3] Malcolm Sawyer, "Income Distribution in OECD Countries," *OECD Economic Outlook: Occasional Studies* (Paris: Organization for Economic Cooperation and Development, July 1976), p. 27.

fourth of all wage and salary employees paid no income tax. Higher incomes are subject to a graduated tax under which those who earn more are supposed to pay more. In this respect, assessments have been more progressive than in the United States and France, but less so than in Britain.

The bottom 30 percent of those who pay anything contribute about 16 percent of income tax receipts — compared to 10 percent in Britain, 18 percent in France, and 20 percent in the United States. The top 10 percent of taxpayers contribute roughly 22 percent, as against 35 percent in Britain and 20 percent in the United States and France.[4] The remainder has increasingly come out of the pockets of middle-income employees. Whereas payroll deductions accounted for only a third of income tax revenues in 1950, they now constitute over half. Increases in wages and salaries have been more than matched by higher levies on such earnings.[5] Inflationary price increases have in recent years amplified the disproportionate tax load carried by middle-income workers. All told, the structure of direct taxation thus favors the richest and the poorest over those in between.

Economic as well as political considerations have led West German lawmakers to rely more heavily on indirect consumption taxes than on direct income taxes when it comes to raising general revenues. Such taxes serve as policy instruments for influencing demand patterns in a supposedly free market economy. In the 1970s, for example, the Social-Liberal government of Chancellor Schmidt raised some consumer taxes steeply in order to put a lid on rising prices, while keeping other taxes low to stimulate production, increase employment, and promote foreign trade.

Indirect taxes also tend to be politically less sensitive than income taxes. West German taxpayers resent increases that reduce their disposable income at least as much as taxpayers in the United States do. And since top- and middle-income

---

[4] See Arnold H. Heidenheimer, Hugh Heclo, and Carolyn T. Adams, *Comparative Public Policy* (New York: St. Martins Press, 1975), pp. 231, 241–45.

[5] Thus, whereas gross income from wages and salaries rose by 97 percent in the 1960s, net income after taxes increased by only 88 percent.

groups are key elements in the West German electorate and are particularly well represented in parties and groups, their sentiments carry a good deal of weight with the decision makers. Indirect taxes, because they are less visible, can be increased more easily without significant political repercussions.

What distinguishes indirect taxes from income levies is, first of all, that they are not graduated on the basis of earnings, but are pegged to the prices of covered goods and services. Accordingly, when prices go up — as they have been doing in West Germany — indirect taxes will go up too. And if the tax rate is increased as well, they will rise even more. Second, indirect taxes on producers are usually passed on to the final purchaser and, therefore, bear most heavily on ordinary consumers. Third, they are more easily administered than income taxes. Most of them are automatically added to the sales price and do not require specific tax assessments, like income levies.

Indirect taxes affect a vast range of goods and services in the Federal Republic. They include levies on beverages and tobacco, sales taxes on clothing and household items, and property taxes included in the rents for offices, stores, and apartments. The most widespread and lucrative is the value added tax (VAT), which West Germany shares with other members of the European Community. It is called a turnover tax. That is, a new levy is added at every stage that increases the cost of goods and services on their way to the final consumer. A person who buys a car, for example, will thus foot the bill for the manufacturing taxes paid in the course of its production from imported iron to last component.

Apart from economic conditions, West German officials can be pretty certain that their tax measures will produce desired revenues. On the whole, the system contains fewer loopholes than the American and French and, therefore, fewer opportunities for tax dodges. Of course, it helps to have a good tax adviser, and that takes money. But outright tax evasion is quite rare. Appropriate regulations are tightly enforced by a large bureaucracy, and infractions carry stiff penalties. Administrative expenses are correspondingly high and absorb as much as 5 percent of tax income, as against 1.5 percent in the United States.[6]

Spending. Government spending, like taxation, reflects as well as affects the policy environment for West German politics. How much money is appropriated by the decision makers and for what purposes thus depends on prevailing socioeconomic and political circumstances. As instruments of public policy, however, budgetary expenditures are also designed to influence these conditions. On both counts, the authoritative allocation of public funds poses constant policy problems and can involve major distributive conflicts.

In the Federal Republic, as in the United States, the total of all public expenditures absorbs roughly a third of the gross national product, and is only partly covered by tax income. Especially local authorities, with a small tax base of their own, must borrow money to meet their expenses (see Table IX.2). Many of the larger municipalities are consequently heavily in debt to banks and such other lending agencies as trust and pension funds. In West Germany, in contrast to the United States, the repayment of such obligations is normally guaranteed by the state or federal government; but these higher

Table IX.2. *West German Public Expenditures and Funding (1973)*

		Funding	
	Expenditures	*Taxes*	*Other sources*[a]
Percentage of GNP	34.8[b]	23.9	10.9
Share of			
Federal government	13.1	12.4	0.7
State governments	12.2	8.3	3.9
Local governments	9.5	3.2	6.3

[a] Loans, income from public enterprises and investments.
[b] In percentages.
Source: Calculated from data in *Statistisches Jahrbuch* (1974), pp. 19, 21.

[6] For these figures, see Heidenheimer, Heclo, and Adams, *Comparative Public Policy,* p. 237.

authorities also wield greater financial control over local governments than in the American federal system.

In considering the patterns of government spending, we need to note two important points. One is that budgetary appropriations from general tax revenues and loans do not absorb a third, but only about a fifth of the West German GNP. Most other public expenditures are social security payments for which public authorities are only the regulatory conduits. A second factor is that government spending includes subsidies to nongovernmental groups and individuals. These allocations provide economic enterprises, political organizations, cultural and educational institutions, and the like, with funds from the public treasury for their private consumption. The same applies to public assistance for needy persons as we will see later.

We must therefore distinguish between so-called transfer payments from persons to persons *through* the public sector and the consumption of goods and services *by* the public sector. And we must also allow for government subsidies, which are frequently concealed in budgetary figures. After making these allowances, we find that the proportion of the gross national product going into public consumption has been considerably smaller in the Federal Republic than in the United States and Britain, about the same as in France, but considerably higher than in Japan (see Table IX.3).

Table IX.3. *Use of the Gross National Product in Major Industrial Countries (1973)*

	Consumption		Savings and investments	Inventories and exports	Total
	Public	Private			
West Germany	13.0[a]	57.5	25.0	4.5	100.0
United States	18.5	61.9	18.2	1.4	100.0
Great Britain	18.8	63.1	19.8	-1.7	100.0
France	12.6	60.3	24.4	2.7	100.0
Japan	8.8	50.8	37.0	3.3	99.9

[a]Figures are rounded percentages.

Source: Statistical Office of the European Community, *Basic Statistics*, 13th ed. (1973–74), p. 27.

Although West German authorities have the power to tax people, they cannot compel them to supply free goods and services to the state. Even soldiers drafted into the armed forces must be paid something. Spending patterns are thus conditioned by (1) the budgetary priorities of the official decision makers, (2) the purchase price of the items they need or want, and (3) the amount of money that can be raised to pay for these items. Current price levels determine the cost of such things as military hardware, the construction and upkeep of public buildings, and supplies and equipment for government offices. Public officials, employees, and government advisers need to be adequately compensated for their services — at levels more or less commensurate with payments for equivalent work in the private sector. And if tax revenues are insufficient to meet such expenditures, money must be borrowed and repaid with interest on terms that compete favorably with those offered in the domestic and international bond market.

Keeping these factors in mind, let us now look at the patterns of budgetary allocations in the Federal Republic over time. Between the early 1950s and early 1970s, a period of rapidly rising prosperity and relatively little inflation, the federal budget grew more than tenfold, that of all public expenditures almost as much. In short, there was an increasing amount of money being appropriated to begin with. Tables IX.4 and IX.5 give us some idea where it went.

Table IX.4 shows that the proportion allocated for general services at all levels of government was almost 10 percent more in the early 1970s than two decades earlier, but only slightly higher than it had been ten years back. Most of the increase can be attributed to more administrative services and higher personnel costs. By 1976, one out of ten employed persons was working for a public agency or enterprise. Though this was still a lot less than the one out of four in Britain, it was more than enough according to conservative Christian Democrats. In their view, fewer but more productive public employees would give the taxpayers better services for less money and provide more funds for private investment and consumption.

A look at Table IX.5 shows that the proportion allocated to general government services in just the federal budget

Table IX.4. *Changes in Federal, State, and Local*
Government Expenditures (1950–72)

	1950	1961	1972
Total budgetary appropriations	28.1 bill. DM	95.3 bill. DM	251.3 bill. DM
Allocations[a]			
General government services	17.7%	23.8%	25.2%
Police and judiciary	4.0	3.9	4.1
Military	16.7	13.8	9.9
Transportation and communications	4.5	7.2	8.3
Health and social welfare	30.6	27.2	25.9
Education, research and culture	7.4	9.5	15.8
Subsidies to economic enterprises	19.1	14.5	10.8
Total	100.0	100.0	100.0

[a]Debt payments included.

Source: Calculated from date in the *Statistisches Jahrbuch für die Bundesrepublik Deutschland* (1975), p. 398.

more than doubled over a twenty-five-year period. This exceptional increase in national service expenditures is reflected in the general growth of the national budget relative to all public expenditures. In 1950, it amounted to about one-third of the total; by 1961, it had increased to almost one-half; and by the early 1970s, it was more than half.

Military expenditures — including substantial payments for allied forces stationed in the Federal Republic — have declined in relation to the total budget but have, in fact, increased. Defense appropriations have been treated as essential by West German policymakers, no matter which parties have formed the Federal Government. The share of the budget allocated for subsidies to economic enterprises — especially for assistance payments to agriculture — has also gone down with the expansion of the federal budget.

The budgetary consequences for a major policy change in the late 1960s and early 1970s show up in the substantial proportionate increases for education, research, and other cultural activities. In this period the Federal Government and espe-

Table IX.5. *Changes in Federal Government*
            Expenditures (1950–75)

	1950	1961	1975
Total budgetary appropriations	11.6 bill. DM	39.7 bill. DM	155.3 bill. DM
Allocations[a]			
General government			
services	9.9%	14.9%	25.4%
Police and judiciary	0.1	0.7	0.7
Military	36.7	32.6	20.5
Transportation and			
communication	3.3	4.2	7.2
Health and social			
welfare	38.4	32.0	35.6
Education, research			
and culture	0.4	4.2	5.5
Subsidies to economic			
enterprises	11.2	9.8	5.1
Total	100.0	100.0	100.0

[a]Debt payments included.

Source: Calculated from data derived from the following volumes of the *Statistisches Jahrbuch für die Bundesrepublik Deutschland* (1955), p. 398; 1963, p. 430; and 1975, p. 399.

cially the state governments put large sums into the expansion of higher education. A similar priority is evident in the increased allocations for transport and communications. Health and welfare expenditures were especially high in the early years of social dislocation after World War II and then declined somewhat. The subsequent increase in federal expenditures in this category resulted from the expansion of national welfare programs in the late 1960s and early 1970s.

Such trends within a country over time are in some ways more reliable and informative than cross-country comparisons because they are based on identical or, at least, similar units of analysis. When we compare national budgetary expenditures in West Germany and the United States with those in France, Britain, and Japan, we need to remember that in the latter countries the central government foots almost all of the bill for public goods and services and in the former it does not.

In Table IX.6 we find that general government services accounted in the mid-1970s for a larger proportion of the na-

Table IX.6. *National Government Expenditures in Major Industrial*
Countries, 1973–75 (in rounded percentages)

	G.F.R.	U.S.	U.K.	France	Japan
General government services	26.4	10.3	19.1	21.7	23.8
Military	22.5	43.2	21.0	18.2	8.1
Health and social welfare	29.7	14.8	27.5	17.3	30.7
Education and culture	5.6	7.5	4.7	24.9	14.6
Transportation and communications	8.0	6.6	6.3	5.9	9.5
Subsidies to economic enterprises	4.8	2.9	10.2	9.1	8.9
Debt payments	3.0	14.7	11.2	2.9	4.4
Total	100.0	100.0	100.0	100.0	100.0

Source: *Statistisches Jahrbuch für die Bundesrepublik Deutschland* (1975),
p. 663.

tional budget than in any of the other major Western
democracies. The percentage for military expenditures was
second only to that in the United States. Health and social
welfare took up a larger share than in any of these countries
except Japan, where it was a bit higher. On the other hand,
the West German government, like that of the United States,
put much less into cash subsidies to economic enterprises than
the governments of Britain, France, and Japan did. These
figures reflect structural differences between these countries,
but they also indicate variations in the policy priorities of
their leaders.

SOCIAL WELFARE

Social welfare policies have generated far less political controversy in the Federal Republic than in many other countries.
One reason has been the widespread agreement that such
policies should ensure a decent existence for all citizens; another has been the presence of sufficient resources to meet the
demand for social welfare benefits.

As in other Western democracies, social welfare measures
include both public and private institutions. The former are

usually autonomous agencies *of* the state run by public officials. The latter are regulated *by* the state and usually supported by government subsidies; the social services provided
by the major religious organizations are, for example, aided by
tax exemptions and tax funds. With rising national affluence,
all social benefit expenditures increased from 17 percent of the
gross national product in 1950 to more than 21 percent in
1972. And although governmental appropriations for that purpose also grew in this period, the proportional share declined
from about a third to a fourth of the total.[7] However, more recently this pattern has changed and policies involving direct
public funding of social welfare have become correspondingly
more important.

The state's ultimate responsibility for the social welfare of
its citizens has been a long-standing principle in Germany,
sustained over various regimes. Now, as in the past, leading
officials place the most importance on measures designed to
prevent widespread social distress and possible political repercussions. The principal policy instrument for programming
and regulating the allocation of goods and services in the
contemporary West German "welfare state" is the social
budget of the Federal Government. Its scope has grown significantly in recent times, largely because of the expansion of
the social security system. The social budget took in 29 percent of the GNP in 1974 — compared to 20 percent in 1962 —
and three-fourths of that represented social insurance payments; the rest went into social services and public assistance.

Social Insurance. West Germany has one of the most comprehensive social security systems in the world. The roots
reach back almost a century to the social insurance laws of
Imperial Germany, which served as models for subsequent legislation in other countries. Government policies determine
who is covered against what risks, who contributes and how
much, and who is to receive what, when, and for how long.
Federal regulations to that effect are implemented by the

[7] Calculated from figures in Presse- und Informationsamt der Bundesregierung, *Gesellschaftliche Daten* (Stuttgart: Klett, 1974), p. 211.

Social Security Administration and other public agencies; disputes over claims are adjudicated by the Federal Social Courts.

As in the United States and other countries, most social security contributions represent enforced savings through payroll deductions. In West Germany, all wage and salary earners are required by law to pay up to 18 percent of such income toward health, maternity, work injury and disablement, and retirement and survivors insurance. In addition, both private and public employers must make a proportionate "fringe benefit" contribution. Self-employed individuals, including farmers, pay the entire premium for their compulsory social insurance.

All told, working people may pay as much as a fifth of their earned income for mandatory social insurance. The size of contributions is much higher than in the United States, but the range of benefits is also more extensive. In West Germany, too, so-called unearned personal incomes from sales, investments, rents, and savings are not subject to social security taxes. Consequently, the more an employed individual gets from such exempted sources, the smaller will be the bite which these taxes take out of total income and the less onerous are across-the-board increases in the rate of personal contributions. Moreover, since benefit payments are based on entitlement, the more an individual has previously earned under the social security system, the more he or she will receive on becoming eligible for disbursements. The same holds for the qualified dependents and survivors of the insured. In effect, these measures place a proportionately heavier burden on the lower than the higher income groups and provide them with smaller financial payoffs.

All of the components of the social security system are designed to be self-sustaining. That is, contributions to the various funds are supposed to exceed or, at least, match payments and administrative expenses. Disbursements to those who are entitled to collect benefits are thus to be met through transfer payments from those who are obliged to pay social security taxes, rather than from general government revenues. As a result, higher expenditures can lead to political conflicts over supplementary payments, as we saw in the dispute over the cost-sharing of medical bills discussed in Chapter VIII. The question of who should pay for the steeply rising health care expenses of insured persons is now once again a major political issue. It has also become increasingly apparent that the seeds for similar controversies are embedded in the unemployment and the old age insurance laws.

Unemployment Compensation. In the mid-1970s, the Federal Republic was suddenly caught up in a worldwide economic recession and the twin problems of rising prices and mounting unemployment that also plagued other Western nations. Massive layoffs — especially in the previously booming construction and export industries — increased the number of jobless almost fivefold within two years; by the end of 1975, the unemployed constituted close to six percent of the labor force. Although there was still a good deal less unemployment than in many other countries, including the United States, for West Germany it was by far the highest level in twenty years.

Foreign observers were impressed by the notable lack of social unrest in the Federal Republic and gave much of the credit to the cushion provided by the unemployment insurance system. But they often failed to see that this system was not designed for extended periods of mass unemployment and that simultaneous inflation both reduced the value of jobless benefits and increased their costs.

The prevailing regulations were devised in an era of full employment, stable prices, and sustained growth in national and personal incomes. There were usually more jobs available than people to fill them, unemployment was on the average less than 1 percent, and far more money flowed into the insurance fund than was taken out. Most benefit payments then went to West Germans who were shopping around for a suitable new position.

These conditions favored legislation that now provides the unemployed with far more generous income-maintenance payments than in any other major Western country. They are entitled to collect up to two-thirds of their last previous earnings

— as long as they are willing to take commensurate jobs. Moreover, West Germans are noted for putting their money into savings and have been encouraged to do so by government policies. They have therefore normally been able to dig into those savings while temporarily out of work. Short-term unemployment is thus not likely to cause serious financial hardships.

However, the fact that far more people were jobless in the mid-1970s than before — and for longer periods — threatened to deplete the cash reserves of the unemployment insurance fund. The Federal Government was not only required by law to make up shortages from general revenues, but to give unemployment assistance to West Germans who had little or no insurance coverage. The latter category included particularly young adults who were just entering the labor market and who had had no time to accumulate any substantial savings.

At the same time, the Federal Government was confronted both with inflating costs for other public goods and services, and with demands from the business community that it help along economic recovery by reducing income taxes and cutting down on "nonessential" expenditures. And it was hard pressed to check both rising producers' prices in the vital export sector of the economy and rising consumer prices that aroused the general public's deeply rooted fears of a runaway inflation.

The response of the SPD-FDP government of Chancellor Helmut Schmidt is instructive; future West German policymakers are likely to take similar actions under corresponding circumstances. On the whole, it emphasized antiinflationary measures designed to raise the levels of productive employment and reduce the costs of unemployment compensation. For example, modest sums were appropriated for public works projects and for subsidies to the construction and export industries. The government stayed clear of raising income taxes and imposing wage and price controls. Instead it encouraged businessmen to keep their prices low and urged organized labor to moderate wage demands. And it took great pains to preserve the strong buying power of the Deutsche Mark in world markets and to maintain the price of export items at an advantageous competitive level.

In addition to general monetary and fiscal measures, the

Schmidt government moved to replenish the resources and halt the bleeding of the unemployment insurance fund. Mandatory employee contributions were substantially increased from two to three percent of wages and salaries. The jobless were allowed less leeway than previously in refusing positions offered through the Federal Employment Office, but were paid special bonuses if they agreed to move to a new job location. Employers were given financial inducements to hire the unemployed, but were forbidden to bring in more foreign workers.

By current indications long-term inflation and unemployment are likely to continue to trouble West German politics and may well cause policy disputes over new and, perhaps, less generous arrangements for the jobless.

Old Age Security. Not long ago, a young woman got into an argument with a much older one at a political demonstration in the Federal Republic and was overheard telling her senior that she bitterly resented having to pay for her old age security benefits. Such remarks point to an emerging new social conflict with major policy implications, according to some observers of West German developments. On one side are said to be the beneficiaries of old age insurance — and that includes not only the elderly, but retirement and nursing homes, which have a vested interest in their care. On the other side are said to be young people who will have to contribute to that insurance for many years before they can collect their share — if they live that long.

Pensions and health insurance for the elderly relieve their families, private charities, and the state of expenses for their care. Here West German social security policies have rested on the principle that old people should live out their days in comfort and dignity and share in the economic gains of the working population. As a result, insurance benefits for the aged are now far more generous than ever before, but their costs are also greater and promise to mount with an aging population, and continuing inflation.

Practically all West German adults are covered by old age insurance for themselves and their survivors. They may begin to draw their full pension when they are sixty-three, or continue to work until they are sixty-seven; most retire at sixty-five. As in the United States, benefit payments are based on previous earnings, and not on an individual's contributions to the retirement fund. In effect, current pensioners may thus be receiving a good deal more money from the social security system than they paid in. On top of this, their pensions are annually adjusted to appropriate wage and salary scales, and recently that has meant upward. Thanks in large part to gains won by organized labor for the employed, old age security benefits almost doubled between 1969 and 1975, whereas the cost of living rose by less than a third. West German pensioners have thus not had to depend on the lawmakers for belated measures to bring their social security income into line with rising prices.

As of the mid-1970s West Germany had a dependent population of some 10 million pensioners — about one-sixth of its citizens — that absorbed roughly a tenth of its national output of goods and services. Moreover, in contrast to dependent children, pensioners could vote; they constituted about a fourth of the electorate. On the other hand, a sizable proportion of young working adults who paid for old age benefits were not yet enfranchised because they were under eighteen. Like the 2 million foreign workers, they had no voting influence over the size and expenditure of their obligatory contributions, whereas the beneficiaries represented a major electoral bloc.

On all these counts, the needs and demands of the aged have carried considerable weight in West German politics and are likely to be even more significant in the future. The increasingly costly terms of the intergenerational insurance contract for old age security bequeathed to the young by elderly policymakers — along with demographic trends — suggest that a new social conflict along age lines may indeed be in the making. It would appear to be even more likely if diminished economic growth should make it more difficult to meet present pension commitments entirely by transfer payments through the old age security fund. In that event, the policymakers may have to fall back on public assistance for the elderly.

Public Assistance. Public assistance, unlike social insurance, is based on need rather than entitlement and comes out of budgetary appropriations from general tax revenues. Policies on that score have been far less controversial in the Federal Republic than in the United States. One reason is that they take in social benefits that are not considered welfare services by Americans. Also, most West Germans subscribe to the notion that public assistance to the needy is neither charity nor a subsidy for freeloaders supported by the taxpayers. It is rather understood as a way to enable fellow citizens who are economically underprivileged and socially disadvantaged, through no fault of their own, to surmount their difficulties.

Social benefits labeled public assistance have in recent times absorbed only a small proportion of goods and services. In the mid-1970s they accounted for about 7 percent of the gross national product and no more than a quarter of the federal social budget. Moreover, most of that amount was for social services and indirect assistance to middle-, as well as low-income groups. For example, public funds and tax benefits provided subsidies for public housing, health care services, labor exchanges, recreational facilities, and vocational training centers. They also supported private welfare agencies, hospitals, nursing homes, and rehabilitation centers. And both low- and middle-income groups received family allowances for dependent children in the form of tax rebates.

At the same time, comparatively few West Germans have been poor enough to qualify for noncontributory public assistance through direct cash payments from government revenues. They must either have no other sources of income — such as savings and insurance benefits — or, as is more often the case, require a supplementary income to maintain an "adequate" standard of living. For instance, chronically ill and physically handicapped persons and destitute widows and orphans may receive financial aid on the basis of appropriate means tests.

Of course, West Germans have found it all the easier to endorse such public assistance since the outlays from general tax revenues have thus far been fairly small. But these benefit payments are particularly susceptible to less favorable economic conditions that cause a drop in government income and narrow the range of preferential policy decisions on the allocation of limited financial resources. Thus, if both the demand for public assistance and its cost should go up without a commensurate growth in public revenues, a West German government would be confronted with a choice between increasing general tax levies or cutting down on "nonessential" expenditures. By current indications, the chances are that the government would raise income taxes very little and would reduce outlays for public assistance ahead of defense expenditures, debt payments, and tax benefits for powerful pressure groups.

ECONOMIC CONCENTRATION

Fiscal and other policy measures for economic growth through private enterprise have, in effect, furthered the expansion of large-scale business establishments. As we observed in Chapter III, the prominence of big business in contemporary public affairs is in large part the product of authoritative decisions taken in the early years of economic reconstruction. Legislation intended to stem the trend toward ever larger corporate mergers has not been particularly effective.

Three-fourths of all business capital and investments flows today through banks, and most of these are privately owned and managed. By far the largest are the Deutsche Bank, the Dresdner Bank, and the Kommerz Bank; a 1967 law that was to curb their preeminence and produce more competition among financial institutions failed to halt the elimination of smaller banks. In manufacturing, 1 percent of West German industrial enterprises account today for 40 percent of the productive output. In this respect, neither the cartel law of 1958 nor subsequent antitrust legislation appear to have been very effective.

Remember, too, that West German agricultural policies — in consonance with those of the European Community — have deliberately promoted the consolidations of farm holdings. Consequently, large proprietors — often members of the old German nobility — have been the principal beneficiaries of subsidies for agricultural development. Moreover, substantial profits from land sales for suburban growth, along with special tax breaks, have helped them (1) to buy out small, marginal farmers, (2) to invest in expensive modern equipment needed for large-scale agricultural production, and (3) to hold on to valuable land for speculative purposes. Here we should not overlook the effectiveness of land ownership as a hedge against inflation. For all these reasons, left-wing Social Democrats have demanded higher taxes on income from land property and closer government controls over real estate speculations, but so far their demands have not been met.

You may also recall that economic consolidation in the private mass media had led to the rapid decline of independent newspapers and periodicals. Even in the case of the favored few who have been aided by overt and covert government subsidies, such aid has frequently not been large enough to offset the gap between rising publishing costs and revenues. Under these circumstances a recent law limiting the size of publishing empires is unlikely to save independent publications from extinction.

Economic concentration in the retail trade accounts for much of the marked decline in self-employed persons. Small shopkeepers have found it increasingly difficult to compete with large supermarket and department store chains that have extended their operations from the inner cities to suburban shopping centers. Current legislation, similar to American "blue laws," provide small shopkeepers with some protection; all stores throughout the Federal Republic are required to close early in the evening and to remain shut on Sundays and holidays. But though this may help the owners of "mom and pop" stores, it also restricts the opportunities of other West Germans for employment and overtime pay in sales and services. Moreover, such legislation makes it most difficult for low-income working people to shop around for bargains before the stores close. Here a 1973 law, vehemently opposed by the small shopkeepers' lobby, is likely to benefit such bargain hunters because it allows large stores to sell popular products at cutrate prices.

ECONOMIC DEMOCRACY

Earlier in this book we noted that former Chancellor Brandt attributed much of the economic strength of the Federal Republic to public policies making for exceptionally harmonious relations between employers and employees. Similar views are frequently voiced by other West German leaders and foreign observers. The latter have been especially impressed by so-called codetermination legislation designed to give both organized and unorganized workers a say in the operation of the enterprises where they work. Such measures have been pushed by the trade unions and have induced big labor to go along with the trend toward economic concentration favored by big business.

Economic democracy through codetermination rests on the notion that West German employers and employees are basically "social partners," rather than adversaries, in the production of goods and services. It is supposed to supplement collective bargaining for labor contracts and takes essentially two forms under federal legislation enacted in 1951, 1971, and 1976. Both incorporate the principles of representation — rather than direct participation — which prevails in other areas of the highly organized society of the Federal Republic.

In every productive and service enterprise with more than five employees, including government departments, the employees elect shop stewards to a works or personnel council.[8] Foreign workers can vote along with West Germans for these representative spokesmen who may, but need not be trade union members. Their chief responsibility is usually to deal with employers and management on the conditions of work in a particular shop, plant, or office. For example, the works council may ask for better safety features or for a reduction in the noise level in a factory. Its consent is required on such matters as changes in working shifts and hours, annual leave arrangements, rest periods, and paydays.

The Codetermination Act of 1951 stipulates that employers and works councils "shall work together in a spirit of mutual trust . . . for the good of the enterprise and its employees, and with due regard to the interest of the community." But although the law may set forth goals and procedures, it takes more than that to give substance to this grassroots form of economic democracy. It can only work if both sides want it

---

[8] The size of the council depends on the number of employees. In a small store or office there may be just one shop steward, whereas in a large plant there may be as many as thirty-one.

to work and if the employee councils do not become the battleground for industrial conflicts, as they did in the Weimar Republic. Particularly in the large public and private enterprises that employ most of the present work force, harmonious relations require mutual trust and shared responsibilities not only between the representatives of management and labor, but between the shop stewards and their clients. The council members are the men and women in the middle; management expects them to be reasonable in their demands and the workers expect them to take care of their grievances. This may not present much of a problem on such matters as the length of coffee breaks and adequate toilet facilities. But when it comes to dismissals not covered by union contracts and to production quotas set by some distant corporate headquarters or public authority, the effectiveness of the employee councils is likely to depend on their determination to have their way and the willingness of management to give way.

The councils are not empowered to negotiate labor contracts, though they have the authority to see to it that the terms are observed by employers. What is more important is that they lack the legal power to block managerial decisions in public and private employment that are supposedly justified by economic conditions, but that may also have a substantial effect on employees. For instance, when cuts in the budget of a government agency require staff reductions, its personnel council cannot prevent the discharge of workers who are not protected by civil service regulations. In privately owned business establishments, employers or management must consult the works council on decisions that are said to be warranted by circumstances in a competitive market economy. But then they do not need its consent to reduce or increase the labor force, capital investments, and production quotas, to introduce technological and organizational changes, or to merge the enterprise or even close it down entirely. In effect, key decisions affecting employment and working conditions in a public or private enterprise are thus made by the owners or their managerial representatives and are not controlled by the employee council.

This brings us to the second and more novel form of economic democracy in West Germany. The enterprises that turn out most of the goods and services in the Federal Republic are owned by private corporations. These are run by supervisory boards of directors who appoint the top management and consider — though not necessarily decide — corporate policies on such important matters as production and investment programs. The board members may control a majority of shares of the voting stock as owners or through proxies for small shareholders and large institutional investors. However, they are not required to own or control any stock in the company under West German corporate law and thus legislation could be passed to place employee representatives on the supervisory boards.

The Codetermination Act of 1951 provides that in the key iron, coal, and steel industry five out of eleven company directors are to be elected by the employees and five by the stockholders; the board chairman is an eleventh "neutral" member, chosen by both sides and empowered to break a tie vote. Under this initial piece of legislation, employee representation in all other companies was limited to one-third of the members of the board in deference to the wishes of the business community. Though the law had been passed under the auspices of the conservative Adenauer government, many of the business leaders felt that it had caved in to pressure from the Trade Union Confederation and professed to be deeply troubled about the consequences for "free enterprise capitalism."

Such concerns turned out to be unwarranted. In subsequent years neither equal nor minority employee representation on the boards caused havoc in the conduct of company affairs. In fact, codetermination at the top evidently contributed to unusually harmonious relations between capital and labor. After twenty-five years a keen American observer concluded that, "The board level intercourse between social partners has reduced strikes, helped real wages to rise, and curbed the feelings of alienation that afflicted workers in other European industrial countries." [9]

[9] Clyde H. Farnsworth, "Schmidt the Lip," *The New York Times Magazine,* May 2, 1976.

By the early 1970s, codetermination appeared to have proven its worth. When the leaders of the Trade Union Federation pressed the SPD-FDP Federal Government for more employee representation on company boards, the big business elite was far more willing to go along than earlier. Its primary concern was to preserve the principle that labor could not outvote capital ownership and that it would not be exclusively represented by trade union officials. The DGB leadership would have liked to do better than that, but was forced to agree to appropriate safeguards in order to obtain passage of a new law.

Both the government and opposition parties in the Federal Parliament voted for the Codetermination Act of 1976. It maintains equal representation for capital and labor, along with a "neutral" chairman, on the boards of coal, iron, and steel companies. For all other companies with more than 2000 employees — which takes in some 650 of the total and about one-sixth of the labor force — employee representation has been expanded from a third to a half. However, one of the ten "labor directors" must be a member of top management chosen by the salaried white-collar staff from a slate nominated by senior company officers.[10] Moreover, the board chairman must be a representative of the shareholders and can cast the decisive vote in case of a deadlock among its twenty members. In short, capital and management retain control over policymaking in these companies.

How far these changes will in fact extend economic democracy is as yet uncertain. Their effect, if any, will not be evident until the 1980s. A great deal will no doubt depend on the stakes that will then be at issue in economic affairs, especially those in labor-management relations. If codetermination continues to serve consensual policymaking in economic enterprises, it may well be adapted in other countries as an alternative to state ownership of the means of production. If it founders in the face of industrial conflicts, it may come to

---

[10] Three of the remaining employee representatives are chosen by the entire staff from a trade union slate and six are nominated and elected by the company's blue- and white-collar workers from their midst.

be viewed as an experiment that was doomed to fail in times of economic trouble.

BRUSSELS SPROUTS

When the Federal Republic became a founding member of the European Economic Community by the Treaty of Rome of 1957, there was a good deal of speculation among interested West Germans over the likely consequences. At one extreme were those who hoped or feared that the EEC headquarters in Brussels would before long become the seat of a supranational European government. At the opposite end were those who predicted either that irreconcilable national interests would soon lead to the disintegration of the Community, or that it would have no significant effect on domestic and foreign affairs.

As we know by now, none of these expectations was confirmed by subsequent events. The promise of a European political union contained in the Rome Treaty has not been realized, but the European Community has also not come to grief. Its membership and the scope of its policy-coordinating functions have expanded over the years and West German leaders have played major roles in promoting these developments. As Chancellor Schmidt pointed out in 1976, the sovereignty of the Federal Republic and other EC states has been reduced to a degree largely unnoticed by the general public. In his view they could therefore no longer afford to act as if their separate policy decisions would have no spillover effect on their partners. And he asserted that very soon their interdependence would reach a point where it would no longer be possible to speak of purely national economic and social policies.

Schmidt's observations were explicitly addressed to his fellowcitizens, but implicitly to the leaders and public of other EC countries less strongly committed to further integration than the Federal Republic — notably France and Britain. For West German policymakers of every political persuasion there is no turning back, but there are strong reasons for pushing onward. We need not go into the details since we have already considered most of them, but to see what is at stake, it may be helpful to recall a few key points. One is that interlocking trade and monetary ties to fellowmembers of the European Community have become major factors in the export-dependent West German industry. A second is that the problems posed by the foreign workers are affected by the fact that migrants from other EC states are not subject to the same restrictions as those from other countries.[11] A third point is that common EC taxes, customs tariffs, and economic regulations have a significant bearing on price and income levels in the Federal Republic. And, finally, remember that as German reunification has been blocked, political ties to and through the EC have become more important.

The bonds with the EC have been forged primarily along two lines. One has been essentially technocratic and has featured functionally specialized, interbureaucratic relations with the High Commission in Brussels and government agencies in other EC countries. The other has been a more general international dimension involving diplomatic negotiations among government leaders of the member states.

The technocratic ties developed most rapidly during the Community's great leap forward in the 1960s. In this period the EC's High Commission, staffed by so-called Eurocrats, became its principal organ for joint economic policy planning and administrative coordination. A particularly important development was that the High Commission acquired the authority to maintain a common pricing system for agricultural products through EC subsidy payments and marketing regulations. For West Germany this development had three major consequences. (1) Its government, and more particularly the Federal Ministry of Agriculture, lost direct control over most policy decisions in this sphere. (2) The Federal Republic assumed the largest share of the financial burden for farm price supports that benefited not so much its own as French agricultural proprietors. (3) Since West Germany depends heavily on agricultural imports, these measures for the pro-

---

[11] Thus far this has involved mostly Italians, but if Spain, Turkey, Portugal, and Greece should join the EC, national control over the influx of foreign workers will become all but impossible.

tection of producers in the Community have kept consumer prices at artificially high levels. West German leaders reluctantly acceded to French demands on this score; they considered the costs for their country steep, but necessary for continuing European economic cooperation.

Of late, West German ties to the EC have been affected by a pronounced leveling-off in the movement toward European integration. There has been a less intensive forward movement along technocratic lines and more of a sideways development on the diplomatic dimension. The High Commission and its Eurocrats are not as much involved in establishing common policies as in the 1960s and the locus of joint decision making has shifted more to the meetings of government leaders. And here — with the inclusion of Britain, Denmark, and Ireland in the Community — policy agreements must now accommodate a wider range of interests. A further shift to the political side may be in the offing with the direct election of the EC parliament by the voters, rather than the national legislatures in the EC countries; direct election may enhance the influence of Community-wide and sectional pressure groups, but it could also prove to be no more than a symbolic gesture toward greater popular participation.

In any event, the Federal Republic is likely to remain for the foreseeable future the foremost industrial, commercial, and financial power in the European Community. It contributes the lion's share to EC budget funds, which not only go into transfer payments to French farmers, but support regional development programs in Britain and Italy and a host of other projects dear to other member countries.

By all indications, West German leaders will do their best to use these resources to nudge, push, and even shove their EC partners toward closer cooperation, especially on monetary issues. They have felt compelled to come to the aid of the British and Italian economies through loans outside as well as within EC channels. But they have resisted pressure from other EC countries for an upward revaluation of the West German currency that would allow those countries to earn more from imports to the Federal Republic and compete more effectively with West German exports. What West German leaders want instead is a common currency for the Community, and they can be expected to become even more persistent in driving for a monetary union if other measures to safeguard the West German economy prove inadequate.

ARMAMENT

On February 27, 1955, the West German Diet voted for the inclusion of the Federal Republic in the North Atlantic Treaty Organization and for a substantial military contribution to the Western alliance against the Soviet bloc. Under a series of agreements with the United States, Britain, and France that ended the last vestiges of foreign control, the heretofore unarmed country was to acquire a "defense force" of some half a million men for its external security.

The policy decision came after years of intense domestic and international controversy on the issue, and observers at home and abroad expected West German armament to have far-reaching political consequences. The proponents held that it would help to maintain peace in Europe and democracy in the Federal Republic; opponents feared that it might lead to the revival of aggressive and autocratic German militarism. Some two decades later, disputes on this issue were conspicuous by their absence. An armed West Germany on the side of the Western alliance had become accepted in international and domestic politics and its military establishment was viewed neither as a threat to world peace nor as a danger to the democratic order of the Federal Republic.

Changes in the policy environment no doubt contributed to this development. However, a good deal was due to the way West German leaders implemented the armament policy. Pressed by the American government to make haste, they chose to proceed with deliberate speed to ensure firm civilian control over the new defense establishment. Here Social Democratic leaders — who had at first opposed the decision to join NATO and arm — collaborated closely with the Adenauer government. All parties wanted to make certain that a military elite would not, as in the past, become an independent and dominant element in German politics.

Accordingly, a good deal of bipartisan effort was devoted to shaping a Federal Defense Force (*Bundeswehr*) of "citizens in uniform" that would be subject to elected officials and support the constitutional order. A civilian screening committee carefully selected the initial cadre of senior officers to ensure its loyalty to the regime. Administrative and command functions in the Ministry of Defense were divided among military men and civil servants. All service branches were put under a civilian state secretary accountable to the defense minister, rather than to a general staff as under former regimes. The administration of military justice was placed almost entirely in the hands of the regular judiciary. To prevent the covert expansion and secret armament of the military establishment, its itemized annual budget and personnel strength were to be submitted to the Federal Diet for scrutiny. The Diet's Defense Committee was authorized to investigate the conduct of military affairs by the Federal Government whenever it saw fit. The office of a special parliamentary plenipotentiary for military affairs was set up to see to it that regulations affecting the armed forces were properly executed and the constitutional rights of soldiers adequately protected.

Not all of these arrangements turned out to be workable once the military buildup got under way. The design for a democratic citizens' army was considerably modified in the name of military efficiency. The supervisory powers of the Diet's Defense Committee proved not as effective, and those of its military plenipotentiary less important, than the reformers had hoped. However, on the whole, the innovations took root — not least because political leaders in the executive branch vigorously asserted their authority over the new military elite. Some initial friction on that score diminished as a new generation of professional soldiers that was more in tune with current trends replaced the veterans.

The present Federal Defense Force bears very little resemblance to past German military establishments and appears to be well integrated into the society and polity of the Federal Republic. The political influence of the military is not only much lower than in former times, but evidently a great deal smaller than in the United States. About half of the some 450,000 men in the army, navy, and air force are short-term conscripts recruited from all walks of life; the rest are regulars who serve for twelve years or more.[12] By all accounts relations between officers and enlisted men are generally good, based on mutual respect, and fairly informal. Sharp differences that once divided the ranks no longer prevail; the proportion of workers' sons among the officers is now not only greater than at any other time, but is appreciably larger than among university students. Most commissioned and noncommissioned career officers, particularly the younger ones, have little use for traditional German military concepts of duty, ideals, and ethics. They see themselves as public employees with specific job assignments in organizations that require hierarchy and discipline for efficient operation. In short, they fit well into the contemporary culture of an advanced industrial society.[13] With rapid advances in military technology, the professional soldiers of West Germany have increasingly become specialists and managers cooperating closely with equivalent experts in other sectors of the society as well as in interallied military bodies.

[12] Conscripts are presently required to serve fifteen months in the military. Since their number by no means includes all the eligible and qualified males and most young West Germans have shown little liking for military service, the demand and need for equity in conscription has had some political importance. Exemptions and deferments for reasons of health, conscience, and family responsibilities have been granted rather generously. But in these cases an alternative form of service — say, as a hospital orderly — is usually mandatory sooner or later. Proposals that the length of military service be reduced to twelve months, as in most other NATO countries, or that conscription be altogether abolished as in the United States and Britain have not found favor with West German decision makers. Their argument is that a shorter term of service would not provide adequate training for conscripts who remain as reserves after their discharge and that an all-professional army would be too costly. But there may be other reasons as well. Conscripts provide a safeguard against the sociopolitical insulation of the military. Furthermore, compulsory military service or its equivalent reduces the demand for jobs and unemployment compensation — and concomitant political pressures — when jobs are scarce, as in the mid-1970s.

[13] Most career officers belong to the Association of the Federal Defense Forces, a special interest association for the promotion of the material demands of its members. In 1970, for example, it staged a noisy demonstration for higher military pay, an event without precedent in German history.

Although armament has not given rise to a new military-industrial complex, it has produced a modest arms production and export industry. By all indications the Federal Republic has honored its treaty commitments not to manufacture or acquire atomic, biological, and chemical warfare weapons, or any other kind of "offensive" armaments. It has evidently not made use of its "nuclear capability" and, along with Japan, remains in this respect a significant exception among the major countries of the world. Moreover, much of the military hardware for the West German army, navy, and air force has been and continues to be bought from Allied countries — especially the United States — and neither economic nor political leaders have thus far expressed any desire to expand West German arms production. This situation might change if arms exports should become more important for the economy or if the supply of American arms should become less dependable.

In international politics West German armament may well have strengthened the external security of the Federal Republic by contributing to the stabilization of a military standoff in Central Europe. Apparently it has not proven to be a critical source of anxiety for West Germany's Communist neighbors and it has led other NATO countries to rely on a West German military contribution for their own defense.

West German troops have become the mainstay of NATO's "conventional" military forces in Europe, and their potential fighting efficiency is rated rather highly by Western military experts. All of the combat units of the Federal Defense Force are under direct NATO command and evidently not equipped with nuclear weapons — in contrast to American, British, and French forces. Questions concerning their disposition, training, logistics, and equipment must be settled by agreement with other NATO countries. And though West German officers have a voice in the Nuclear Planning Council and other NATO military organs for the defense of their country, it is by no means a dominant one among the fifteen members of the alliance. Now, as before, West German policymakers depend on an American nuclear umbrella for the Federal Republic and on American leadership of the North Atlantic Treaty Organization. Armament may have enhanced their position in the Western alliance, but it has also carried with it exceptional restraints on the use of force, or even its threat, in relations with other countries.

UNANTICIPATED CONSEQUENCES

In the mid-1960s, West German policymakers came under growing public pressure to open up the highly restrictive system of free higher education to far more students. At that time, the proportion of university students and graduates in the population was appreciably lower than in other advanced industrial countries and opportunities for upward mobility into high status and income white-collar positions were correspondingly more limited. Although government revenues had greatly increased with rising national affluence, the share of government expenditures for higher education had not. There was a severe teacher shortage, and educational experts pointed with alarm to a lack of all sorts of university-trained specialists. The Federal Republic was said to face a "cultural catastrophe" if drastic action was not taken to remedy the situation quickly.

The policymakers responded to demands for action with a massive program for the expansion of higher education. The state governments established many new universities, and the Federal Government took a major hand after the Social and Free Democrats came to power in 1969. By 1970, the Ministry for Education and Science had worked out a national master plan in collaboration with the state ministries of education and sundry quasigovernmental advisory bodies. The Federal Parliament approved vast new appropriations for student aid and university construction. Federal matching grants, in turn, induced the states to step up their own outlays for higher education. Altogether, these outlays accounted for much of the increase in public funding for education and research from 9 percent of per capita governmental expenditures in 1961 to more than 15 percent in 1971.

As it happened, the answer to one policy problem produced new problems that had not been anticipated by West German decision makers. By 1974, one of the principal planners was forced to conclude that they had tried to do too much in too short a time and had failed to take full account of possible consequences and unfavorable economic developments. The release of previously pent-up demands for a free higher education swamped the universities and university-preparatory schools. On top of that, an unexpected economic downturn led to a reduction in government funds for higher education and in the demand for university graduates in the job market.

In 1974, three times as many students attended institutions of higher learning than in 1960. For 1975, the master plan of 1970 had projected an enrollment of 665,000, but the actual number turned out to be 842,000. The substantial increase in teaching personnel and facilities proved to be more costly than expected and the absorptive capacity of the most popular university departments proved unequal to the demand load. Moreover, the educational planners had failed to anticipate that the expansion of the universities would have a significant effect at lower levels of the educational system. The number of students in the university-preparatory schools jumped from 850,000 in 1961 to 1.7 million in 1975. The proportion that graduated increased from four of ten in 1971 to six out of ten in 1975 — that is, from 11 percent to 15 percent of their age group — while the proportion wanting to go on to the university remained fairly constant at nine out of ten. Consequently there were about 155,000 secondary students seeking a higher education in 1975, compared with 87,000 only four years earlier.

The policymakers were confronted not only with the inability of the most popular university departments to take care of the mounting student body, but with a potentially serious political problem. As the number of university graduates increased, more and more would be unable to find the sort of jobs they had been trained for and thought themselves entitled to. Under these circumstances there loomed a threat that an underemployed, if not unemployed academic proletariat of disaffected status seekers might before long cause trouble for the present regime, as it had for that of the Weimar Republic.

In the light of these conditions and their possible outgrowth, West German policymakers decided to abandon the traditional principle of open admission to institutions of higher learning and to apply tighter performance criteria. Whereas in the past any graduate of a university-preparatory school was able to matriculate, a centralized national computer system now selects those with the highest grades for whatever spaces are available in disciplines of their choice. In addition, measures have been instituted to limit the number of years a student can stay at a university at the taxpayers' expense without passing required examinations. In short, who can study what, where, and for how long has become less a matter of personal preference and material resources and more a matter of academic achievement and state control.

The lessons of this case can be applied to other policy processes in West Germany and elsewhere. Policy formulation and attendant political conflicts focus on a future state of affairs, and decision makers need to consider what consequences are likely to follow from their actions. Eventually, the question becomes: Will the policy outputs of executive and legislative bodies sell? Satisfied policy consumers are likely to ask for more of the same, whereas dissatisfied ones are likely to seek different policy products and, perhaps, policymakers.

Of course, leading West German officials will, and usually do, claim to know all the answers. But, more often than not, they are by no means all that sure. Selecting one policy over another is usually a gamble. Authoritative decision makers will proceed on the basis of what they expect to happen; but they can never be entirely certain that the outcomes sought will be realized in fact, no matter how carefully a measure has been planned and crafted.

As in the above instance, a policy move may unleash unforeseen demands that give rise to new political issues and disputes. We have observed such policy feedbacks throughout this book. Recall, for example, that government regulations for rapid economic growth in the early years of the Federal Republic gave rise to new policy problems, such as urban congestion, industrial pollution, and the social tensions created by the mass influx of foreign workers. Or consider that energy programs providing for a massive shift from native coal to foreign gas and oil supplies failed to allow for a sudden, steep increase in the cost of these imports. As a result, policy decisions taken in the 1960s came to haunt leading West German officials in the 1970s.

Another problem for decision makers is that their policy products may not be bought by their intended consumers at home or abroad. Restrictions incorporated in the new abortion law may be widely circumvented and prove unenforceable. The Basic Treaty with the German Democratic Republic may not induce East German leaders to become less truculent toward the Federal Republic. And recent trade agreements with Communist and Third World countries may yield neither appreciable economic nor diplomatic gains for West Germany.

THE NEED FOR CAUTION

Looking backward and forward, we find that one factor is clearly basic to any consideration of policy outcomes and their actual or potential effects on West German politics. As has been emphasized repeatedly, the performance of particular public officials and agencies is judged by the affected elites and nonelites in terms of the perceived costs and benefits. But beyond that, the operation of the entire regime is ultimately evaluated by West Germans on the strength of its evident ability or failure to promote their personal well-being and that of their children.

Thus, the authoritative leaders must at all times be able to adapt their policies to changing conditions without appearing to yield simply to the force of circumstances. Above all, they must be prepared to diffuse highly charged political issues. If these should blow up, it will do little good to plead ignorance of their being loaded. In this regard, the future may well reveal explosive charges that are presently concealed in the domestic and foreign environment.

CHAPTER X

Conclusion

WEST GERMANY'S RISE TO EMINENCE in international affairs brings to mind a little-known variation on the familiar story of the ugly duckling that grew into a majestic swan. The tale concerns a Great Dane that thought itself a little dachshund — and an ugly one to boot — because people refused to take it into their laps and pet it. Then came the day when the creature came across a mirror, realized its true identity, and henceforth played the big dog, looking down its nose on smaller ones.

The sudden recognition that the Federal Republic is not what it used to be has in recent times startled both West Germans and foreign observers. West Germany is no longer merely an object of power politics, but a leading actor in European and world affairs. Its regime no longer appears to be tenuous and fragile, but well established and stable. The once troublesome "German problem" no longer bedevils East-West relations, and West German leaders have become less concerned with fond feelings for their country abroad and are more assertive in promoting its international interests.

The new-found status of the Federal Republic is directly related to the reduction of tensions in Central Europe and to West Germany's increasingly important position among economically interdependent states. It matters today not so much that the Federal Republic is not a military superpower as that it stands in the front rank of the richest industrial and commercial countries. This fact alone gives ruling elites in other Western, Communist, and "Third World" nations strong reasons to watch West German politics closely. What, then, are the main strands that have emerged from our analysis?

TAKING STOCK

During our tour through West German politics we have repeatedly addressed two major questions. One is comparative: How heavy is the German accent? What distinguishes policy-relevant attitudes and processes in the Federal Republic from those in other advanced industrial societies with democratic regimes? The other question concerns the future development of West German politics: Will there be significant changes or will present patterns continue? Both questions proceed from present conditions in West German politics and require us to look at the key developmental factors. Let us consider first the evolution of the system over three decades.

The politics of the 1950s were those of reconstruction. Economic recovery was underway, but had not yet led to general affluence. A "provisional" new state and regime had been imposed on West Germany by the former occupation powers and had still to take root in the political culture. The persistence of traditional authoritarian patterns was reflected in the autocratic style of Chancellor Adenauer and other leading policymakers, as well as in deferential popular attitudes toward authorities in state and society.

The politics of the 1960s were the politics of transition, marking the end of a beginning. National prosperity was no longer in doubt and came to include most West Germans. The constitutional order was more firmly established, and authoritarian traditions were on the wane. However, vivid memories of past conflicts continued to impinge on domestic and foreign politics. The Nazi legacy kept cropping up, and relations with the Communist countries were troubled both by West German fears of Communist aggression and by West German demands for the reunification of the former Reich and the return of "lost" territories.

The politics of the 1970s bear the imprint of a different political climate and new policy concerns. The specters of yester-year are fading away as a new political generation comes to the fore. The accent is on preservation — of prosperity and political tranquillity at home, of diplomatic, economic, and military stability abroad. Policy conflicts are more subdued than in the United States and Britain and less ideologically divisive than in France and Italy. Reunification, in particular, is no longer an emotionally charged issue. All told, the policy course is essentially conservative.

Now let us review major elements affecting the operation of the present system:

1. Political relationships are generally shaped by elaborate formal rules for the formulation and implementation of public policies. The constitutional framework provides for a representative, liberal democratic regime and for a division of powers between (a) national and regional authorities and (b) executive, legislative, and judicial bodies.

2. The policy environment is marked by the general characteristics of an advanced industrial society and by a particularly close relationship between domestic and foreign affairs. Economic prosperity rests heavily on stable, sustained economic growth through private enterprise and extensive international trade and investments. External security arrangements are based entirely on membership in the Western NATO alliance and on the protection of an American nuclear umbrella.

3. The general public supports the established political system, largely because it identifies that system with general affluence and the rejection of authoritarian forms of government. Most West Germans are law-abiding, low on sentiments of national community and patriotism, and disinclined to become involved in public affairs beyond turning out for elections. They look to their authoritative leaders to safeguard their collective concerns, principally for external, internal, and economic security.

4. Patterns of socioeconomic stratification and political learning sustain a graduated distribution of influence over policymaking. The rules and practices of representative democracy allow ordinary citizens the least say, a small political public of organized, middle-range participants more, and the elites of the top policy stratum the most.

5. Political relations among leading actors in the system are marked by a common commitment to the present regime, fundamental agreement on major policy ends and means, an exceptional amount of interelite collaboration, and pluralist bargaining on controversial issues. The accepted rules of the game stress stable, orderly, and effective arrangements for the management of policy disputes and favor discrete compromise solutions.

6. Party government, competition, and cooperation are basic elements in the operation of the political system. The principal parties are not set apart by fundamental ideology cleavages, and they emphatically endorse the constitutional order. Between them they control the election and appointment of key public officials, aggregate and reconcile diverse policy demands, and integrate political activists into the system. A steady expansion in the number of independent voters has gone hand in hand with increasingly general campaign programs, and electoral considerations have constrained militant extremists in the major parties.

7. Interest associations complement the parties, linking a pluralist society to authoritative organs of the state. They are the principal channels for the legally regulated flow of special interest demands into the policymaking system. Pressure group politics focus first on executive agencies; second on party and legislative organs. Organized business and labor groups have the most influence; the influence of agricultural and religious associations over public policies is waning.

8. The official processing of policy demands and production of policy measures reflect the pluralist and integrative elements of both the organization of public authority in the Federal Republic and West German society and, more particularly, its policymaking stratum. The diversity of the political system and its democratic features restrict the power of the ruling elites; on the other hand, the extensive, hierarchical organization of socioeconomic and political affairs enhances their policy influence.

9. The cumulative effect of public policies has been to promote the institutionalization of the political system, increase the scope of governmental economic and social welfare measures, reduce friction with Communist countries, and solidify

ties to allies and trade partners in Western Europe. Regulatory measures have failed to stem business concentration but have advanced economic democracy.

From a comparative perspective, these patterns indicate quite a close resemblance between the contemporary bases and nature of policy processes in the Federal Republic and those in the United States. We can go even further: they differ in particular but not in general, more by degree than in kind, from the patterns prevailing in all other advanced industrial societies with capitalist socioeconomic systems and liberal democratic regimes.

West German politics of course have distinctive features and may be shaped by unique environmental factors. Indeed, we underscored these in preceding chapters. But we should not exaggerate their significance. In the final analysis we have to realize that the German accent is now decidedly less pronounced than in years past and that it may well become even less distinct in years to come. The notion that politics in the Federal Republic are largely formed by factors attributable to the cultural peculiarities of a singularly German "national character" is anachronistic. Political modernization spells adaptation to new conditions for policymaking, and public affairs have become less "Teutonic" as they have become more closely enmeshed with those of other countries in Europe and elsewhere.

PROBLEMS AND PROSPECTS

Political forecasts are not prophecies; they are at best educated guesses based on imperfect information. Developments, especially long-range ones, are usually not as evident to contemporary observers as to later historians. Too close a focus on dramatic current events can therefore all too easily obscure our view of the road ahead for West German politics. At the same time, the further we seek to peer into the future, the more we are limited to broad speculations about conceivable, but by no means certain, developments.

It is safe to say that the politics of tomorrow in the Federal Republic will be different from those of today. But exactly how different we cannot really tell. The clues we have are too few and too ambiguous to let us predict the nature, direction, and magnitude of coming changes. We have noted some signs that point to an unspectacular evolution of policy-relevant attitudes and processes and others suggesting that we should not rule out major transformations. In any event, the dynamics of the international policy environment are bound to introduce new elements whose effect cannot be readily anticipated when we project present domestic patterns.

In short, when we contemplate what may happen over the next decade or so we can do no more than consider possible developments. For that our preceding analysis allows us to identify some pending issues that are likely to have a particularly important bearing on political continuity and change in West Germany.

Military Security and Peace. We can expect defense problems to remain leading policy items as long as key West German decision makers consider the threat, if not the use of force by other states a distinct possibility. Under these circumstances, further rapid advances in weapons technology will require increasing military expenditures. If most West Germans continue to view the Soviet Union as a potential menace to world peace and stability, they will probably endorse higher defense outlays. And the more they fear for their military security, the more likely they are to accept a resulting tax bill with little protest.

Public opinion will most certainly continue to demand and support policies that promise to keep the Federal Republic out of military encounters, not only between the superpowers, but between any other countries. If more countries should acquire atomic weapons, such policies may eventually call for a West German nuclear deterrent force. What seems more likely is that West German leaders will seek and, perhaps, achieve greater control over the deployment and use of British and French atomic weapons through tighter political integration of the European Community. But even if they should obtain it, they are unlikely to rely much more on the collective military power of the European Community's members than they do now and less on American security guarantees. And if political developments in other European NATO countries — say, Communist participation in French or Italian governments — should threaten to undermine the Western alliance, West German policymakers would probably strive for even closer defense arrangements with the United States.

However, these speculations assume that a combination of basic factors in the external security environment of the Federal Republic will remain essentially constant. This means, first of all, that there will be no significant shift in the Soviet-American military standoff; a marked destabilization favoring either side would undoubtedly have a great, but unpredictable effect on West German politics. Second, we presuppose that the Soviet Union will continue to play a predominant role in Eastern Europe in general and in East Germany in particular; a change in this condition would create an entirely new situation for West German defense policies. Third, we take it for granted that American policymakers will stand convincingly by present United States commitments to protect West Berlin and defend the Federal Republic; if they do not, adroit Soviet moves might well promote a massive upsurge of neutralist sentiments in West Germany that would shatter consensual support for the alliance with the United States.

In any event, external security developments are bound to have a major effect on socioeconomic policy issues. West Germans have not yet had to choose between more guns and more butter thanks to an almost uninterrupted expansion of their national income. Whether this will continue to be the case depends, therefore, not just on the scope of military security demands, but on economic developments.

Economic Security and Growth. We may count on it that West German governments will be hard pressed to safeguard domestic prosperity and prevent economic stagnation or decline. What is less certain is that they can ensure substantial productive growth over the long run and that they will continue to adhere to fairly restrained measures for steering the private sector of the economy.

The public in the Federal Republic can be expected to push for steady growth as long as most citizens define "the good life" in terms of economic security and abundant goods and services. Perhaps such "materialistic" values will in time give way to more "idealistic" standards for the general welfare and personal self-fulfillment, but such change will come only very slowly.

Today's young adults were raised in an age of increasing national affluence and may not be quite as much preoccupied with bread-and-butter issues as older groups. But the incoming generation does not seem to be appreciably less attached to comfortable living standards, less interested in secure, well-paying jobs and "welfare state" benefits, or less committed to sustained prosperity. Some left-wingers may discount or ignore any contingent need to choose between guns and butter and question the desirability of much further economic growth. Their programs for a more equitable distribution and "beneficial" public utilization of the national income assume nevertheless that the gross national product will continue to expand rather than diminish.

Growth issues, as we have seen, enter into most aspects of West German domestic and foreign policy. Compared to the economic problems of less prosperous countries the West German concern may strike an outsider as no more serious than that of a fat man who must watch his weight to stay healthy. But to some observers in the Federal Republic the potential social and political consequences of economic development at home and abroad provide little reason for complacency and a good deal for alarm.

To be sure, the West German economy appears to be strong enough to withstand considerable buffeting. But it is highly doubtful that the fortuitous combination of circumstances that have furthered its growth will persist. The era of spectacular economic expansion, ensured full employment, and rapidly rising affluence is evidently over. And as in other rich, non-Communist states, rulers and ruled now confront unavoidable public policy decisions on just how much and what sort of further growth is necessary, desirable, and feasible.

These issues may contain the seeds for bitter domestic and international disputes over the mobilization and allocation of scarce economic resources. At home they involve, for instance, such controversial policy questions as what constitutes the "best" tradeoff between technological progress and consequent unemployment, between the costs and the benefits of mandatory pollution controls, between the use and the conservation of natural resources, and between the consumption and the reinvestment of economic products. In foreign affairs policymakers differ largely on what is the most advantageous policy mix between economic competition and cooperation with other industrially advanced countries, on how much and what kind of aid should be given to less developed nations, and on the problems raised by the increasingly important role of multinational corporations and transnational, intergovernmental agencies in promoting or inhibiting domestic growth.

Although these problems are not unique to West Germany, a number of closely related factors underscore their significance for political developments in the Federal Republic. One is the particularly pronounced association in its political culture between a generally high level of prosperity and democratic processes in state and society. Elites as well as nonelites have come to view steady economic growth as a necessary, though not sufficient condition for the smooth operation of the complex system of checks and balances embodied in the prevailing constitutional order. By all accounts, if there should be less to go around, presently muted party and interest group controversies over economic policies will become more virulent, and demands for decisive conflict resolution by executive agents of the state will increase correspondingly.

A second key factor is that West Germans are not united by strong bonds of national community that transcend socioeconomic and political cleavages in the United States and other countries. Public officials therefore find it harder to invoke overarching patriotic sentiments to obtain voluntary compliance with unpopular austerity measures "in the national interest."

A third factor is that the heavily trade-dependent West German economy is highly vulnerable to protectionist policies of other countries and to unfavorable international conditions of demand and supply. The most promising growth sectors are especially dependent on low-cost imports at stable world prices and ready access to foreign export markets. Here we should take note of two developments affecting future growth. One is the increasing pressure from allied, but economically competing countries for a slowdown of the West German export drive. The other is the increasing insistence by less prosperous countries for more generous financial assistance from the Federal Republic and for measures that will allow those countries to sell their products in West Germany more easily and more profitably. In both cases the West German policymakers face a dilemma: they risk strong internal opposition if they accede to these external demands at the expense of powerful domestic interest groups. However, future international conditions inside and outside the European Community may leave them no other choice.

Growth policies are also likely to be complicated by the fact that an increasing number of West Germans object to what they take to be qualitative social shortcomings of quantitative economic gains. For example, many employees are no longer reconciled to the "human costs" of high-speed assembly line processes and monotonous working conditions, but major improvements on this score might require policy measures that would reduce productive output. Fears of atomic contamination are feeding an emerging protest movement against the construction of nuclear power plants, but without such energy resources the West German economy will be all the more dependent on increasingly costly and uncertain foreign oil and gas supplies.

Whether and how all of these matters can be resolved by future policymakers remains to be seen. It now seems that persistent demands for more West German industrial and commercial expansion and mounting obstacles to further productive growth at home will have two major political consequences.

West German foreign policies are likely to feature intense diplomatic efforts for closer trade relations with Communist and wealthier "Third World" countries and more "hard-nosed" endeavors to make the European Community yield maximum benefits for the Federal Republic. In domestic affairs the signs point to much more overt and covert state intervention in what is now essentially a capitalist economy. Here present indications suggest three developments: (1) more extensive and intensive regulatory efforts by the Federal Government to structure the domestic consumer and labor markets and to restructure "private enterprise" production and capital investments, (2) more far-reaching and centralized policy planning by executive authorities, and (3) more emphasis on policy-implementing understandings among collaborating government, business, and trade union leaders, bypassing legislative bodies.

Internal Security and Civil Liberties. The possibility that conflicts on military or economic security issues might seriously strain, if not tear the established political fabric accentuates a crucial problem for the present regime. In a fairly open, pluralist polity, disputes over internal security curbs on personal freedom are bound to arise even under the best of conditions. A decisive question for future West German political developments is whether the prevailing libertarian conception of a Rechtsstaat — a liberal democratic state under law — can be reconciled with persistent demands for domestic peace, stability, and order.

As we noted in Chapter II, constitutional principles call for as much personal freedom as possible and for as much collective internal security as necessary. The Basic Law contains an extensive catalogue of fundamental civic rights, including general guarantees for freedom of speech, association, personal privacy, and equality of opportunity under law. However, it also requires executive, legislative, and judicial authorities to take all necessary steps for safeguarding both the constitutional order and the public welfare.

What sort of balance should be struck between the two sets of provisions has long been a sticky political issue. Recall, for example, the intense controversy in the late 1960s over emergency regulations for contingent crisis situations. By current indications, difference over the "legitimate" scope of internal security regulations will prove no less problematical in the future and may prove even more so.

The scope of the state's internal security tasks can be broadly

defined to include practically all aspects of West German political, economic, and social relations. Authoritative constraints
on individual freedoms in the name of the collective interest
may thus take in not only regulations for the protection of
life, property, public health, and safety, but for the preservation of esteemed cultural values as well. In a narrower and
currently more immediate sense, internal security measures
focus on the permissible limits of political opposition and
dissent.

By some accounts there is a clear and present danger that
aspiring Communist and militant socialist "counterelites" will
abuse their civil liberties to undermine the constitutional
order from below — ostensibly to achieve more participatory
democracy, but in fact to create a leftist dictatorship. According to other accounts West German democracy is threatened
by the gradual erosion of civil liberties through autocratic
measures from above — ostensibly for the good of all, but in
fact to maintain the power of the ruling few. The former view
stresses the pressing need for effective internal security controls *by* public officials, the latter the urgent necessity for
more adequate popular control *over* public officials.

These tensions are highlighted in the sustained controversy
over the effects of a 1972 decree of the Federal and state governments barring subversives from public employment. The
questions at issue are what should be considered proof of
actual or potential seditious activities, whether the decree
should apply equally to all positions in the public service, and
how far it infringes on civil liberties. Conservatives, who
sought and welcomed the measure, press for its most rigorous
enforcement; they see it above all as a means of curbing what
they consider the ideological corruption of West German
youngsters by radical leftist teachers. Critics of the decree
hold, however, that it stifles unorthodox opinions, intimidates
opponents of the ruling establishment, and promotes the inva-
sion of personal privacy by internal security agents of the
state; some leftists even assert that it confirms a general trend
toward an increasingly authoritarian capitalist regime.

The alarming pictures projected from the more extreme
positions on both sides of the internal security–civil liberties

issue may strike us as rather stark and overdrawn. To be sure, Communist subversion and espionage — especially from East Germany — and the sporadic terrorist acts of small anarchist groups do pose internal security problems that might become more serious. And public authorities have no doubt imposed constraints on the civil liberties of not only leftist, but rightist dissidents; such curbs might indeed become more extensive and restrictive if outright opposition to the present regime should increase substantially.

But as matters stand now, at least, West Germans do not appear very close to losing their liberties to either a "capitalist" or "socialist" police state. They may be more attached to law and order and less to maximum freedom for all citizens than people in countries with older libertarian traditions. However, it has been argued as well that the warning examples of Nazi and East German autocracy — and a pronounced individualistic outlook — have made West Germans, particularly young West Germans, all the more resistant to the notion that the inevitable price of internal security is less personal freedom and privacy.

Suggestions for Further Reading

This bibliography, limited for the most part to relatively recent studies in English, is designed for readers who wish to delve more deeply into topics surveyed in this book.

For new titles, see *The American Political Science Review*, *International Affairs* (London), *International Political Science Abstracts*, *ABC Political Science*, *Comparative Political Studies*, *Revue d'Allemagne*, *Neue Politische Literatur*, *Politische Vierteljahreshefte*, *Zeitschrift für Politik*.

For current events, see the German weeklies, *Die Zeit* and *Der Spiegel*, *The German Tribune* (a weekly translation of articles from the German press), and reports published in German by Inter Nationes (Bonn-Bad Godesberg).

GENERAL STUDIES ON GOVERNMENT AND POLITICS

Balfour, Michael. *West Germany*. London: Benn, 1968.

Ellwein, Thomas. *Das Regierungssystem der Bundesrepublik Deutschland*. Köln-Opladen: Westdeutscher Verlag, 1973.

Löwenthal, Richard, and Hans-Peter Schwarz (eds.). *Die Zweite Republik: 25 Jahre Bundesrepublik Deutschland*. Stuttgart: Sewald, 1974.

Tilford, R.D., and R.J.C. Preece. *Federal Germany: Political and Social Order*. London: Wolff, 1969.

CONTEMPORARY SOCIETY, ECONOMY, AND CULTURE

Bolte, Karl Martin et al. *Deutsche Gesellschaft im Wandel* (2 volumes). Opladen: Leske, 1970.

Clässens, Dieter, Arno Klönne, and Armin Tschöppe. *Sozialkunde der Bundesrepublik Deutschlands* rev. ed. Düsseldorf: Diederichs, 1973.

Dahrendorf, Ralf. *Society and Democracy in Germany.* Garden City, New York: Doubleday, 1967.

Wurzbacher, Gerhard. *Leitbilder gegenwartigen deutschen Familienlebens.* Stuttgart: Enke, 1969.

THE COLLECTIVE PAST

Bracher, Karl D. *The German Dictatorship: The Origins, Structure, and Effects of National Socialism.* New York: Praeger, 1970.

Childs, David. *Germany Since 1918.* New York: Harper, 1972.

Dill, Marshal. *Germany: A Modern History.* Ann Arbor: University of Michigan Press, 1961.

Grosser, Alfred. *Germany in Our Time.* New York: Praeger, 1971.

Schoenbaum, David. *Hitler's Social Revolution.* New York: Anchor, 1967.

Schwarz, Hans-Peter. *Vom Reich zur Bundesrepublik.* Neuwied: Luchterhand, 1966.

POLITICIZATION AND PARTICIPATION

Baker, Kendall L. "Political Alienation and the German Youth," *Comparative Political Studies.* 3 (1970): 117–30.

———. "Political Participation, Political Efficacy, and Socialization in Germany," *Comparative Politics* 6, no. 1 (October 1973): 73–98.

Beyme, Klaus von. *Die Politische Elite in der Bundesrepublik Deutschland.* München: Piper, 1971.

Inglehart, Robert. "The Silent Revolution in Europe," *American Political Science Review* 65 (1971): 991–1017.

Jaeggi, Urs. *Macht und Herrschaft in der Bundesrepublik.* Frankfurt: Fischer, 1969.

Jaide, Walter. *Jugend und Demokratie: Politische Einstellungen der Westdeutschen Jugend.* Müchen: Juventa Verlag, 1970.

Pappi, Franz Urban. *Wahlverhalten und Politische Kultur.* Meisenheim: Hain, 1970.

Schramm, Glenn. "Ideology and Politics: The Rechtsstaat Idea in West Germany," *Journal of Politics* 33 (1971): 133–57.

Schweigler, Gebhard L. *National Consciousness in Divided Germany.* Beverly Hills, California: Sage Publications, 1975.

Watson, Gerald G. "The Structure of Opportunity in West German State Politics," in *Sozialwissenschaftliches Jahrbuch für Politik,* III. München: Olzog, 1972, pp. 367–91.

POLITICAL PARTIES AND ELECTIONS

Conradt, David P. "Social Structure, Voting Behavior and Party Politics in West Germany," *Sozialwissenschaftliches Jahrbuch für Politik*, III. München: Olzog, 1972, pp. 175–230.

————. "Electoral Law Politics in West Germany," *Political Studies* 28 (1970): 341–56.

————, and Dwight Lambert. "Party System, Social Structure, and Competitive Politics: An Ecological Analysis of the 1972 Federal Election," *Comparative Politics* 7, no. 1 (October 1974): 37–60.

Dittberner, Jürgen, and Rolf Ebbighausen (eds.). *Parteiensystem in der Legitimationskrise*. Opladen: Westdeutscher Verlag, 1973.

Edinger, Lewis J. and Paul Luebke. "Gross Roots Electoral Politics in the German Federal Republic," *Comparative Politics* 3 (1971), pp. 463–98.

Fishel, Jeff. "On the Transformation of Ideology in European Political Systems: Candidates for the West German Bundestag," *Comparative Political Studies* 4, no. 4 (January 1972): 406–37.

————. "Parliamentary Candidates and Party Professionalism in Western Germany," *Western Political Quarterly* 25 (1972): 64–80.

Gunlicks, Arthur B. "Intra-Party Democracy in Western Germany: A Look at the Local Level," *Comparative Politics* 2 (1970): 220–49.

Guttsman, W. L. "Elite Recruitment in Britain and Germany Since 1950: A Comparative Study of MPs and Cabinets," in Ivor Crewe (ed.), *Elites in Western Democracies*. New York: Wiley, 1974, pp. 89–125.

Kaack, Heino. *Geschichte und Struktur des deutschen Parteiensystems*. Opladen: Westdeutscher Verlag, 1971.

Merkl, Peter. "Coalition Politics in West Germany," in Sven Groennings et al. (eds.), *The Study of Coalition Behavior*. New York: Holt, 1970, pp. 13–42.

Segal, David R. "Social Structural Bases of Political Partisanship in the Federal Republic of Germany and in the United States," in William J. Crotty (ed.), *Public Opinion and Politics*. New York: Holt, 1969, pp. 216–35.

Zohlnholler, Werner. "Party Identification in the Federal Republic of Germany and the United States," in Kurt L. Shell (ed.), *The Democratic Political Process*. New York: Ginn, 1969, pp. 148–58.

PRESSURE GROUP POLITICS

Ackermann, Paul. *Der Deutsche Bauernverband im politischen Kräftespiel der Bundesrepublik*. Tübingen: Mohr, 1970.

Braunthal, Gerard. *The Federation of German Industry in Politics.* Ithaca, N.Y.: Cornell University Press, 1965.

Freye, Charles E. "Parties and Pressure Groups in Weimar and Bonn," *World Politics* 17 (1965): 633–53.

Huddleston, John. "Trade Unions in the German Federal Republic," *Political Quarterly* 38 (1967): 165–76.

Willey, Richard J. "Trade Unions and Political Parties in the Federal Republic of Germany," in *Industrial and Labor Relations Review,* 28, no. 1 (October 1974): 38–59.

POLICY PROCESSES AND ISSUES

Altenstetten, Christa. *Health Policy-Making and Administration in West Germany and the United States.* Beverly Hills, Calif.: Sage, 1974.

Arndt, Hans-Joachim. *West Germany: Politics of Non-Planning.* Syracuse, N.Y.: Syracuse University Press, 1967.

Gunlicks, Arthur B. "Representative Role Perceptions Among Local Councillors in Western Germany," *Journal of Politics* 31 (1969): 423–84.

Hanrieder, Wolfram F. *The Stable Crisis: Two Decades of German Foreign Policy.* New York: Harper and Row, 1970.

Hirsch, Joachim. "Scientific-Technical Progress and the Political System," in Klaus von Beyme ed.) *German Political Studies,* I. Beverly Hills, Calif.: Sage Publications, 1974.

Johnson, Neville. *Government in the Federal Republic: The Executive at Work.* Oxford: Pergamon, 1973.

Kaiser, Karl, and Roger Morgan (eds.). *Britain and West Germany — Changing Societies and the Future of Foreign Policy.* London: Oxford University Press, 1971.

Kelleher, Cathryn M. *Germany and the Politics of Nuclear Weapons.* New York: Columbia University Press, 1975.

Kommers, Donald P. *Judicial Politics in West Germany.* Beverly Hills, Calif.: Sage Publications, 1975.

Loewenberg, Gerhard. *Parliament in the German Political System.* Ithaca, N.Y.: Cornell University Press, 1966.

Massing, Orwin. "The Federal Constitutional Court as an Instrument of Social Control," in Klaus von Beyme (ed.) *German Political Studies,* I. Beverly Hills, Calif.: Sage Publications, 1974

Mayntz, Renate, and Fritz W. Scharff. *Policy-Making in the German Federal Bureaucracy.* Amsterdam: Elsevier, 1975.

Röhring, Hans-Helmut, and Kurt Sontheimer (eds.). *Handbuch des deutschen Parlamentarismus.* München: Piper, 1970.

Schmidt, Helmut. *The Balance of Power.* London: Kimber, 1971.

Schwertzer, Carl C. "Emergency Powers in the Federal Republic of Germany," *Western Political Quarterly* 22 (1969): 112–21.

Whetten, Lawrence L. *Germany's Ostpolitik: Relations Between the Federal Republic and the Warsaw Pact Countries.* New York: Oxford, 1971.

Ziller, Gebhard. *Der Bundesrat.* Frankfurt: Athenaum, 1966.

Index